Acclaim for *It's Not Just Who You Know*

"Tommy Spaulding has done something quite amazing. He has combined a deeply moving personal memoir with a practical tutorial on building genuinely enriching relationships. *It's Not Just Who You Know* is an open, honest, and authentic book by a talented teller of real-life tales about one of the most fundamental of human truths. You'll be moved, uplifted, and educated. You'll find yourself laughing, crying, and nodding in agreement. *It's Not Just Who You Know* is a one-of-a-kind masterwork, and you need to buy it, read it, and give it to your friends and family. You will be thankful that you did."

> —Jim Kouzes, coauthor of *The Leadership Challenge* and *The Truth About Leadership*, Dean's Executive Professor of Leadership, Leavey School of Business, Santa Clara University

"Tommy Spaulding teaches us the joy and value of investing in relationships!"

> —James H. Maynard, chairman and cofounder, Golden Corral Corporation

"Someone once told me that your students do not care how much you know until they know how much you care. This is true in all relationships; and this book provides the tools needed in cultivating your relationships at any level. Tommy's book is a homerun. *It's Not Just Who You Know* is a must read if you are interested in transforming your life.

> —Frank DeAngelis, principal, Columbine High School

"A remarkable collection of insights that teaches how generosity, humility and thankfulness will take your business and personal relationships to the next level!"

> —Jason Jennings, bestselling author of *Hit the Ground Running* and *Think Big, Act Small*

"I didn't want the book to end. I found myself hanging on every word and making notes in the margins as I connected the concepts to my own experiences. This book presents so many deep truths about transformational leadership in a way that is easily understandable to any audience. I will give every member of my staff a copy of *It's Not Just Who You Know*."

—Dr. Barney Forsythe, president, Westminster College

"Tommy Spaulding is masterful at building relationships that matter. In *It's Not Just Who You Know*, he shares powerful lessons and weaves them into a fascinating modern-day follow-on to Dale Carnegie's *How to Win Friends & Influence People*. I only wish that I had this book early in my own career."

—Richard R. Eakin, chancellor emeritus, East Carolina University

"Nothing is more important than our connection with other people. It's what's behind everything we do. With this book, Tommy inspires us with his first-hand experiences and insight to reach for those deeper relationships that make everything more worthwhile. Read this and you'll be better for it."

—Sam Parker, bestselling author of *212° the extra degree*

"Inspiring and moving! Tommy is someone who truly understands the human heart. This is a book that I will not only give to all our teachers and staff, but more importantly, all our students."

—Dr. Jill Scheulen, principal, Crestview Middle School

"Tommy lives, teaches, and leads from the heart. The message and tools in this book will not only change your organization and your career, but your life.

—Jared Polis, U.S. congressman and founder of Proflowers.com and Bluemountainarts.com

"Truly compelling! As I have watched my friend Tommy live out these principles and faith journey, I have seen it not only transform his life, but those around him. This is THE BOOK on authentic servant leadership."

—Mark Schultz, GMA Dove Award– and Platinum Award–winning singer/songwriter

It's Not Just Who You Know

Transform Your Life (and Your Organization)
by Turning Colleagues and Contacts into
Lasting, Genuine Relationships

Tommy Spaulding

Broadway Books • New York

Published in the United States by Broadway Books, an imprint of the
Crown Publishing Group, a division of Random House, Inc., New York.
www.crownpublishing.com

BROADWAY BOOKS and the Broadway Books colophon are trademarks of
Random House, Inc.

Library of Congress Cataloging-in-Publication Data

Spaulding, Tommy.
    It's not just who you know : transform your life (and your organization)
by turning colleagues and contacts into lasting, genuine relationships /
Tommy Spaulding.
        p. cm.
    1. Success in business.   2. Success.   3. Interpersonal relations.
I. Title.

HF5386.S7512 2010
650.1'3—dc22

                                                            2010012355

ISBN 978-0-307-58913-2

Printed in the United States of America

Design by Lauren Dong

10 9 8 7 6 5 4 3 2 1

First Edition

Dedicated to my father, Tom Spaulding Sr.,
the greatest man I have ever known.

In loving memory of Anthony D'Aquanni,
Tom France, Paul Gillett, Keli McGregor,
and Lori Nolan.

Contents

Foreword

My dad graduated from Dale Carnegie's first course in 1927, so I grew up on *How to Win Friends & Influence People*. Carnegie's concepts are timeless in terms of beginning relationships. And yet Tommy Spaulding realized there was more. He has learned a lesson that I think only comes with age: you finally become an adult when you realize that life is all about serving rather than being served, giving rather than getting, and, as Zig Ziglar often says, "Realizing that people don't care how much you know until they know how much you care."

Tommy's teaching in this book is about developing genuine, lasting relationships. These are the kind of people who, if you're hurting and call for support, are out the door to help you—no questions asked. They show up to cover your back when the going gets rough. In short, they're there for you. Why? Because they know you'd do the same for them.

I'm a big fan of Tommy Spaulding and *It's Not Just Who You Know*. Read this book. Apply its wisdom and live its principles. I guarantee the payoff will be amazing for you and the people whose lives you touch. You'll generate what Tommy calls *Return on Relationship* or ROR. Practicing these principles not only improves the financial health of individuals, organizations, and communities—it brings joy and fulfillment as well.

Life is about more than winning friends and influencing

people—it's about serving others. When you make a difference in other people's lives, guess what? It makes a difference in your life, too. Thanks, Tommy.

—Ken Blanchard, coauthor of *The One Minute Manager*® and *Helping People Win at Work*

Introduction

Standing on Carnegie's Shoulders

It was Dale Carnegie and his book *How to Win Friends & Influence People* that got me started on nurturing and developing the relationships that have been so central to my life. I kept a copy of the book on my nightstand next to my bed as I made my way through high school, college, graduate school, and into my business career. I lived that book—I lived it, I would argue, like few others. Why? Because it resonated with my every instinct.

I became obsessed with sending handwritten notes, with returning phone calls, with sending birthday cards, with using people's names, and with recognizing other people. To this day, anytime I'm reading the newspaper and I come across a positive article about someone I know, I cut it out and I send it to that person with a handwritten note. If their mother is alive, I'll write, "You might want to send this to your mom. She'd be proud to put it on her refrigerator!" I do that a couple of hundred times a year, and I doubt that will ever change.

For years it seemed like the things I had learned in that book would open every door in every hallway that ever came my way. Carnegie's message, after all, survives even today because it works. Do what he teaches and, in fact, you will win friends and influence people. You will grow your Rolodex like kudzu in Mississippi, and you'll get more Christmas letters than Saint Nick. And isn't that how you build a career? Isn't that how you advance in business? Isn't that the heart of the message "It's not *what* you know, but *who* you know?"

Well, as I have come to learn, there is more. What you know is important, and who you know is critical. But real success is about much more than what or who you know. Indeed, it's the *more than* that really matters when it comes to advancing your career and building a business or an organization. It's the *more than* that allows you to find satisfaction in your life, both at work and at home. It's the *more than* that can bring meaningful change to your community. And it's the *more than* that can change the world.

Why set small goals, right?

Carnegie helped start me on that ambitious path. But his groundbreaking book—an international bestseller even today, more than seventy years after it was first published in 1937—could only take me so far. I knew that I'd never stop using the techniques and principles he taught, but then I began digging much deeper into the value of great relationships and the ways to go about developing them.

And the more I've examined and dug, the more I've come to realize how much individuals and organizations—corporations, small businesses, foundations, governments, non-profits, churches, etc.—can benefit from the skills and attitudes that are essential for building deep, meaningful professional relationships. I'm not talking about relationships that get you a Christmas card. I'm talking about relationships that get you invited to Christmas dinner.

By standing on the shoulders of Carnegie's masterpiece, we

can live out a greater version of his message in the twenty-first century. We can use those timeless principles in ways that move beyond the tactical to the transformational. We can create customer loyalty that produces greater outcomes than ever imagined. We can discover how to make our influence matter—and how to win friends whose influence matters—throughout our organizations, with our clients and customers, and across our communities.

This level of commitment and loyalty is more important than ever. Carnegie wrote his book in the 1930s partly to fill a Depression-era void among the participants in the classes he taught on public speaking and human relationships. It started as a textbook, and the techniques, skills, and principles he offered unapologetically met the needs of its readers. It promised individual success in an era marked by massive failures.

Though the world has changed dramatically over the last seven decades, our economic climate compares all too closely to that of Carnegie's day. Failed financial institutions, depleted investment accounts, high unemployment, and a thick pall of uncertainty permeate the landscape. In such times, relationships—deep, lasting, "call me at 3:00 a.m. no matter what the reason" relationships—are the ultimate lifeline for people. Sometimes, in fact, our relationships with each other are all we've got.

Carnegie's principles and techniques seem timeless. And most are. That's why his book has sold more than 15 million copies. But it's time to broaden the scope and influence that were central to his message. It's no longer enough to just strategically use someone else's name. It's no longer enough to avoid an argument. It's no longer enough to talk about people's interests. Those are nice qualities and giving qualities. But you can't win long-term loyal friends and customers just by smiling, remembering people's names, and paying them compliments. There has to be more.

In our fiercely competitive world, those who separate themselves from the pack define the interests of *others* and work tirelessly to help them advance. Today, you need to go beyond the obvious all the way to what I call "Penthouse" relationships—relationships that move up from surface level of facts and social niceties (First and Second Floor relationships), past the exchange of opinions (Third Floor) and feelings (Fourth Floor), and into the Fifth Floor, the Penthouse reserved for complete transparency and marked by long-standing loyalty.

These types of relationships are possible. I've created dozens of them, many with customers, clients, neighbors, colleagues, and co-workers who started out as complete strangers. People see me as a connected and networked person, and that's true. My contact list runs long, but it's the quality and not the quantity that makes the difference—the mutual depth and devotion found in so many of them, and the rewards that come from seeing everyone—not just the high and mighty—as the potential next guest on the Fifth Floor.

I'll share the stories behind many of these relationships as we move throughout this book, from Mrs. Singer, the teacher who challenged and inspired me in high school, to the CEOs of some of the most successful organizations in the world. They all have influence that matters, and I've been fortunate to develop a level of influence with them.

Through their stories and the principles they represent, you'll see that taking your relationships to a higher level isn't just nice theory, but something everyone can and should internalize and live out on a daily basis so that it transforms your life, your organization, and your community.

Most people, of course, already understand the basic, practical importance of strong professional relationships. They willingly take advantage of all the technologies that weren't around in Carnegie's day. They have the latest software that tracks and mines every possible piece of data they can record about their customers and clients. They link-in, tweet, Facebook, blog, and Skype their way toward each new deal. And, of course, they feel as lost as a duck in the desert if they leave home without a cell phone that will text and e-mail and connect them to all their social networks on the Web. They know that there will always be another worthwhile "networking" tool on the horizon, and they'll use it like crazy when it comes out. But many people lack the skills, confidence, or motivation to build professional relationships that go beyond mere networking.

Some see themselves as relationship-challenged, not realizing that they're just as capable of building valued relationships as a dyslexic teenager was of earning two master's degrees (and writing a book!). Some just need direction and a gentle kick to get started. Some are "there" but can still grow, because we never really get to where we could be. Most, however, simply get by with whatever works because that's what they know.

It's comfortable.

It's safe.

And it's hollow.

Today's business world often suffers from "reactive syndrome." Building meaningful relationships is something we fall back on when we are in trouble. We "network," but we never move beyond our shallow, immediate needs. We never experience the fullness of deep, meaningful relationships. That, my friends, involves taking risks, and living well beyond the borders of reasonable expectations. It's about really understanding and caring about the aspirations of others, and asking what we can do to help them meet or exceed those aspirations. And then actually going out and doing those things.

When I look back at how the power of relationships lifted me—a skinny kid with a lisp, below-average grades, and a learning disability—out of a middle-class community and put me in leadership positions that took me all around the world, I can boil it down to this: It's not about me. At every turn, whether it was in student government, playing football, working as a waiter during college, traveling internationally, selling software for Lotus Development, leading organizations, starting my own companies, or consulting with the leaders of large corporations and institutions, the most powerful benchmarks of my success involved relationships in which my focus was on helping others.

That type of focus generates what I call Return on Relationship, or ROR, and the power of ROR is great and varied. For the organization, it's an economic driver, not some motivational HR mandate. For the individual, it's not only a quicker path up the corporate ladder, but a more joyful, fulfilling experience along the way. For the community, it's greater outreach, more sincere participation, and, most of all, a positive force for change.

That's the *more than* that can make all the difference.

That's the *more than* that can make the world spin better.

Relationship Discoveries

Chapter 1

An Unlikely Prodigy

Every father hopes for a child prodigy—the next great physicist or musician or artist or athlete or scholar—and I suspect my dad was no different. But, smart man that he is, my dad realized early on that my ticket to success would take me on a different train.

It was pretty clear that I wasn't going to win a Nobel Prize for physics, paint any modern masterpieces, write any critically acclaimed concertos, or make it as an infielder in the major leagues. But he saw the glimmer of another gift in me. And that's why he picked out the book he put in my hands during my early teens. That's when the other boys had growth spurts that I didn't. That's when the testing my parents had done confirmed I had a learning disability and that I trailed my peers in such areas as reading comprehension by as much as two years. Reality whispered a message into my dad's kind ears. My father, the schoolteacher, knew what lessons I most needed to learn, and they had little to do with conjugating verbs or solving complex mathematical problems or memorizing historic dates.

"Son," he told me, "your mother is going to insist that you read one book—the Bible. And I'm going to ask that you read this one." And with that he handed me a copy of *How to Win Friends & Influence People* by Dale Carnegie.

I was in college before the experts accurately diagnosed my

disability as dyslexia. As a result, reading any book in junior high made my head spin. I doubt I read more than three or four books before I graduated from high school. But because it was a gift and a request from my father, I read this one cover to cover; the quick-hit principles and insights in Dale Carnegie's classic self-help book gave me exactly what I needed as I pressed on through high school, encountering hurdle after hurdle along the academic track. The book provided a road map that eventually took me to levels of success I never would have envisioned. But to understand the importance of Carnegie's book in my life, you need to understand where I came from and a few of the relationships that shaped me.

My journey—in academics, in business, and in life—took some interesting, nontraditional, and, quite frankly, painful twists and turns. I struggled with (and still struggle with) many of the things most people say are essential for success—readin', 'ritin', and 'rithmatic, for starters. But I learned at an early age how to leverage my strengths and overcome my weaknesses. I learned the value of a fourth "R"—relationships.

I not only learned the art of winning friends and influencing people, but of *mastering* relationships, personally and professionally. This book is about creating those kinds of relationships— the kind that can change your life, change your organization, and change your world. Because business is about relationships. Success is about relationships. Leadership is about relationships. Life is about relationships.

The village of Suffern, New York, sits peacefully near the base of the Ramapo Mountains just twenty-six miles northwest of New York City. The eleven thousand or so residents form a community within a patchwork of other tight-knit towns and villages, where a mix of blue-collar workers and big-city commuters represent the best of colonial heritage and urban grit.

My parents raised me there on a steady diet of traditional family values that placed high importance on serving others, and a great emphasis on hard work and education.

The serving and hard work came easily. The education, however, was another matter—nothing melted my spirits faster, like hot asphalt on an August day.

I feared being called stupid by my teachers and classmates—because I believed that was what my grades indicated. I failed classes outright, or passed by the skin of my teeth, only to fail the end-of-year standardized tests and have to attend summer school to make up the credit—all while working on my homework and studies as hard as, and usually harder than, the other kids I knew.

My self-confidence took a beating. The more embarrassed I became by my grades, the more I tried to compensate by achieving things in non-academic areas—participating in athletics, running for student government, earning Eagle Scout honors. In much the same way as a blind person experiences sensory compensation, I seemed to make up for my academic limitations with a heightened ability to communicate with and connect to other people. I don't know how much of this was in my nature and how much was nurtured by those around me (and by Dale Carnegie's book), but it was as real as rain.

I had the ability, it seemed, to make friends with *everybody*.

I didn't smoke, drink (much), or do drugs, but I chatted easily with those who did. I wasn't into Dungeons & Dragons, but those who were treated me like a brother. (You can befriend all sorts of kids in the school Resource Room.) I wasn't physically gifted, but I was captain of the ski team and played soccer, baseball, and football. I was in the school's show choir and in musicals. I mixed as easily with the students in the chess club as I did with the jocks on the athletic teams. Every clique was my clique. I was elected senior class president and voted "most friendly" and "did most for Suffern High" by my peers.

And it wasn't just with the students. All the teachers at Suffern High knew my name, and I knew theirs. I knew the janitorial staff. I knew all the secretaries and administration. And I knew most of their family members.

Building those relationships came naturally to me. But seeing relationship-building as a gift, and not as a crutch to compensate for my academic weakness, was part of a maturation process that took years of painful struggle.

I learned early on that my educational path would be different from those of most of my friends. As early as elementary school, I became intimately familiar with the Resource Room— that place where those with special needs went to get extra help. For three years, in fact, I spent part of each school day making the embarrassing walk to that room, trying to correct a lisp by placing a device between the tip of my tongue and the roof of my mouth.

And the "regular" classroom wasn't a refuge. I remember the heart-gripping fear I felt whenever our teacher decided to have the class do a little "round-robin reading." We'd get out our books and a student in the front of the class would begin by reading a paragraph aloud. Then the next student would read the next paragraph aloud, and the next student the next paragraph, until we'd worked our way through all the students and finished whatever passage the teacher had selected.

Sweat would cover the palms of my hands, and a knot the size of a football would form in my stomach as the other kids read. I knew I'd stutter and stammer through my passage, and everyone would see further evidence that I was the only person in the class who couldn't read. From my seat near the back of the room, I'd count the sixteen kids who sat ahead of me. Then I'd count seventeen paragraphs into the passage to find my paragraph. I'd block out the noise of the other kids reading. I'd focus intently on my paragraph, willing myself to make out each word, and I'd commit them to memory before the class got to me. My memory often carried me through. When I looked at the words on the pages, the letters spun around out of focus like images in a kaleidoscope. But if I had enough time to memorize the paragraph, I'd be able to sail through and disguise my inability to read. If not, I'd *feel* a deep-rooted shame as my peers fought to hold back their giggles and stares and embarrassment.

Dyslexia is not something you can fix; you live with it every day. That reality hit me painfully, for example, when my grandmother died in 2009. About an hour before the service, one of the nuns—my aunt, Sister Loreen—asked if I'd do one of the three scripture readings. When she showed me the verse, all I could make out were a bunch of big and unfamiliar words, and my hands immediately turned cold and sweaty. I looked at my aunt apologetically and begged off, saying, "I'd rather not."

Just a few months shy of my fortieth birthday, I still found myself—an accomplished public speaker—overcome by my fear of *reading* in public. Given more time, I would have memorized the verse and "read" it without looking at the pages. Instead, I missed an opportunity to honor a woman I dearly loved.

Away from the books, meanwhile, I always flourished. Like most young boys, I had a high energy level, but I was well-mannered and worked hard, so my teachers loved me, and I got along with all my classmates.

As I moved into the junior-high years, it became clear that my learning struggles weren't just the mark of a late bloomer.

Numbers and letters looked as if they'd been pulled randomly from a bag of Scrabble tiles, and my visits to the Resource Room became like a scarlet letter sewn across my backpack. Looking back, I probably was fortunate not to take more teasing from my peers. But my own battles with self-doubt at times felt like more than I could bear. Even when the other kids said nothing, I knew that they knew, and that was bad enough.

While my friends played baseball and went to summer camps, my dad drove me to summer school following ninth, tenth, and eleventh grades. I took some classes because I had to, and others because I needed to improve my end-of-course test scores to have any hope of getting into college.

For most people who knew me (and my academic record), the idea of college seemed a foolish dream. At the start of my senior year, in fact, I found myself sitting in the office of David Tilton, one of the guidance counselors. Because he didn't frequent the Resource Room and I'd never gotten into any trouble as a student, this was the first time I'd met Mr. Tilton. I walked into his office to find a tall, thin gentleman wearing a navy blue plaid suit and a tie with a big, poorly made knot. His hair shot out in a million directions. I eased into a chair, not knowing what to expect from him. I was a little surprised when he said, "So tell me where you want to go to college." Maybe I'd found an advocate, I thought. I told him I wanted to go to Notre Dame or Boston College, and that I was interested in business and politics.

Mr. Tilton pulled out my file. He looked at my transcripts and then looked at me. I knew what was coming. "Do you know what your GPA is?" he asked. I did: not good. "Do you know your SAT score?" I did: not good. (Even after taking an SAT prep course, I'd only managed to improve my original 640 score to a 680 out of 1,600.) "Do you know your class ranking?" I did: not good.

Then, as nicely as possible, Mr. Tilton talked about what I'd need to get into college. And by the end of the conversation he was gently suggesting that a junior college or trade school might better fit my needs. He wasn't being mean; he was just telling me my grades indicated I wasn't ready for the academic rigors of a university.

I went home totally deflated, not because I thought I was too good for junior colleges or trade schools. They serve a great purpose, and for many people they are the perfect fit to help them achieve their dreams. In some ways, I had a wrong-headed notion that I "had to go to college" to be successful. And I also rightly believed that I'd have a better chance of achieving my personal goals with a college degree. Mostly, though, Mr. Tilton's message unwittingly reinforced my self-doubt.

I had experienced similar days when the SAT scores arrived and all the other kids were announcing their results while I did my best to hide mine. I knew my grades weren't good. But all of my smart-kid friends were talking about going to Michigan or Cornell or other top-flight schools, and the reality of my situation hit me like a locomotive.

I remember telling my dad how disappointed I was that I wasn't going to get into a good college. But my father kept encouraging me. Forever my biggest fan, my father would always tell me three things: first, living with goodness in your heart counts more than good grades; second, you have an obligation to make a contribution to this country. Democracy isn't free. Instead of focusing on your grades, focus on what your contribution will be. And, third, those people in your class who are making A's and B's—they're going to work for you one day. (He turned out to be right. I've hired a lot of people who went to Ivy League schools and earned impressive grades and SAT scores.)

By the time of my senior-year visit with Mr. Tilton, however, I'd already come to grips with my academic weaknesses, and such setbacks didn't keep me down for long. The more rejection I experienced, the harder I worked.

My personal tipping point had come during my sophomore year, when I was enrolled in Mrs. Deanne Singer's semester-long merchandise marketing class. I liked Mrs. Singer. She was inspiring and full of energy. She was a bit eccentric, but she made class fun. She knew all the students' names. She cared. Also, I did pretty well in her class. I had a C average, which was a *very* good grade for me, when she assigned the final exam project—to come up with an idea for a company and write a seven-to-ten-page business plan for it.

For the first time, I found myself energized about an academic project. I'm someone who has a hundred ideas a day for businesses, but I had never written anything down, much less come up with a marketing plan or done a competitive analysis or thought through pricing. I just dreamed up business ideas, filed them away in my mind, and then moved along to the next one. Now I had a chance to pull one out and see if it might really work.

My dad grew up in Saratoga Springs, New York, home of the oldest thoroughbred racetrack in America. So one of my business dreams was to open a restaurant in Saratoga Springs called Winners & Losers—a five-star restaurant separated by a glass wall from a pub on the other side.

Gamblers who won at the racetrack could order escargot, steaks, and fine wine served on real china, while seated at linen-covered cherrywood tables surrounded by plush red-carpeted floors. The waiters would wear jockey outfits, and the walls would be decorated with pictures of famous horses, jockeys, and owners. On the pub side, patrons who were less flush could order hot dogs, hamburgers, and nachos. The concrete floor would be littered with peanut shells and torn-up betting tickets.

I went to work writing a business plan for the restaurant. My dad drove me three hours north to Saratoga Springs to do a competitive analysis of the restaurants there. Amazingly, none of them at the time had betting or racetrack themes. We even found the perfect location for our restaurant, an old Victorian house across the street from the racetrack that was for sale for $74,000. (Today that property's worth more than a million. Clearly we should have bought it!)

I covered everything. I even wrote out a SWOT analysis (Strengths, Weaknesses, Opportunities, and Threats). I was more excited about that project than about anything I'd done in school—well, anything that didn't involve sports or girls.

About two weeks after handing in the project, Mrs. Singer returned it with my grade: an A-plus. An A-plus! I'd never gotten an A of any sort before. I'd never gotten a B before, except maybe in gym. I was standing as tall as the New York City skyline. Then I looked underneath the grade and read Mrs. Singer's note: "Tommy, this is excellent work. Whoever did this for you, please tell them they did a great job. —Mrs. Singer."

I was upset. I mean, really angry. I had worked my behind off on this project. OK, she was right, my friends usually helped me through my course work. But I did the work on this project completely on my own. I stormed up to her after class, and said, "Mrs. Singer, this is crazy! I did all the work on this project myself." She only half-believed me. She said, "Tommy, you haven't demonstrated this kind of work all semester. I don't know how you did this, because this is exceptional work." And I looked directly into her eyes and said, "I swear, Mrs. Singer, I did this myself."

"If you did this," Mrs. Singer said, "then you have to join DECA."

DECA (Distributive Education Clubs of America) was the club for students interested in marketing and business. So not only did I join the club, but I entered my business plan in the DECA state championship against the plans of hundreds of other students. My fifteen-page plan grew to more than seventy pages, and I took it to the Concord Hotel in upstate New York, where I spent my first night in a hotel without my parents. And I returned home with a trophy for second place!

I'd never won anything academically before, and suddenly I was one of two students from New York State who had qualified for the national competition. A few weeks later I was getting on a plane for the first time in my life, to Atlanta, where I would compete against some of the brightest students in the nation.

I went to Atlanta expecting nothing more than a great field trip. I got to see a Braves baseball game, and visited the world headquarters of CNN and Coca-Cola. But to my surprise, my business plan for Winners & Losers finished in the money—third place in the nation! Figuratively speaking, I was on the winner's side of the academic glass for a change!

It was the first time I began to recognize entrepreneurship as my gift. When I spoke to the committee of business leaders who had volunteered to act as a mock venture capitalist group, I realized that my ability to communicate verbally extended to groups of people, and that other people were drawn to my passion for my ideas.

Mrs. Singer was the first teacher to see my raw abilities and urge me to reach higher. A lot of teachers gave me a passing grade because I was a nice kid, I was well respected, I never got in trouble, and I did all of my homework. But Mrs. Singer brought out something more in me. If she hadn't given me an A-plus and written that dismissive comment, I wouldn't have been pissed off and she never would have challenged me to join DECA. Mrs. Singer saw something in me that I didn't see in myself; she encouraged me to take risks and become a leader.

At the same time, I was already becoming a leader in non-academic circles. In my sophomore year I earned the rank of Eagle Scout, the youngest in our troop to do so. I'm told only two percent of all Boy Scouts become Eagle Scouts. If anything, it's a reflection of how driven I was to prove myself outside the classroom, but I learned a great deal along the way.

For my Eagle badge, I organized the renovation of an old carriage garage of our church parsonage. The church often ran food and clothing drives for the needy; I put together work crews and we gutted the unused garage, built shelves, and turned it into a pantry for food and clothing. I found people from all over town and from all walks of life to help. In the process I learned you can't do all the work yourself, nor do leaders have all the answers. But they do have to get other people involved.

Between my sophomore and junior years, I also was one of two students picked for the Rotary Youth Leadership Academy (RYLA), a five-day leadership camp that significantly shaped my thinking.

There were about a hundred kids at RYLA, from all the schools in the district. Probably the single most important lesson I learned there came from a speech by Tom France, the Rotarian who had nominated me for RYLA. "The world consists of three types of people—leaders, followers, and critics," he told us. "The most important question you have to ask yourself is which one are you going to be."

I had never thought of leadership as a choice rather than as something we were born with, but it was a message I quickly embraced with newfound energy and passion.

Back at school, I was elected vice president of my junior class, beating out a popular girl who had held the office during our sophomore year. I started thinking about school in a different way. I had a sense of confidence and purpose. My grades didn't improve during junior and senior years, but I had decided I wasn't going to let my grades, my GPA, and my SAT scores define me. I shifted my attention to what I could do, rather than getting caught up in what I couldn't.

During my junior year, I took an accounting class from Mrs. Dizzine, an older woman with a strict temperament, whose personality must have been surgically removed at an early age. I got a D, barely passing her class. At the end of the semester, she pulled me aside to talk about my future. When I told her I wanted to go to college and then go to business school, she looked me in the eye and said, "Tommy, you'll be lucky if you get into college, much less business school."

In that moment, I couldn't fight off a sense of discouragement. So I slunk with my tail between my legs to see Mrs. Singer, who quickly set me straight. When I ran into people who didn't believe in me, she told me, "Tell them to kiss your ass!" It was a typical "Singer zinger."

Mrs. Singer recognized and cultivated my leadership potential. When I ran for senior class president, she and my father helped orchestrate my campaign. Mrs. Singer ran the school store and used the printing machine to make buttons (VOTE FOR TOM FOR A GREAT PROM) and T-shirts promoting my candidacy. My father made papier-mâché flowers, each featuring a different one of my "Thomas's Promises." And I easily defeated the guy who had been class president our junior year.

Somehow, though, I knew that the goal wasn't to be popular. It wasn't *just* to win friends and influence people. I didn't fully understand what *more* there was, but I knew my popularity—that precious foundation that provided stability for my fragile self-confidence—came with an equal measure of responsibility. "Ego biscuits" were nice, but there had to be more to living a life of purpose than just feeding my self-esteem.

I began to learn that relationships led to influence, and it was what I did with that influence that mattered. It wasn't just about winning an election; it was about getting things done that helped other people.

When we wanted to hold a junior prom, I led the team that organized it. And when I realized our senior prom had grown too expensive for many of the students to attend, I went to the administration and pitched an idea for a fund-raiser—a competition pitting the top garage bands from our school against each other. Our vice-principal didn't think the idea would work, but he gave us a green light to go ahead with it. And we raised more money than any fund-raiser in school history.

When I didn't find leadership opportunities, they seemed to find me. That's how I ended up on the school's football team in my senior year, and that's how I found myself speaking at a tense school board meeting.

I was an average soccer player at Suffern High; my position was left bench. The coach hardly ever put me in the game, and if he did, it was usually for the last two minutes in a lopsided victory. What mattered to our coach was how we performed as players—he wasn't interested in our development as individuals.

I didn't realize what a disadvantage this was until I got to know Bob Veltidi, the Suffern varsity football coach. Coach Veltidi approached me in the hallway near the end of my junior year and asked me to come to his office. I didn't know the football coach, had never played football, and didn't know why he wanted to meet with me. When I arrived in his office, he asked me if I liked playing soccer. I respectfully said no. He asked me if I'd ever tried kicking a football. No, I told him. Then he asked me, "Would you like a chance to be a part of my football team?" I thought it over for a few minutes and said, "Sure. Why not?"

Coach Veltidi gave me a bag of footballs and a kicking tee and told me to practice kicking field goals. He told me football tryouts were at the beginning of August, and he expected me to be there, ready to play. He told me he believed in me. I had never heard those words from a coach before—certainly not from the varsity football coach.

That summer I went to the football field every day, seven days a week, rain or shine, and practiced kicking the football for hours. I kicked hundreds of footballs, and eventually I started kicking the ball through the goal posts—from fifteen yards, twenty yards, twenty-five yards, even thirty yards out.

My little sister, Michele, often came to the field to catch or fetch the balls. One time she sprained her thumb while trying to catch a ball, and, to my embarrassment, I made her wait until I was finished kicking all two hundred field goals before we went home.

When I showed up at tryouts in August, I was ready. I put on a football uniform for the first time, and some of the other players teased me a bit. But they shut up when they saw me kick a field goal from thirty yards out. Coach Veltidi was impressed enough to give me jersey number one and put me on the varsity team as Suffern High School's starting field-goal kicker. It was the first time in my sporting career that I felt like I mattered.

Coach Veltidi always asked about my activities before and

after practice. Because he treated me like a leader on the team, I eventually became one. He always told us that being a football player was more about leadership off the field than on. I believed him, and I believed in him. And he believed in me.

After working so hard all summer practicing to make the squad, I was excited about playing in our first game. There was just one problem: as the start of the fall term neared, a strike by the teachers' union threatened to keep the school doors locked.

Mrs. Singer encouraged me to attend a school board meeting just a few days before the scheduled start of classes. I was the incoming senior class president, but I also was a veteran of many summer school classes and I knew my 2.0 GPA wasn't going to impress the board. But I went anyway—partly because I didn't want us to forfeit our first home football game.

I'd never been to a school board meeting before, but even I realized that this one was particularly tense. Teachers and employees of the school filled the auditorium, and they were pretty much at war with the twelve people on stage—the board of education. Anger and contention filled the air as each side argued its points and dismissed those of the other. It quickly became clear there wasn't going to be an agreement that evening.

At the end of the meeting, however, school board chairman Scott Vanderhoef asked if anyone had anything to say. I'm pretty sure I was the only student in the auditorium, and I know I was the only person to raise a hand. Standing in front of the microphone, I spoke for about twenty minutes about the fact that both of my parents were teachers, and how some of the greatest people in my life were the teachers at Suffern High School who believed in me. I told them we were about to start the new school year and play our first home football game, and that we needed a united school. We needed to get the contract done and put it behind us.

My unrehearsed twenty-minute pep talk received a standing ovation. And after my speech, they reopened new business and approved a contract for the teachers. The next day's newspaper even gave credit to me for inspiring the board to finish its work on the contract.

My role in the events of that night made me proud, of course, but I also realized something bigger. You can make a real impact if you speak from the heart. I didn't go up there with a grand strategy for changing minds and inspiring action. I just shared the feelings in my heart. And because I'd developed relationships of trust and respect—based on who I was as a person, not on how I performed in the classroom or on the athletic fields—the board took me seriously.

We played and won that first home football game of the season. In fact, we had a great team that year. Danny Munoz was one of the best quarterbacks in school history, and we won the first seven games. Although I kicked a lot of extra points, I went the first three games without even attempting a field goal because Danny Munoz's arm always put Suffern High in the end zone.

Then came the Saturday afteroon showdown with the Clarkstown North Rams.

Fans packed the Clarkstown North stadium, and, as expected, the game was a close one. Clarkstown North had a 21–19 lead with just twenty-two seconds left to play in the game. We had the ball at the Rams' twenty-yard line, but it was fourth down. Coach Veltidi had to decide between a Hail Mary pass by all-star Danny Munoz and a thirty-seven-yard field-goal attempt by Tommy Spaulding—my first of the season.

I nearly had a heart attack when he called the kicking crew onto the field. I went to Coach Veltidi and told him he should put Danny Munoz back on the field. I had never kicked a winning field goal before, and certainly had never kicked a thirty-seven-yarder. And I had missed an extra-point attempt earlier in the game. Then he whispered some of the most significant words I've ever heard in my life: "Spaulding, I asked you to be on this team because I believed in who you were as a person, not just as a player. I saw that you were a leader. I saw that you had character. I saw that you had tenacity. Now go out there and kick that field goal and win this game for us. I believe in you, son!"

As I walked onto the field to the roar of the mostly hostile home crowd, I could nearly taste the bile in my stomach. The Clarkstown North coach called time out to "ice" the kicker—me—and I stood in the middle of the field for a few more minutes, waiting for my big moment in front of a thousand people. My legs were shaking. My heart was beating like the pistons in a racecar. But my mind was peacefully relaxed, back on the practice field with my little sister kicking field goals on a hot summer day.

When the whistle blew, the ball was snapped, and I kicked it.

"The kick is GOOD!" shouted the announcer. "The kick is GOOD!"

Suffern High won the game 22–21. I was carried off the field like a conquering hero and made the front page of the local newspaper: SUFFERN WINS ON SPAULDING'S KICK. The game became a legend in our school and in our town's history.

All these years later, however, what has meant the most to me wasn't the football game or the kick or the accolades. What has meant most to me was my relationship with Coach Veltidi. He gave me the opportunity to play football in my senior year; he gave me an opportunity to be a part of something greater than myself. And, most of all, much like Mrs. Singer, he gave me the opportunity to believe in myself and to respond to his belief in me.

Ten years after I graduated from high school, I saw Coach Veltidi again and I asked him why he had invited me to try out. There were several kids on the soccer team he could have asked who were much better players than I was. He said, "I wanted to build a team around leadership, and you were the most respected leader in the school."

When it came time to look at colleges, only two—Johnson & Wales University and Springfield College—showed an interest in me, Springfield because I could kick field goals and Johnson & Wales because of my involvement in DECA. My two best friends in high school—Corey Turer and Lori Nolan (who also was my first love and my longtime sweetheart)—were heading to Springfield College, so that's where I planned to go.

Part of me realized Mr. Tilton was right about how well prepared I was for college, but my mind was fixed on that goal even if I didn't have many options. Then, out of nowhere, the door of opportunity literally stood open right in front of me.

One February day in 1987, Lori and I were walking down the hall when we heard music coming from the school auditorium. We peeked in and saw the cast of Up with People rehearsing for its performance.

Up with People is a nonprofit that puts together casts of young people who perform all over the world while building community service and leadership skills. I knew they were in town because I did the morning announcements over the school PA system and because my family had signed up to host two of the cast members. I remembered watching an Up with People group perform during halftime at the 1986 Super Bowl between the Chicago Bears (I was a huge fan of Jim McMahon, the quarterback of the Bears) and the New England Patriots. But I had yet to meet the two cast members who were staying in our home, so I knew very little about how the organization worked. And I had no idea about how big a role Up with People would play in shaping my life.

As we stood in the auditorium doorway, one of the cast members looked at us and yelled, "Hey, Number One" several times until I finally realized I was wearing my football jersey that day and that he was talking to me. So we walked over and met Brian Kanter, a twenty-three-year-old from Kinston, North Carolina, who was working the sound system in the back.

Brian, with his bulging biceps and an accent straight out of Andy Griffith's Mayberry, was the opposite of the stereotype I had in my mind for an Up with People cast member. We talked for several minutes and made an immediate connection, and Lori and I promised we'd be there for the show.

The next night, Lori and I sat up front as a hundred young adults from twenty-five countries sang and performed. Seeing all these very different people on stage working together, I couldn't help wondering why the world couldn't work together like that—black, white, Asian; people from all different countries, religions, and backgrounds.

I'd never been out of the country. I'd only been on a plane a couple of times in my life. Heck, my exposure to other cultures came mainly from movies. But as Brian sang the closing song—"We'll Be There"—I leaned over and told Lori, "That's what I want to do."

At the end of the show, the cast interviewed anyone between the ages of seventeen and twenty-six who thought they might be interested in traveling with Up with People. So I watched a twenty-minute video, interviewed, and filled out an application. Two months later I got a letter from Glen Shepherd, the director of admissions with Up with People. Out of eight thousand annual applications, I was one of five hundred from around the world selected to participate in one of the five international casts.

For a guy who had applied to dozens of colleges and had been rejected by all but two, this was a huge deal. So I went to my parents and asked if I could take a year off before college; thank God, I had parents who saw the bigger picture. The only obstacle was the cost. The tuition was $7,300 (a lot of money back in 1987). Also, I needed a round-trip ticket to Tucson and spending money. My parents didn't have that kind of money. If I wanted to go, my parents said, I'd have to raise the money myself.

Up with People encouraged fund-raising and sent me a pamphlet with more than a hundred ideas on how to do so, but by now it was April, so I only had about ninety days to come up with the $8,000 I needed. It turned into a huge lesson in the power of the relationships I had built during my young life.

Tom France and the Suffern Rotary Club supported a fund-raising spaghetti dinner that I held. My father and I produced an "Up with Tommy Pancake Breakfast Show" at our church. My mother led the crew that cooked pancakes and sausages, and the priest and nuns directed patrons from the early services down to the basement cafeteria. McDonald's, one of the places I had worked while in high school, donated the food. Around five hundred people showed up. My next-door neighbor, Mrs. Warren, who worked at PepsiCo's world headquarters, encouraged me to write a letter asking Pepsi to be a sponsor. In exchange for their sponsorship, I told them I'd wear Pepsi-Cola T-shirts, place Pepsi bumper stickers on my suitcase, and spread the word about Pepsi-Cola to people worldwide. And Pepsi came through—they gave me $3,000. We raffled off a Sony Walkman and a year's worth of Domino's Pizza (another place where I had worked), and the football team sold tickets. I even sold stock in myself, sending letters to a hundred relatives and friends saying that "Tommy Spaulding Inc." was going to change the world. That was the dividend they could expect—that I'd give back to the world. And I raised $1,000 with my stock offering. The bottom line—three months later I had the $8,000 I needed.

I left to join Up with People in July 1987. I spent a year traveling the world as the youngest member of a cast of one hundred people from twenty countries. It helped me gain an incredible sense of confidence and learn lifelong lessons about working with people of different backgrounds, races, and cultures. The group became very close, building tremendous trust between us. I was able to take risks, fail, grow, and find my own path for the future. I built friendships that made good times better, but that also loved me through my first significant tragedy.

We were in Palm Springs, Florida, when the cast manager told me I had some news from home and took me to the staff hotel for a phone call. This was before cell phones, and because the cast traveled every three days, phone calls were rare and often brought bad news. I feared something had happened to my grandparents. When I got on the phone, both of my parents were crying. They told me that Lori Nolan, my first love and the girl I had dated since seventh grade, had died of meningitis while at Springfield College—just one day after her nineteenth birthday.

Lori was more than a first love. She had been my best friend. She was extremely popular at our school. An athlete, Lori played basketball, field hockey, and lacrosse. Our high school retired her number when she died. She was inducted into the school's athletics hall of fame. An overflow crowd of friends and family came to the funeral; I couldn't stop the tears from rolling down my face as I saw her lying in the casket, barely nineteen years of age, wearing the same violet dress and lace collar that she'd worn to the prom. It was the first time anyone that I was close to had died. It brought home to me that I couldn't take anything for granted in life. Tomorrow isn't promised to any of us.

Springfield College had given me a year's deferral in terms of starting school so that I could keep my commitment to Up with People. After Lori died, however, the last thing I wanted to do was go to Springfield. When I rejoined Up with People in Florida following Lori's funeral, I told my good friend Brian Kanter that I wanted to enroll in a new college and live in a different part of the country.

Brian asked if I'd heard of East Carolina University. As it turned out, I had a cousin, Joey Welsh, who was a senior there. It sounded like a great place, but I told Brian I didn't think I had the grades to get in. Brian called his father, and he helped get me a one-on-one interview. So I made my way from our tour stop in Columbia, South Carolina, to Greenville, North Carolina, where my cousin picked me up and took me to a meeting with the admissions counselor. They agreed to accept me that fall, after my tour with Up with People was over.

At every turn, it seemed to me, the power of relationships had influenced my direction. My relationship with Brian Kanter couldn't have been more unlikely. In many ways, we are complete opposites. I'm a Christian; he's Jewish. I'm a Republican; he's a Democrat. I'm a Yankee; he's a Southerner. I'm a New York Giants fan; he's a New Orleans Saints fan. And yet a chance meeting at a high school auditorium provided the seeds that blossomed into a lifelong friendship. Twenty years later, Brian is the closest thing I have to a brother.

Those types of relationships—hundreds of them through the years—have helped me grow from a doubt-filled adolescent who survived largely on the hopes that others would like me, into a confident leader who has learned that the power of relationships is not in what those relationships can do for me, but in what they can do for others.

That's the measure of true success.

In fact, the single greatest accomplishment in my life has nothing to do with earning academic degrees, how much money I've made, starting and leading companies and organizations, or winning awards. No, here's what it would be: a fund-raiser for Lori Nolan.

In July 2005, eighteen years after I graduated from Suffern High and flew to Tucson to join a cast of one hundred that included Brian Kanter, I stepped into the role of president and CEO of Up with People. The organization, dormant for three years because of financial problems, hired me to bring it back to life. We still had offices in four countries, but we shrank our staff to fewer than one hundred people and the budget down to about $10 million a year. In addition to making cuts and reorganizing the business, I spent much of my time rebuilding relationships with donors and working to get our shows back into high-profile events.

One of the first initiatives I worked on was getting Up with People a performance in the 2007 Macy's Thanksgiving Day parade in New York City. At the same time, I was responsible for organizing the twenty-year reunion for my high school class because I had been president of our senior class. So we held the reunion that Thanksgiving weekend, and I brought the Up with People cast from New York City to Suffern High for a fund-raiser performance to benefit the scholarship fund in Lori's name.

That night, we honored Lori's memory and replenished the near-empty scholarship fund with thousands of dollars. My parents were there. Tom France was there (the Suffern Rotary Club was a sponsor of the event). Mrs. Singer was there. Hundreds of my high school classmates and friends were there. And most of Lori's family members were there.

I handed her parents a program with a photo of Lori on the cover, then walked them into the packed auditorium, down the aisle, to the two end seats on the fourth row—the very seats Lori and I had sat in that night almost twenty years earlier when we watched Up with People perform. I sat next to Mr. and Mrs. Nolan, and we watched the show together. The three of us cried. And as we sat together, tears in our eyes, smiling, I was struck by the meaning of it all: You don't have be a prodigy to change the world.

Chapter 2

The Bartender

The restaurant bar in upstate New York felt like a morgue, which seemed appropriate at the time since I felt like I was about to die.

Even a short but good night's sleep at my parents' nearby home in Suffern, New York, couldn't cure the jet lag I had from sitting in economy class for nearly thirteen hours straight. I had endured the 6,744 air miles from Tokyo to JFK and driven to the restaurant bar for one reason and one reason only—to take my shot at winning the prestigious Rotary International Ambassadorial Scholarship. I needed to clear the cobwebs from my head and put on my game face before my turn came to interview with the scholarship's selection committee.

Nine recent college graduates sat scattered around the room, each sitting alone, one to a table, but collectively giving off enough cold vibes to turn the restaurant into a meat locker. I might have struggled reading books like *War and Peace*, but I could read their faces: "Stand clear," they said.

As finalists for the scholarship, the ten of us were hanging out together—or alone but in the same room—as we awaited our turn with the selection committee.

Until I walked into that bar/morgue, I had felt pretty confident. I was one of ten finalists, after all. They wouldn't have asked me to fly home from halfway around the world if they hadn't seen me as a top contender. Then I noticed the name tags worn by the other nine competitors—Harvard, MIT, Princeton, Penn, Cornell, Dartmouth—and I looked down at mine. East Carolina University.

This was no slam-dunk.

After scanning the room, I followed their verbal cues and found my way toward the only friendly face I saw—the one behind the bar.

This was 1996. I had no laptop, no Blackberry, no access to the Internet, no handheld game player, and no music player loaded with a thousand songs. And I wasn't one to sit alone flipping through a magazine or a book for what I knew would be a long wait. My last name starts with an *S*, which meant I'd be among the last to go in for the interview. So I ordered a Diet Pepsi and kept company with the bartender as he went about his routine chores.

As it turned out, the bartender owned the restaurant, just like his father before him and his father's father before them both. And it seemed very likely the four-year-old boy playing behind the bar would one day own it too.

It was a good life, the bartender told me as I nursed that Diet Pepsi. He told me all about growing up in a restaurant family in upstate New York, about the joys and perils of parenthood, and about the trials and rewards of running a small business. He broke out the family photo album as he told me all about his life, and—although I had no idea at the time—he changed the course of mine.

I was just grateful for the diversion that came with sitting on that barstool. Listening to his stories, if nothing else, would keep me from thinking too much about my own anxieties.

After all, I was in the restaurant bar as part of Plan B in the Tommy Spaulding Master Plan for Success. Naturally inclined to take risks, I had risked everything I had to get there. And after eyeballing the Ivy League opposition sitting in the room, moving on to Plan C, whatever that might be, seemed highly likely.

Plan A hadn't been so modest—I had decided to become governor of New York. I always saw politics as an honor and a privilege—a chance to really serve others. And after successful stints as senior class president in both high school and college, I dreamed of going to law school and then climbing the political ladder until it took me all the way to Albany.

I hit a few bumps along that road, however. I had a 4.0 grade point average in high school and college, for instance, but only if you added the two together. While I was living in Japan and teaching English in Kisofukushima-machi, a village of about eight thousand people nestled in the Nagano Alps, I rode a train two and a half hours each way on the weekends to take a course to help improve my score on the law school entrance exam. I studied and studied, and still my score came in well below the average.

Realistic but undeterred, I began applying to law schools back in the United States. To increase my odds, I applied to the bottom thirty accredited law schools in the country. (At fifty bucks a pop for the application fees, and with only about $1,800 in my savings account, I couldn't afford a thirty-first application.) I even applied to North Carolina Central University School of Law, where I hoped the admissions committee might take me on as a "minority" student at the predominately African-American campus. It didn't. In fact, in 1995 the Japanese mailman delivered to Mr. Thomas J. Spaulding Jr., teacher of English in Japan, aspiring attorney and would-be governor of New York, thirty rejection letters.

"Thank you for your interest, Mr. Spaulding, but we regret . . ."

"We are sorry to inform you . . ."

"After careful consideration, the selection committee has declined your application . . ."

I didn't even know there were thirty different ways to tell someone to take a hike.

With Plan A in the trash bin, I got on a plane and headed to Bali, Indonesia, for some snorkeling, scuba diving, and soul-searching. Those rejection letters were a crushing blow to my hopes and dreams, and frankly I wasn't sure what to do next. My confidence wasn't shattered, but it was severely cracked. There were sleepless nights when I wondered if I would have been better off staying back in Suffern. Had I just set myself up for failure after failure, I wondered.

One day, however, I took a day trip to Lovina Beach, on the northern coast of Bali. I figured a walk along the sandy shores, some snorkeling, and a chance to swim with the famous black dolphins might lift my spirits. And it did. But what really revived them was a conversation on the boat with Chuck Colman and Sarah Gay, a couple from Atlanta who had also signed up for the excursion.

I felt almost immediately comfortable with this couple, and before I knew it I was telling them my life story. I shared and they listened, and I figured that little bit of therapy was worth the price of the snorkel trip. Then Sarah gave me an unexpected gift: "You have to meet my sister, Carolyn Gay," she said. "She lives in Washington, D.C., and works for the Department of Energy. She's a Rotarian and very involved with their Ambassadorial Scholarship program. That program has your name written all over it."

I was familiar with Rotary, but I had no idea it offered such a prestigious scholarship—full tuition and expenses to a graduate school overseas in return for representing Rotary International. The scholarship, she said, factored in academic achievement, but what it really sought were "global ambassadors."

The idea of Rotary considering me a "global ambassador" fit me like a glove. In addition to my world travels with Up with People, I had backpacked all across Europe and Southeast Asia. And not only was I teaching English in Japan, but I was also helping with the preparations for the 1996 Winter Olympics in Nagano. I had come to see myself—in fact to define myself—as just that: a global ambassador. My outgoing personality and a track record for hard work also seemed like advantages that just might offset my less-than-stellar academic achievements.

So I took down Carolyn's address and wrote her a letter. She responded a few weeks later, encouraging me to apply for the scholarship. She even included an application form for me to fill out and send to my hometown Rotary District. As I mailed the application, the thought of getting that scholarship renewed my hope in the future.

Three months later I received a letter from Rotary District 7210 in Rockland County, New York, but this time it wasn't another right hook of rejection. This one informed me that I was one of ten finalists, and that I needed to come the following month for an interview with the selection committee. So I depleted my savings to buy a plane ticket, headed back to the United States, and parked my butt on a barstool until my turn came to dazzle the Rotarians.

When that chance came, the ten-member selection committee drilled me with questions about my travels throughout Europe, living in Asia, and my worldwide tours as a cast member with Up with People. They also asked about my academic record, and I did my best to turn that lemon into lemonade by shifting the focus back to the relationships that had helped define me as a leader.

I told them stories about how I'd actively cared for people like my college fraternity brother. As a freshman, Chad Harris dove into the shallow water of a pond, suffered a broken neck, and became a quadriplegic. For the next four years, Ed Davenport and I lived with and cared for Chad, feeding him, dressing him, bathing him—helping him in every way imaginable (and in some ways I never could have imagined!). Then, during the summer prior to our senior year in college, Chad's parents gave the three of us an early graduation gift—round-trip airline tickets to Europe. We backpacked from city to city, sharing in Chad's joy as he experienced things most quadriplegics never dream of—ascending to the top of the Eiffel Tower in Paris, visiting the Berlin Wall, taking boat rides through the canals of Venice.

I told them stories about how I'd worked hard to succeed despite my learning disability, and I drew comparisons to famous people who overcame obstacles before they achieved success. I talked about how Michael Jordan's coach cut him from the varsity basketball team when he was in the tenth grade and how Thomas Edison was labeled mentally slow by a teacher and had to be home-schooled by his mother. I talked about how Dwight Eisenhower finished at the bottom of his class at West Point.

And I told them about famous people who were also dyslexic—business leaders like Henry Ford, William Hewlett, and Charles Schwab; politicians like Winston Churchill and John Kennedy; scientists and inventors like Edison, Alexander Graham Bell, and Albert Einstein.

I gave the sales pitch of my life, and then I left my fate in the hands of those ten Rotarians and headed north in a rainstorm to visit my grandmother upstate in Saratoga Springs.

The committee, meanwhile, began sifting through the applicants and soon narrowed the field to two finalists—an Indian girl who had graduated from Harvard University magna cum laude and me, Thomas Spaulding Jr., who graduated from East Carolina University "thank God Almighty cum laude!"

Half of the selection committee was high on Miss Harvard University with her perfect 4.0 GPA and her life-goal of ridding the world of AIDS. The other five were impressed with my passion, my love for people, my travels, my leadership experience and, most of all, my desire to make a significant contribution to the world.

Five for Harvard and five for Spaulding!

They had debated for about an hour with nobody budging when the chairman called for a recess. The group headed to the bar, ordered drinks, and informally resumed the debate. No matter what was said, however, the vote remained tied—five for Harvard and five for Spaulding.

In frustration, the chairman turned to the bartender. "Barkeep, we're at a dead split," he said. "You spent the entire afternoon in the same room with the ten young candidates. You must have met them all. Which candidate were you most impressed with?"

"Well, sir, I didn't meet all ten candidates—just one," the bartender said. "Only one person came up to the bar and introduced himself. That Tommy Spaulding has to be one of the nicest kids that I have ever met!"

The bartender cast the deciding vote.

The Rotarians awarded me the $25,000 scholarship to attend Bond University in Queensland, Australia, where I earned my MBA, setting the new course for my life.

I left that interview feeling like I had given it my best effort, but unsure the committee would pick me over the other well-qualified candidates. With each mile I drove up Interstate 87 in the pouring rain, I replayed the interview in my head. Finally I pulled off the highway, found a pay phone, and called the only person I knew on the committee—Tom France, the same Rotarian who had helped me go to the Rotary Youth Leadership Academy (RYLA) when I was in high school.

By the time Tom got to the phone, my heart was beating faster than a thoroughbred making a stretch run at Saratoga. But I braced myself for the likely event that the news wouldn't be good.

"How are you, Tommy my boy?" Tom said when he took the phone from his wife, Lu.

"I don't know, Tom," I said. "You tell me."

Then he said six words I'll never forget: "You won, Tommy boy! You won!"

I'd won in athletics and I had won student government elections, but I'd never won anything like this—an academic scholarship. For a guy who loves to talk, I hardly knew what to say. I thanked him over and over and over, then hung up the phone, fell to my knees, and cried like a baby—in a phone booth on a highway in upstate New York as rain poured all around me like tears from heaven.

It took me a few minutes to pull myself together, but then I made one more phone call before getting back on the road. I called the person I always called first when something wonderful happened to me—my father.

When he picked up the phone, I didn't even say hello. I just said, "Dad, I won!" Whenever I've won or lost in life, my father's always responded with words of affirmation, and this night was no different. "Of course you won, son," he said. "You are changing the world!"

Chapter 3

Relationship Economics

It was a year later that Tom France told me about the bartender's impact on my life. The revelation shocked me. I didn't even remember the guy's name. I had simply shown a genuine interest in him, much as I show a genuine interest in everyone I meet. I remember the sense of humility and gratitude that washed over me as I considered the impact of that simple chance meeting.

The bartender taught me lessons that have been reinforced hundreds of times over the course of my career—lessons about life and, more specifically, lessons about the power of *relationship economics*.

Economics deals with how things like "production, distribution, and consumption of goods and services" shape the financial and material welfare of people. So relationship economics emphasizes the human aspect of that. It sounds simple enough. But no part of our economic system gets less attention from the so-called experts. No part of our economic system is more greatly undervalued or, worse, wrongly valued. Too many authors, leaders, and managers treat relationships as a commodity. Therefore, no part of our economic system is more worthy of our understanding and attention.

The realities of relationship economics are, in many ways, exemplified by my encounter with the bartender. He and I had a minimal financial transaction. I bought a Diet Pepsi in exchange for an agreed-upon amount of U.S. legal tender (about $1.25, as I remember it). But our relational transaction—an investment of a few hours of our time—paid huge dividends for me; and, who knows, he might have gained something beyond that buck and a quarter.

From such relationships, I began discovering the laws that govern relationship economics. In the world of monetary economics, there are realities so universally accepted that they're considered laws. The Law of Supply and Demand, for instance. Or the Law of Diminishing Returns. Or the Law of One Price. Or Gresham's Law. As we move throughout this book, we're going to explore a number of laws that govern relationship economics.

My relationship with the bartender is an example of **the Law of Random Relationships**: an investment in a short-lived and seemingly random encounter can produce unforeseeable yet significant benefits. It's important not to dismiss what happened with the bartender as a one-in-a-million, never-would-happen-to-me encounter. Indeed, such encounters happen to all of us more frequently than we realize. If Tom France hadn't shared the story about the bartender, I never would have known about his influence on my life.

Many times, however, the power of these random relationships is quite clear, as was the case with Sarah Gay—the woman I met while snorkeling in Bali. Because of that unexpected one-day connection, I ended up applying for a scholarship that changed my life. Not only that, but I became friends with her sister Carolyn, and we still visit whenever I'm in D.C.

In fact, there are many examples of long-term partnerships that illustrate the Law of Random Relationships. In retrospect, it's easy to see many great partnerships or business deals as preordained, but what if Bill Hewlett and Dave Packard had never gone with friends on the two-week camping trip in Colorado that launched their friendship? Would the two Stanford grads have launched one of the world's pioneering technology companies? What if Steve Jobs hadn't met Steve Wozniak while sitting in on some Hewlett-Packard workshops? What if Harvey Firestone hadn't been working as a salesman at the Columbus Buggy Works in Detroit on the day Henry Ford walked in looking for some tires that might work on the low-cost car Ford hoped to build? What if Ben Cohen and Jerry Greenfield hadn't been assigned the same seventh-grade gym class?

The point is, we can't afford to dismiss casual encounters. The one we ignore might be our Hewlett (or our Packard), our Jobs (or our Wozniak), our Firestone (or our Ford), our Ben (or our Jerry)—it might even be our bartender!

Economists, authors, and business leaders love to talk about ROI—Return on Investment—and well we should. When it comes to relationship economics, I'd like to introduce a different concept—Return on Relationships (ROR). My investment of time with the bartender, without my even realizing it, was an investment that produced an incredible, life-altering return—exactly the type of Return on Relationship anyone can pursue.

Such ROR comes in all sorts of forms, and it should be as important to you and your organization as profits, revenues, and ROI—because without generating ROR, the ROI won't matter.

If you're building a career or running a company, there's an opportunity for ROR throughout your organization with your clients, colleagues, employees, vendors, management team, and customers. If you're running a nonprofit, there's an opportunity for ROR with your volunteers, your donors, your stakeholders, and your staff. If you're a student, there's an opportunity for ROR with your classmates, teachers, coaches, and professors. If you're a politician, there's an opportunity for ROR with your constituents, with the civil servants who actually run much of government, and, of course, with voters.

And ROR works from the bottom up as well as from the top down. Wherever you are in the organizational flow chart, increasing your ROR provides opportunities for the types of successes that not only advance your career, but also provide meaningful satisfaction in your work.

This isn't a reality some business leaders willingly embrace. Maybe you work with or for some of those people. Or maybe you work for wonderful people who love and respect you. But even wonderful managers and leaders in highly successful organizations often miss this big idea. When that happens, they lose out on an opportunity for even greater success. In fact, chances are the leaders you know who devalue ROR simply do so out of ignorance or inattention or habit. You might even be one of those leaders.

Our Western culture promotes executing business at the speed of light, which often leaves the wrong things dead along the side of the road. Pressed by the tyranny of the urgent and the perceived demands of the "bottom line," all too many leaders—even those who actually believe in the importance of ROR—end up neglecting it, and eventually it costs them.

It's impossible to build a successful career or organization in a silo; relationships, in other words, aren't optional, they're essential—internal relationships (up, down, and across the organizational chart); external relationships (with clients, vendors, and customers); financial relationships (with stockholders, investors, and donors); personal relationships (with spouses, partners, family, and friends) and peripheral relationships (with the community).

This isn't news to most modern leaders. Ask any leader or manager, and you'll hear all the corporate buzzwords about the importance of people. They're every organization's "greatest asset." It's right there with the other "values" that are framed on the lobby wall or gathering dust in a binder on a shelf. But while leaders generally understand the importance of the relationships that affect their organizations, many fail miserably when it comes to truly developing a corporate culture that lives out that value.

Tom Rath, who leads Gallup's Workplace Research and Leadership Consulting division, put together a team that dissected years of Gallup's data. They found, among other things, that only one in thirteen people is engaged in his or her job if he or she doesn't have a best friend at work. They found that if you have at least three close friends at work, you're 96 percent more likely to be extremely satisfied with your life. And they found that if you have a close relationship with your manager, you're more than 2.4 times more likely to be satisfied with your job. And yet only 18 percent of us work for organizations that provide opportunities to develop such relationships on the job, and only 17 percent of employees report that their manager has made "an investment in our relationship" in the past three months.*

Even the best-intentioned leaders struggle with how to make this "value" come alive. What does it look like? How does it work? How can we get people to buy into it and not see it as just another program or platitude? How can we take it from a "good

---

* This research is reported in Rath's book *Vital Friends* (Gallup Press, 2006).

and noble idea" to an intrinsic attitude that permeates the organization's culture? And eventually the money question drags them down: Can we afford it? When it comes right down to it, can building this type of relationship culture increase profits—is the ROR bringing an ROI?

That last question represents what I've come to see as the greatest myth about building deep, meaningful relationships throughout an organization: that anything more than a nominal effort in that direction will hurt the bottom line. The reality is just the opposite. In fact, it's never been more important to figure out how an organization can give more than lip service to the idea of building a culture that values authentic relationships, because relationships have become the currency of the modern economy.

The world's "economy" evolves with each rotation of the planet. We've seen it represented as an agricultural economy, an industrial economy, a service economy, an experience economy, and a knowledge economy. Some say we're moving, or have moved, into a green economy. More accurately, we've moved into a servanthood economy—one in which our greatest value is found in how we serve each other and our greater communities. To build a sustainable organization in the twenty-first century, we must add value to something and someone other than ourselves. We might do that by "going green" or by mentoring a junior executive or by organizing a fund-raiser for a micro-lending bank or by helping a close friend through a career change.

Don't misunderstand me: skill and talent remain important, as does experience and knowledge. Competition is fierce for the essentials to success—information, talent, customers, investors, and on and on. But when competing forces clash, what separates one from another is almost always relationships. I've found this to be true whether I've been working in sales for a corporate giant, building a statewide leadership program for teens, running one of the most influential nonprofits in the world, or consulting with leaders of for-profit companies.

Think about it. If you're picking between two vendors or clients who want your business, two nonprofits that need your donation, or two investors who are considering funding your venture, what factors do you consider? Quality is important. Price matters. But what about integrity? Trust? Loyalty? Whom do you *really* know? Who *really* knows your needs? Who breathes energy into your soul and your organization rather than sucking the life out of it? And it always comes down to this most important question: Whom do you have the *relationship* with?

Organizations that succeed in relationship economics—that generate significant ROR—are marked by what I call "relational competence." And I believe any organization that isn't marked by relational competence is marked for extinction. It simply can't survive for long.

What's more, successful "organizations" are nothing more than a collection of the people within them. Individuals who excel in relational competence stand the greatest chance of advancing toward their career goals, while also advancing the goals of the organization. So relationships matter regardless of whether you are an emerging leader who is just beginning to blaze a trail, or a veteran leader responsible for the ultimate vision and bottom-line decisions that can make or break the organization.

Profit has always been an important factor in economic history, and shareholder value has been in the mix for a few hundred years. But American capitalism has been at its best when it has balanced those desired outcomes with noble motivations—that is, when business has found ways to improve lives and make a profit at the same time.

Success isn't always about profit. In fact, the most important question an organization must ask itself is this: How do we define success? And the answer must go beyond profits.

Innovation and entrepreneurship are born of the desire to identify needs and fill them, but somewhere along the way we lost the balance of power. Profit became a dictator. Relationships, the key to cultivating a desire to help others, became secondary. The results haven't always been pretty. Consider any organization that's fallen on hard times, from companies like Countrywide Financial, Washington Mutual, or Enron, to entire industries (banking, mortgage lending, health insurance). The root cause is that they put profits ahead of people. Companies and industries that rose to the top by valuing relationships, fell to the bottom by abandoning those relationships in the name of greed.

If profit is king, it must share the crown. Profit and relationships are not always equal, but they need to be in balance. Each in its own way is essential to building a sustainable and significant organization. And despite the way that most organizations see it, they aren't mutually exclusive. They not only respect each other, they can't live without each other. And when they work together, they not only change lives and organizations but entire communities.

Dozens of organizations of all sizes prove this point, from the TOMS Shoes program that gives away shoes to needy children to the billions of dollars given in corporate and foundation donations.

Many great companies understood this long before "corporate responsibility" became a buzzword. In 1943, just before his family-built company went public, Robert Wood Johnson crafted a now-famous corporate "credo" that starts off by saying, "We believe our first responsibility is to the doctors, nurses and patients, to the mothers and fathers and all others who use our products and services."*

The Johnson & Johnson credo goes on to talk about respecting the dignity of workers and their families and being responsible to the community. And not until the fourth and final paragraph does it mention the responsibility to stockholders to make a profit. "When we operate according to these principles," Johnson wrote, "the stockholders should realize a fair return."

The cost of poor relationships shows up all over the balance sheet in great big strokes of red ink. It shows up as lost sales, of course, and inefficient partnerships, and don't forget the cost of turnover. What does it cost to replace the employee who was fired because he didn't do his job well or who simply left for a job somewhere else? And what are the underlying costs related to his departure? Was he an underperformer because of the poor management and leadership around him? Or did he leave because he had no reason to stay loyal to the company? And what did it cost the company in terms of decreased productivity that comes with landsliding morale?

A 2007 *Gallup Management Journal* survey estimated that "actively disengaged workers" cost the U.S. economy about $382 billion. Around 24.7 million workers eighteen years of age and older—about 18 percent of the workforce—fall into this category. They aren't just unhappy, but they're "acting out their unhappiness." Another 56 percent are considered "not engaged," meaning they are putting in their time at work, but without

---

* http://www.jnj.com/connect/about-jnj/jnj-credo/

"energy or passion." Only 26 percent of workers are fully "engaged" in their work, according to the survey.

Well-managed relationships generate a return in opportunities for greater profits and shareholder value. And while some poorly managed relationships might generate positive outcomes in the short term, they are always the cracks that eventually break the dam. This applies on the organizational level and for each of us as an individual.

My motivations with the bartender weren't based on my own profit. The ROR came naturally from my focus on the relationship, random as it was. In that case it was unexpected, but more often it's the result of intentional effort to invest in others with an understanding that there's a potential—but not guaranteed—benefit.

If I had known what the bartender *could do* for me, would I have treated him differently? I think not, but there's no way to know for sure. And that's the thing: you never know when the next relationship will be the most important of your life, in your career, or in your organization.

I learned this (again) when Leader's Challenge, the nonprofit I founded in 2000, began to experience some growing pains en route to becoming Colorado's largest youth leadership program.

Every year we had more and more graduates of the program, which meant our graduation ceremony quickly outgrew most of the smaller facilities in Denver. One year we realized we'd have as many as two thousand graduates, friends, and family attending that event. Our board authorized me to find a larger facility, and I went to work going over a list of places that were big enough.

Very quickly, however, I hit a roadblock. Lions Club International, a community service organization much like Rotary, had booked almost all of the city's larger facilities on the date we needed because Denver was hosting the group's annual convention.

We had made too many plans to shift our date, but I could find only one available venue big enough for our graduation: the historic and palatial Paramount Theater in downtown Denver. There was only one problem. I called the manager of the facility, and he told me the price for the Paramount was $25,000—and that was the "nonprofit" rate!

Our budget: $2,000!

I did my best to negotiate a lower price, but the manager never budged. My spirits sank as I hung up the phone with no good options for a place to hold our biggest and most important event of the year.

My wife, Jill, and I were still dating at that time, and that night we dressed up and I took her to dinner at D'Luca's, one of Denver's best Italian restaurants. I looked forward to sitting with her at a nice, romantic table by the front window, eating a great meal with a beautiful woman, and forgetting all about my venue crisis.

As we were taking our seats, however, I took off my jacket and inadvertently put my elbow in the ear of the middle-aged bald guy sitting at the next table. As I was begging the man's forgiveness, Jill was making friends with his wife and family.

Now, Jill is the only person I know who looks at the dessert menu before ordering her entrée. She looks like she eats nothing but salads and rice cakes, but she's actually a lover of great desserts. So while I was apologizing, she was moving the conversation away from my social blunder by inquiring about the scrumptious-looking chocolate cake the family had ordered. Before I knew it, our tables were joined and we were talking about life with Larry and Debra Melnick and their children.

Larry, I discovered, worked for Stan Kroenke, the owner of the Denver Nuggets, the Colorado Avalanche, and a handful of music venues in town. More specifically, Larry was an executive with KSE-CCE Promotions. And KSE-CCE Promotions owned the Paramount Theater. So, despite my elbow to his ear—or perhaps because of Jill's charming personality—we experienced the Law of Random Relationships. By the end of dinner, Leader's Challenge had found a friend who helped us get the Paramount for the graduation at a price that was within our budget.

Larry and I never formed an intimate friendship, but we have a great relationship that started with me elbowing him in the ear and him offering to help an event that honored more than a thousand students in our community.

If relationships are so important that even seemingly random meetings offer huge potential, why are so many of us—and, thus, so many organizations—so poor at cultivating intentional relationships with co-workers, clients, customers, and employees, much less discovering the hidden value of random relationships? Why do surveys tell us that so many people are unhappy with their work, or that they distrust their employers? Why are cynicism and skepticism the hallmarks of most organizational cultures, and not meaningful relationships? And how can leaders bring about change that takes this core value from a well-meaning platitude and puts it into action?

We have to face this challenge by taking a fresh look at the importance of relationship-building, taking steps to live out relational competence in all of our daily interactions, and, if we're in a leadership position, offering innovative solutions that will energize the organization's culture. First of all, look at where the organization needs to go. In other words, start with the end in mind, as Stephen Covey would suggest. To create an organization with a culture that's steeped in relational competence— that is committed to deep, meaningful relationships—you need to start with each individual within the organization. It starts with you. And that change has to move the individual up the grid of the Five Floors of Relationships. As the individuals begin to move along this grid, so too will the organization. In some organizations the change will be led from the top down. In others it will start from deep within the organization and expand throughout it. Regardless, there's no excuse for shifting the responsibility to someone other than ourselves.

We're going to dive deep into the heart of relationship economics—how we can define relationships that matter, how we can create relationships that matter, and how we can grow relationships that matter.

We're going to explore the keys to relationship economics, relational competence, and ROR. And when they are put into practice, they will help you retain clients, supercharge your career, create loyal colleagues and customers, grow business—all the bottom-line measures of a successful business.

But there's something even more important about relational competence. It will spawn the kind of random relationships I've had with the bartender, Sarah Gay, and Larry Melnick, as well as deep, long-lasting relationships such as those I've had with Mrs. Singer, Brian Kanter, Tom France, and many others you'll meet in the coming pages. Those types of relationships will change you and your life for the better. They'll change your career. And they'll change the organization you work for. And by doing that, they can—and will—change the world.

How to Build Relationship Capital

Chapter 4

The Five Floors of Relationships

I know thousands of people, and many of them wield tremendous influence. If life and business were all about "who you know," then I'd be set. But none of those relationships took on extraordinary value unless I approached them with the idea that they mattered for something above and beyond the transaction. I didn't set out to make the bartender a lifelong friend, for instance, and that type of friendship never materialized. But I also didn't settle for what I call a First Floor relationship.

I think of relationships in terms of a five-floor building. The deeper and more meaningful a relationship, the higher the floor it resides on. My closest, deepest relationships are Fifth Floor, or Penthouse, relationships.

Let me be clear—relationships seldom fit neatly into a box (or a building). They're far too dynamic. Some overlap on different floors, and others seem to move up and down floors like an elevator. But the Five Floor plan helps give me a reference point and allows me to think about the boundaries that define my relationships, so that I can continually work to make them stronger and more rewarding. I try to develop strong relationships at every level. And because my relationships with others matter so much to me, and because I come to them intending to help others, many of these relationships develop into something more meaningful than anything I had imagined.

Most relationships start on the First Floor. We meet and we greet. We exchange business cards. It typically involves a transactional exchange. We need something specific from the other person—an airline ticket, or lunch, or help with a question. After we get what we want, we move on.

"How are you today?" I might ask the clerk behind a counter, without really expecting much of an answer. And, likewise, the clerk may respond, "Fine, thanks for asking," even though the truth is he may be anxious about unpaid bills or a sick relative or a car that needs to be repaired.

We engage in dozens of First Floor relationships each day— with clients, colleagues, the postal clerk, the receptionist at the dentist's office, the waitress at the restaurant, the flight attendant on the airplane.

This is where most relationships start. But all too often we allow our relationships to stay there. We meet the new hire in our department one morning and forget her name by lunch (if not before). If people aren't essential to our jobs or our daily lives, we don't make the effort to get to know them better. We only make a minimal investment of time and effort; the vendor on the phone who takes an order is a faceless voice.

The next level of relationships—Second Floor relationships—is where we begin sharing more information. But it's very basic information, the type we dispense out of social obligation or because it's a job requirement, not because we're offering some insight into who we are.

At work, "positional authority" often guides these kinds of relationships. We interact because the other person's position, or our position, requires it. But Second Floor relationships also result from casual friendships with people whom we know to a degree, but not particularly well. Perhaps you catch a football game together, or get together for a holiday gathering. These are people with whom we hold polite conversations, but the level of intimacy seldom moves beyond NSW—news, sports, and weather.

Unfortunately, many of us have friends we think of as "close" who, in reality, are only on the Second Floor. We seldom reveal things to them about ourselves that would make us vulnerable or open; we seldom take emotional risks. If someone else mentions such an acquaintance, our instinct is to say, "Oh, I'm friends with so-and-so." But when we really peel back the onion, all we have is an NSW relationship. We would never count on them for help, or for a big favor. I have a number of friends who live in an NSW world. Whenever I talk to them, everything is perfect—their family is perfect, business is perfect, life is perfect. That's all they let you see—the perfect parts. They never talk about the things in life that challenge or really define them. And as a result, they never rise above the Second Floor.

In Third Floor relationships, people develop an emotional comfort level that goes beyond facts and information. Instead of resting on NSW conversations, we begin sharing opinions and feelings. It's not uncommon to feel safe enough to exchange competing viewpoints, and not just on trivial matters like who was the best clutch hitter in the history of baseball. (As a Yankees fan, I have to go with Derek Jeter, even over Reggie Jackson and Mickey Mantle; and, yes, I realize that some fans don't see this as a trivial question!)

In business, positional authority remains the primary guiding force in Third Floor relationships. Our position at work requires us to say what we think, rather than just present data, because our opinions can help shape decisions. The higher we move up the organizational chart, the more our opinions and concerns about issues matter.

In Third Floor relationships, we learn about the lives of our co-workers, vendors, clients, and other professional associates, and we begin to understand something about who they are as people, even if we don't necessarily agree with all of their opinions. And we're sharing personal information about ourselves— our ideas and feelings.

But it's also in Third Floor relationships that we discover what I call a "wall of conflict." Relationships often stall here because the inevitable conflict acts as a locked door to the staircase leading up. But it also presents opportunities to foster the type of interactions that can lead to much deeper relationships.

Genuine relationships aren't based on our position or on a hierarchy. When we follow someone because she is the boss, we're responding to her positional authority. When we follow someone because we trust and respect her, we're responding to our feelings about her as a person. That's "relational authority." Darlyne Bailey, in *The Leader of the Future 2* (Jossey-Bass, 2006), calls this type of authority a defining characteristic of genuine, authentic leadership: "Positions of power are just that—positions. True leaders know that who they are is much more than what they do."

In a Fourth Floor relationship, the relationship takes on deeper, more significant meaning. We share common interests, goals, beliefs, and causes. We've also learned to work through conflicts, and we're responding in ways that show that we value the relationship for its own sake.

The increased trust and respect we share in such relationships also leads to greater vulnerability and openness. We might confide that our marriage is failing, or discuss private, sensitive details about our finances with such a friend, both in an effort to share our dreams and fears, as well as to ask for their advice and support.

We still may not share all of our flaws and insecurities with Fourth Floor friends, and they don't yet share all of theirs with us. But we don't judge each other the way we did in the early stages of the relationship. We've dropped our guards; we're well beyond deciding on whether or not we like the other person—at this stage we're looking for ways to take the relationship even further and maintain the close connection we feel. We're more comfortable telling each other about the things that are important in our lives, that help shape who we are. We've gone way beyond NSW relationships.

Fifth Floor relationships—the Penthouse of relationships— go well beyond anything discussed in Dale Carnegie's *How to Win Friends & Influence People*. In Fifth Floor relationships, vulnerability, authenticity, trust, and loyalty are off the charts. They are relationships based on a shared empathy—an intuitive understanding of each other's needs, even those that aren't necessarily expressed. We literally "feel" another person's state of mind. It's a relationship based more on giving than on getting. But that kind of giving gives us more than we could possibly imagine.

In Fifth Floor relationships, we become confidants, advisers, and partners in helping the other person achieve their greatest potential.

Yes, Fifth Floor relationships are uncommon, if for no other reason than the amount of time and energy required to develop and maintain such relationships. But our tendency is to put unnecessary limits on our Fifth Floor relationships. We may think we only have room for two or three such relationships, when in fact we can easily embrace a dozen or more. Or we think only certain types of people can relate to us on a Fifth Floor level. We think we can't have a Penthouse relationship with, say, a homeless man we met at a soup kitchen, or with our spouse's ex-spouse. But that's simply not true. There is no limit to our ability to reach out to others.

I'll share plenty of examples with you later in the book, but I don't want to get ahead of myself. Before we can get to the Penthouse, we first have to learn how to get off the First Floor.

All relationships require hard work, patience, understanding, and, yes, tactics and strategies designed to make them blossom. But don't confuse that with manipulation. We can have tactics and strategies for building relationships, just as we have tactics and strategies for marketing, selling, advertising, production, distribution, and customer service.

The key to creating a rich network of relationships, however, is understanding this deep and basic truth: motives matter. If all we care about is using others to advance our career and our net worth, our relationship will have no lasting value. It may work for a time, or in a few specific situations, but the foundation on which you build your relationships will be unstable, and the relationship ultimately will collapse—likely when you need it the most. Yes, at times we live in a dog-eat-dog world, but acting in kind will destroy your soul and, in the end, your career. Moreover, regardless of what your bank statement says, you'll leave a legacy, a footprint on life, of insignificance.

By building meaningful relationships, without sacrificing our integrity or treating other people as a means to an end, I'm convinced we not only can achieve our goals but move beyond them, personally and professionally. Here are the nine key traits that I've found help us to achieve real relationships:

authenticity	confidentiality	generosity
humility	vulnerability	humor
empathy	curiosity	gratitude

I don't pretend that these traits are all-encompassing, but my experience suggests they offer a reliable filter in evaluating the tactics and strategies we use to build relationships.

These traits relate more to "who you are" than to "what you do." They are deeply personal. That's because who you are is far more important in building relationships than what you do. The things we "do" in reaching out to others typically flow out of our inner character. Our actions reflect our character. If we don't examine the qualities of our character, we're like a yacht owner who only cares for the part of the boat that's above the waterline, while letting the hull rot away from below. Sooner or later, if the hull is untended, the best-looking boat in the harbor will become worthless and sink.

That's not to say what we do isn't important. Indeed, we have to take specific actions to move a relationship from the First Floor to the Second or Third. Many people—regardless of their motives or character—struggle when it comes to figuring out how to reach out to people and develop meaningful relationships. They feel a strong inward pull to *do something*, but they don't know what to do or how to do it.

The trick is to combine the two—who you are and what you do—into a powerful approach that not only expands your network, but gives that network, regardless of its size, real meaning.

After all, it's not just who you know.

Relation*Shifter*

All relationships fall somewhere within the five-floor structure. The goal is to develop the ability to build relationships at
all five levels. That means developing the traits that define
"who we are," as well as identifying and practicing the actions
we need to take.

THE FIVE FLOORS OF RELATIONSHIPS*

Relationship Levels	Marked by	Examples
First Floor Relationships	Transactional in nature—people who do things for you because it is their job. Interactions are based on fulfilling a need.	Clerks, service employees, people who help not because of their relationship with you, but because of the nature of their position or job.
Second Floor Relationships	Sharing some personal information, facts. Conversations typically start with news, sports, and weather, and seldom move beyond the superficial or topical. At work, such relationships are based on positional authority.	Casual relationships and acquaintances, most boss-employee relationships; peers in unrelated departments, people you encounter at parties or functions whom you know casually, but with whom you aren't truly friends.
Third Floor Relationships	Sharing opinions, learning to deal with conflict. For the most part, however, such relationships are relatively superficial, and kept at arm's length.	Peers who interact regularly to reach common goals. You know some details about their personal lives and professional hopes and dreams, but are not asked or invited to give advice or feedback.
Fourth Floor Relationships	Sharing emotions and feelings; ability to work through conflict; willingness at times to put the other person's needs ahead of your own. Conversations consistently move beyond news, sports, and weather.	Mentor, good friends, close colleagues, people you care about in your job, industry, or community.
Penthouse (Fifth Floor) Relationships	Shared values, high level of openness, candor, and vulnerability; focusing on the other person's needs.	Your closest and most intimate relationships.

* This model is retrofitted from the five levels of communication commonly studied in communications theory.

Chapter 5

What You Do

I had nothing against Denver when I moved here in 1999 as director of corporate affiliates for Up with People. But I have a confession: I arrived with no particular passion for getting to know the city or her people. Denver was just a temporary stop on a journey back home to New York.

I had traveled with Up with People as a cast member prior to college, and I had worked as a traveling staff member after graduating from East Carolina University. After stints of teaching English in Japan and working on a political campaign, earning an MBA, and working in sales for IBM Lotus, I returned to Up with People in a senior-level position.

My job gave me an opportunity to work with CEO Bill Lively, one of the most influential and successful fund-raisers in the world. But when my one-year appointment was over, I expected to move back to New York and start a business or a nonprofit and perhaps eventually go into politics.

I found a place to live in north Denver close to the Up with People headquarters, and I immersed myself in my work. My primary responsibility was raising financial support within the Denver community. I met with high-profile business leaders, including several who were on the Up with People board. But initially I made little effort to engage the community or expand my circle of acquaintances.

Fortunately, that limited view didn't last.

Six months later, Bill Lively resigned as president and CEO of Up with People. Lively's departure bolstered my decision to leave Up with People after that first year. I had taken the job because I loved the organization, as well as to study at Lively's feet. And as much as I loved Up With People's mission, I could see the internal conflicts that had hamstrung its board and leadership teams. I wasn't surprised in late 2000 when the organization shut down for several years, to regain its bearings.

I continued working hard on behalf of Up with People, but I decided not to extend my contract. I started dreaming about the next phase of my life. For the first time, however, I began to toy with the idea of calling Denver home.

My move from north Denver to a downtown loft jump-started my engagement with the Denver community. I joined an athletic club and the Denver Rotary Club, and I started making friends outside of Up with People. The more I got to know Denver, and Colorado, the more I liked it.

A couple of months before my contract ended, I began putting together a business plan for Leader's Challenge, a nonprofit that would provide a leadership program in high schools. I showed the plan to my friends to get their input and advice, telling them that I planned to move back to New York to launch the program. Several came back to me with the same response: Why don't you launch it here in Denver?

So I did.

Why the sudden change in plans? I'd grown to love the climate, and the mix of big-city amenities and surrounding natural beauty. But most of all, I loved the people. I now have dozens of close friends in and around Denver. It's where I met my wife.

Today, we in America live in a transient culture. There's a

temptation to avoid putting down roots, as we contemplate the next move. One of my biggest regrets is that I didn't start investing more of myself in Denver from the day I arrived. How many relationships and opportunities to serve did I miss because I arrived with one eye on my job and the other on New York? And the fact is, even if I had moved, I never would have regretted building more relationships.

Once I realized I was staying in Denver, my relationship motor kicked into high gear. Frankly, the key relationships I had built through Up with People and the fact that I was launching a nonprofit combined to give me an advantage in expanding my network of relationships. But the fact is each of us has advantages of one type or another; we just have to identify them, and draw on them. The lessons I learned, and the approaches I used, can be adapted to any number of circumstances.

I knew three people outside of work when I moved to Colorado, and one of those was my sister. How did I turn three relationships into several thousand?

In one sense, I believe it all comes back to the traits that make you who you are. I'll come back to those traits shortly, because if you lose sight of them, you're never going to change the world, no matter how big you grow your network or your bank account. But there are also practical actions you can take to expand your network of relationships. There are lessons I believe all of us can draw upon, specific tactics and strategies that will help you expand your network of relationships, whether you are a shy person or an extrovert, whether you want to create a circle of five close friends, or a social community of five thousand. And if you combine them with the traits that I'll talk about later, you can exponentially expand your influence and change the world.

Chapter 6

Don't Shoot the Moose

More than 2.5 million people live in the greater Denver area. It's home to all the glass, steel, and concrete you'd expect from a metropolitan region of that size. But the heart and soul of Denver isn't in its skyscrapers or toll roads or shopping malls; it's in the land—the nearby Rocky Mountains and the region's wide-open high plains.

People first began settling along the confluence of the South Platte River and Cherry Creek in the late 1850s and early 1860s, mostly to look for gold around Pike's Peak or to start a new life along the Western frontier. Many people stayed, and more came. Homes became neighborhoods that expanded out into suburbs. Businesses and industry took root and thrived. The arts arrived. Professional sports came in. And Denver went from a cozy settlement to a bustling town to a lively city to a vibrant metropolis that serves as the hub of a region.

Denver experienced all the typical growing pains. But it has never lost its Western charm and personality; it has never tried to become a financial or media center like New York, or a cosmopolitan tourist destination like San Francisco, or the center of the movie industry like Los Angeles. All are wonderful cities, but they just aren't Denver.

When I decided to stay in Denver, I knew I needed to meet more people in town, especially if I was going to become a successful entrepreneur. But as I began to reach out to others, the most important decision I made was to take a cue from Denver itself: I learned to stay true to myself.

I was a kid from suburban New York. I knew nothing about the Wild West. I'd never owned a pair of cowboy boots or worn a bolo tie or a cowboy hat. To make this new life work, did I need to reinvent myself? Did I need to create a Tommy Spaulding 2.0? Did I need to throw myself at the Rocky Mountains, taking up fly fishing, mountain climbing, and elk hunting?

Now, trying new hobbies and experiences is a great way to expand your network of people. Discovering our interest in something we never knew existed can open us up to an entirely new circle of friends, both personal and professional.

It's important to remember who you are, however, and never try to fake an interest in things just to try to meet people you think might be valuable to your career. It's a lesson I learned firsthand at the most unlikely of places: a hunter education course.

Blanton Belk, the founder of Up with People, introduced me to two people when I first moved to Denver, and both became close friends. One was John Gart. His family founded Gart Brothers Sporting Goods, which grew to become the second-largest sporting goods retailer in the country. The other was Tate McCoy, executive vice president of an insurance company.

John and Tate were about my age. They were also independent, successful, smart, and very talented. Although they came from well-off families, they worked hard to make their own ways in the world. They were great guys, and important people for me to know, both personally and professionally.

Tate loves duck hunting and goes just about every chance he gets. So Tate suggested that I take up duck hunting. I could join him and his friends on their outings, and meet some of the influential leaders in the Denver area. A large number of the business and political leaders in Colorado love to hunt and fly-fish—it's one of Denver's great attractions—and they often spend their free time together on the weekends in remote mountain cabins, or at a hunting club, fishing or hunting during the day, and hanging out in the evenings by a warm fire. It's a great opportunity to get to know people beyond the typical news, sports, and weather conversation of parties and water coolers.

So I decided I would take up hunting. To do that, I first had to get a hunting license. And to get a hunting license in Colorado, one has to complete an all-day hunting education course. My only experience firing a weapon came as a teenager when I was earning the rifle-shooting merit badge as a Boy Scout. I had never shot at a live target before. And by the end of that day-long class, I knew I had no interest in shooting animals with a gun. It just wasn't in my nature.

So I finished the class and got my certificate, but I never went hunting. Although I was invited many times, I would always politely decline—it just wasn't me. And if I had tried to fake it to meet some of the movers and shakers I desperately wanted to meet, I'm convinced it wouldn't have worked; they would have seen through my insincere efforts in a heartbeat.

My point? You have to be true to yourself. It is rule number one. One of my passions, I realized, was running. So why not use *that* in reaching out to others? When I learned that John Gart was a runner, I suggested that we run together. So we did. Eventually we trained together for half-marathons. Our morning runs around Washington Park or the High Line Canal were a great way to spend time together. I can't tell you how many terrific conversations we had about ourselves and life.

Meeting new people, I quickly figured out, had to begin with making sure I remained true to myself. I've never been afraid to try new things—it's one of the great adventures of life. But I needed to stay true to who I was.

Our natural interests and passions can lead us to all sorts of opportunities to meet new people. Do you love hiking, or golf, or tennis? The opera, or the theater? There are opportunities to join book clubs, chess clubs, cooking clubs, and gardening clubs. Or why not help out in the community? I believe community involvement should play some role in all of our lives.

If you have special interests or hobbies, you can find others who share it. And those interests, those passions, are great places to begin with when looking to reach out to others. Listen, as well, to what others tell you about their interests. If they sound appealing, don't be shy about expressing an interest and looking for ways to do things together. Go online and do a little research about activities in your region. Take action.

On the flip side, just because the person you want to meet loves country music and you don't, that doesn't mean you can't develop a relationship. Look for other interests that you share. Although I have never been hunting with Tate McCoy, he's one of my closest friends. Tate and I love to go to sporting events together. He served as chairman of the board for the Leader's Challenge, the nonprofit I founded. My son's nickname is Tate. So look for the things you *do* have in common— don't get fixated on the ways in which you are different.

Relation*Shifter*

Never try to fake an interest in things just to try to get close to someone. Build your network of relationships around shared passions. When your relationships are built on things you don't truly enjoy, they likely won't last for long.

Chapter 7

Do Your Homework

Every successful business venture, from a one-time project for a department of a mega-corporation to launching an entirely new company, involves planning. You wouldn't start a marketing or creative project without planning it out first. A company wouldn't start a new product line without thinking it through and mapping it out. You would never create a new business strategy without weighing the pros and cons, and ironing out the details.

The same is true about reaching out to new people to expand your community of contacts. For most of us, the way we meet new people and build meaningful relationships relies on serendipity—it is simply a by-product of our daily interactions with colleagues, customers, clients, and vendors. It is the Law of Random Relationships in action. To make friends through such casual contacts, all we need to do is develop an attitude of openness toward the unexpected, approaching every person we encounter with an awareness of the hidden potential to develop a relationship.

But we shouldn't leave all relationships to chance. If we know there are certain people or groups we want to meet, reach out to, and get to know, we need to be proactive; we need to plan specific approaches to help bring them into our world. Why wait for the mountain to come to us, when we can go to the mountain? As the Roman philosopher Seneca put it, "Luck is what happens when preparation meets opportunity." That's not being manipulative—that's being purposeful.

In other words, to meet the kinds of people you'd like to become friends with, or valued associates, you need to do your homework. Now, my academic record was hardly stellar, but one thing my dyslexia pushed me to do was to develop a strong work ethic. Because I didn't read or write so well, I invested a lot of time identifying and memorizing important details, words, and speeches. I overprepared for everything I did, because I had to if I wanted to succeed. I use the same approach in reaching out to others to create the relationships I want in my life.

Whenever I start a new project, begin a new job, or prepare to launch a new initiative, one of the first things I do is to make lists of the people I think I need to know. I don't just focus on the people who can "help" me, but the people I can help, as well. One of the keys to establishing strong relationships, I feel, is to think about what we can do to help each other. I try to imagine what success for both of us would look like.

How do I know which people to reach out to? I ask others on my team, I take colleagues in the same industry or sector out to lunch and ask them who *they* think I should know. I invite others to help me identify the people who can help me, and who I can help. And I suggest people I think they should know, in return.

Another way to find out whom you should consider reaching out to is to read industry publications or journals. Go to the relevant websites and blogs. Contact industry organizations. Pay attention to the world around you.

When I was starting Leader's Challenge, I needed to develop relationships with key people in the community who were in a position to advance the vision I had for the organization.

That included reaching out to donors. But there were thousands of people in Denver wealthy enough to donate money to my cause. I needed to be more targeted in my approach. So I identified the people who shared a passion for the mission of Leader's Challenge. In other words, people who valued education, leadership, investing in youth, service, and bridging cultural gaps.

I needed to develop a circle of key advisers—people who could tell me what I didn't already know about starting and running a nonprofit organization or who could help me structure the organization so that it would most effectively serve high school students. Because the organization's goal was to build a local leadership program for high school students, I knew I also needed to develop strong relationships with Denver area parents, teachers, principals, and superintendents.

So I began creating lists. I started by researching the top one hundred companies and top one hundred nonprofit organizations in Colorado. You can find this type of information online, as well as by asking people who have lived and worked in the region or community longer than you have. Most cities of any size have a business journal that collects and reports this type of data.

The information I gathered about the mission statements of those organizations, and the people who led them, proved invaluable. First, it got me started on another list—the "fifty most influential people in Denver." I made it a point to learn as much as I could about the people on this list, and then find ways to meet each of them in person. Why? Because these were the people who had the resources and contacts to help me launch a nonprofit. All were potential donors, of course, but they were also the people whose opinions and decisions helped shape the opinions and decisions of everyone else in local government and the community. They were influencers and tended to know a lot of other people toward whom they could point me.

I printed this list and kept it with me. Whenever I discovered that someone I knew knew someone on my list, I would ask their help in introducing me. And as I met some of these people, I would ask *their* help in meeting one or two others on my list. Most of the time, the person I had met would make a call for me to encourage the next person to take my call. Other times she would give me permission to use her name in reaching out to someone I didn't know—"So-and-so suggested that I get in touch with you about a program I am creating." Each relationship became a link to reaching out to others to launch new relationships.

Of course, I reach out to others differently in pitching the message of a nonprofit than I do a business venture that is for a for-profit company. I can ask for more help with a nonprofit, because the "cause" isn't me—it's helping others. So, while coming up with lists is important, you do have to recognize when and when not to use them. If you're selling a product or service, you want to be very careful not to abuse your relationship with one person in an attempt to build another. (I'll discuss this in chapter 12.)

In addition to researching companies, organizations, and community leaders with influence, I made a list of the top charity fund-raising events around the state. Attending those events gives me an opportunity to meet more of the people on my lists. Look for events in your profession or industry you can go to. You can find much of this information online, as well as in business journals and by asking others.

Doing my homework didn't just help me identify the people I needed most to meet—it also helped me in building the relationships I hoped to establish. When I identified a person who

I felt might share my interests and values, I tried to learn as much about the person as possible: her company, her career accomplishments, the boards she served on, her hobbies, her family and her friends, where she went to college, her church, and what she said when she gave a speech recently to a local civic organization. I wanted to know *everything* I could to help me establish a relationship with her.

But isn't that manipulative? Why? If I know I'm interested in bringing the other person into my circle of friends or professional contacts, why not know as much as possible about the other person in advance, to find out the things we have in common? As long as your purpose is honorable—you're not out to undercut or use the other person—why not spend some time looking for ways to connect, rather than groping around blindly when your initial approach might be a fleeting one? I want the chance to show the other person how our interests align. How can they decide whether or not I am a person they should be interested in investing time with, if they aren't afforded a chance to get to know me?

That homework also helps me find ways to meet other people. If I know I want to meet the president of the Denver School Board, and I know she serves on another board with someone I know, I might ask my friend to introduce us, and put in a good word for me. Once I am introduced, of course, it is up to me to try to build a relationship. But knowing something about the person usually helps me in initiating a conversation. After initial small talk, I am able to move quickly to topics of mutual interest. In other words, it allows me to accelerate the process of creating a relationship, and possibly help both of us to discover mutual interests, and ways we can help each other.

Jared Polis, for example, was on my initial list of people that I wanted to meet in the Denver area to talk about Leader's

Challenge. As a nineteen-year-old student at Princeton, Jared cofounded an Internet company, American Information Systems. He then helped turn his parents' Boulder-based greeting card company, Blue Mountain Arts, into a multimillion-dollar online sensation by cofounding bluemountainarts.com. He later founded, grew, and then sold ProFlowers.com.

When I met Jared in early 2001, he was only twenty-five years old, but he had already been named an Ernst and Young Entrepreneur of the Year, and listed as one of the top ten young entrepreneurs in the country by *Success* magazine.

Jared's business success made him a potential donor, of course, but that's not why I wanted to meet him. He hit my radar because he had just been elected to the state board of education, and because his private foundation listed "educational opportunities" as one of its strategic initiatives. In other words, Jared was passionate about helping kids in school get a better education.

I combed through my Rolodex until I found someone I knew well who also knew Jared. Rather than using my friend's name as a calling card, I actually got my friend to call Jared and recommend that having a meeting with me would be worth his time. Then I called Jared's assistant, and she set up a time for us to have lunch at Strings, a wonderful Denver restaurant whose owner had agreed to give me complimentary meals when I was there on Leader's Challenge business.

While I had done enough homework to identify Jared as someone I needed to know, I did even more research on him and his interests before we went to lunch. As a result, when we sat down that first time, I didn't start off with general, information-gathering questions like "So, Jared, tell me about yourself." We didn't begin with NSW. Instead, I asked him informed questions about what it was like growing up with an artist father and a poet mother, and about what life was like at Princeton. I asked him what challenges he faced starting up his own company, and about his ideas on reforming education. In other words, I showed I was interested enough in him to have found out a little about him before our meeting, and it allowed our conversation to advance far more rapidly.

We were very different politically in many regards, but I also knew we had like-minded interests, especially when it came to improving education. Our first lunch led to another. Six months later he invited me to Washington, D.C., to meet some of his political friends. He encouraged me to change party affiliation and run for office. (Jared is now a Democratic U.S. congressman.)

As it turned out, our trip to Washington was scheduled for September 11, 2001. We took a red-eye from Denver, landing at Dulles Airport at 8:00 a.m., just an hour before the terrorist attacks. The meeting we had set up was abruptly canceled. As word spread of the attacks, the airports, train stations, and bus stations all shut down, and there were no rental cars available. We were stranded, with no way home. So we took a taxi to a Ford dealership, where Jared bought a car so we could drive back to Colorado. (Traveling with a multimillionaire can have its perks.)

Driving across the country together in the wake of such a searing tragedy gave us a ton of time to talk further and deepen our relationship. We debated ideas, shared stories, and talked about the experiences that had shaped our lives. And we encouraged each other. We found more and more common ground. We talked about the things in life that were important to each of us. It helped us to take our relationship beyond the Second and Third floors.

But none of that would have happened if I hadn't done my

homework first. Is that manipulative? I would argue if you truly want to meet someone you think has the potential to become an important figure in your life, why would you *not* want to do a little legwork to prepare the ground? I see it as a compliment to take the time and learn something about people before you spend time with them.

Today I have less homework to do before reaching out to new people. But that kind of preparation, that kind of homework, never really stops. As the Eagle Scout in me would say, you always want to be prepared.

We can't build close relationships with everyone we know. But doing our homework can help us to figure out where we should best invest our time and energy. My homework, for instance, almost always includes something I call the "Black-Berry Scroll."

Pull out your BlackBerry (or whatever PDA or other device you use to manage your contacts). Scroll through the list of people you know. What's your immediate reaction to each name you encounter? Is that person a "giver" in your life, or a "taker"? How about you? Are you a giver in that person's life, or a taker? On what floor would you place each relationship? Do you have far too many NSW relationships? Which of those relationships would you like to move up to the next level?

This simple exercise can be an eye-opener in terms of where you stand in your relationships. Print out your contact list; spend an hour going over it, marking each name with a *G* for "giver" or a *T* for "taker," and a number to represent what floor your relationship is on. Mark it with an "up" arrow if you think the relationship has potential for growth or improvement. Later, you can simply scroll through your list while waiting on a flight, or during the time you have for personal reflection.

The point isn't to rate or judge the people in your life, but to honestly assess your relationships with them. It is a window into your life. When I practice this exercise, I learn far more about *myself* and things I need to improve than I learn about the people on the list. But I also finish with a clearer focus on the relationships in my life that have the most potential for mutual growth.

Relation*Shifter*

You can and should be intentional and strategic about building relationships, and that starts with doing research that helps you decide where to focus your time and energy. Proactively researching potential relationships helps you identify the people you most need to know, make introductions, and launch those relationships in a positive way.

Chapter 8

Breaking the Ice . . .
and Stirring It Up

Bob Barbour and I met in Greenville, North Carolina, while watching a college football game.

Garry Dudley, my best friend from college, had invited me to tailgate with him and some friends before an East Carolina University game. Bob and his family were among the group who had gathered with Garry for the pre-game meal in the parking lot at Dowdy-Ficklen Stadium.

Bob is a humble leader who built eight successful car dealerships across eastern North Carolina. He's not the sort of man who immediately opens up with the details of his life, but I knew I wanted to know him better. I wanted to see if he and I might build a relationship that could last much, much longer than the football game.

How did I know that? For starters, Bob was on one of my lists. At the time, I was the "leader-in-residence" for East Carolina University. That's a fancy title for a consultant hired to help the university launch a campus-wide leadership initiative. That year, I spent a week each month on campus, which is why I happened to be in town for the football game. As a part of my duties, I made it my job to know as many leaders on campus and throughout the community as possible. By every measure,

Bob was one of those leaders—a successful businessman with a reputation for integrity and service to others.

I didn't approach him with any specific agenda; he just seemed like a guy ECU's leader-in-residence should know. But I was confident there were ways he could help ECU, and ways ECU could help him. The only way to find out was to get to know him. I didn't know in advance that he was one of the friends Garry had invited to the tailgate party that Saturday. But I was thrilled when he was introduced to me. It gave me a perfect opportunity to make a connection with him.

But how do you do it, you might ask. For many people, of course, therein lies the big, brick wall with no obvious doors or windows. As one friend put it, "What do you say to break the ice with someone you'd like to meet?"

The answer is simple, if perhaps a bit unexpected: news, sports, weather.

You may think I see no value in NSW relationships. They are shallow. They are confined to the First or Second floors of relationships. We want to move most of our relationships beyond that, right?

True enough. But there's value in NSW conversations exactly because they belong on the First and Second floors. After all, that is where most relationships begin!

Small talk—the essence of NSW relationships—is an important emotional glue in bringing people together, and creating common bonds. It's like stretching before a workout. If you don't stretch, you'll pull a muscle. But if all you do is stretch for thirty minutes, you'll never get much of a workout in. Eventually you have to get your heart rate higher.

Every relationship is different. Some relationships require more stretching than others. Some people are able to move quickly into deeper-level conversations. Others prefer to move more slowly. How I start a conversation with someone depends largely on what I know about the other person and the vibe I pick up from him about how fast he wants to move things along.

When I meet someone for the first time, I introduce myself and tell her honestly that I'm honored to meet her. Then I always try to start with compliments. *It's a beautiful day . . . You live in a wonderful city . . . I met your son earlier. You must be extremely proud of the man he's become . . . Those are amazing shoes. My wife has a pair just like them . . .*

To know what to compliment, of course, I pay attention to the details of our exchange. My hope is that such compliments will lead to natural questions I would like to ask the person I'm meeting. *Do you spend a lot of time outdoors? What's your favorite thing about living here? When did your son realize he wanted to study biology? What is your favorite shoe store in the area?*

The questions I ask—and the compliments I give—reflect a part of me while demonstrating my interest in the other person and his or her world.

I've learned along the way that what I don't ask can be as important as what I do ask. In Australia, I discovered that people almost never talk about their careers or vocations. Two guys can sit at a bar sharing drinks for hours and never realize one is the CEO of a huge corporation and the other works in construction. In America, successful people are often defined too narrowly by their jobs or for "something" they've done—the singer for her music, the preacher for his church, the umpire for his calls in the World Series, the manager for the department she leads, the surgeon for his medical expertise. Those things are real and important, but most people enjoy talking about "something else"—just about anything other than the things that "everybody" asks them. When I meet someone for the first time, I often intentionally avoid the very thing I think they get asked about the most—and ask, instead, about *them.*

I had done my homework; Bob was one of the top business leaders in Greenville. But we'd just met. He was there with his family and friends, enjoying time together and thinking about the upcoming football game. He didn't know me. If I had started out asking him questions about his business success, I suspect he would have run for cover! I know I would have.

So I let our relationship start with some stretching—some NSW conversation as we all stood around the tailgate of the car before the kickoff of an afternoon college football game. Frankly, I don't really remember much about what I told him. But I remember thinking that I wanted a chance to learn more about him.

Sometimes a second meeting comes weeks or months after an initial meeting, and it may require considerable intentional follow-up, as we'll discuss in chapter 14. At the time, I figured I would call him or send him a letter and try to set up lunch with him the next month when I was back in town. As it turned out, however, an opportunity arose later that same evening.

When the game ended, Bob invited us all to his house for dinner.

Bob has a beautiful home and a generous, welcoming family. They made me feel right at home from the moment I walked in. We all sat around inside, talking about local politics and people in the community as Bob prepared burgers and carried them out to the grill on his deck. It seemed like the perfect time to get to know Bob better. So, while the others stayed inside, I slipped out to talk with Bob.

"I've heard a lot about you from Garry," I said. "He's told me that you've done a lot for the community."

It was the sort of icebreaker that honors two people, both

my friend Garry and Bob. But I wouldn't have brought it up if it weren't true.

Bob responded with the expected reaction. He was friendly yet humble. While I think he appreciated the compliment, Bob remained modest and unassuming. But it did set the tone for a question that almost always gets people to talk about themselves.

"Do you mind if I ask you a personal question?"

If I had asked that at the tailgate party, I suspect Bob would have given me an awkward look and said, "Well, I probably do mind." But several hours later, in the relaxed comfort of his home, the question was far more appropriate. He had to wonder what kind of "personal" question I might ask, but by then he trusted me enough to find out.

Now, I could have blown it right there. He agreed to let me ask the question, but, like anyone, he was listening cautiously before actually answering it.

My first "personal" questions to someone aren't usually that personal. I just want to move the conversation gradually in a personal direction. In this case, everything I'd learned about Bob from Garry and my research had led me to believe that Bob wasn't born with a silver spoon in his mouth and a private jet. He was a self-made man. So I asked how he'd ended up in Greenville, and gotten into the car business. It wasn't an invasive personal question, but it invited him to take a step beyond strictly business; it gave him an opportunity to share something about himself, if he was open to letting me know more about him. But it left the next step up to him.

He told me a little of his background. I asked if his father had been in the car business. No, he said, he was twelve when his father died. He was the youngest of three children, and the family had very little money.

"That must have been hard," I said. "What was it like growing up without your father?"

Later we talked about the death of his son, Robbie, who was killed in a car accident at seventeen, and Bob gracefully shared how he struggled with the grief of that loss.

You can see where this was heading. I wasn't pushing too hard, and we were establishing some trust. I wasn't focusing on what he had earned in life—the beautiful home, the car dealerships, the nice boat. I was interested in him as a person. And he was inviting me to peel back the layers of his life.

What I expressed was a genuine desire to learn a little more about him. I have a relative who tends to jump right in with probing personal questions before she's gotten to know someone or without any sense of what's appropriate to ask. And I've seen more than one person emotionally shy away. They're just not ready to make themselves so emotionally available to her.

I think Bob sensed that I was genuinely interested in him partly because I was open and vulnerable about my life and my ups and downs as I listened to him share about his. I stayed at Bob's house well past midnight, learning about how Bob started mowing lawns to make money after his father died, and how he dropped out of school at sixteen to help feed his family. He worked from 7:00 a.m. until 9:00 p.m. Monday through Saturday at a local grocery to make ends meet. Each Saturday evening Mr. Spence, the owner, handed him an envelope with his pay—$33.10, in cash.

Imagine the sense of pride he experienced years later when he took ownership of his first car lot and walked his mother onto the lot and told her, in gratitude for all she'd done for him, "Pick the one you want."

Bob struggles to read and write; like me, as it turns out, he has dyslexia. Nonetheless, he became one of the most successful car dealers in North Carolina. As you can see, how he got there is far more interesting than where he ended up. People today often see him for what he has, rather than for who he is. And they're missing out on the best of Bob Barbour.

I returned to Greenville several times over the next eight months, and each time I got together again with Bob. On my last visit as part of my contract with ECU, Bob invited me to breakfast. He said, "Tommy, there are very few people who know me like you do. I've never opened up to a friend as much as I have opened up to you."

We no longer had to stretch—no more news, sports, and weather; we had become friends. Our relationship, I knew, would outlast a lifetime of football games.

Relation*Shifter*

Before diving too quickly into potentially sensitive personal questions, first develop a rapport. Do some "relationship stretching." Get to know the other person by asking simple, non-intrusive questions. Patiently explore deeper ground together.

Chapter 9

Back of the Business Card

I didn't have a business card when I was twelve, but here's what it would have said if I did: TOMMY SPAULDING, KID.

That tells you something about who I was. But it doesn't tell you enough to know if you'd like to get to know me. What sort of "kid" was I? What did I like? What were my hobbies? What did I dream of doing with my life?

Frankly, the business cards I've carried as an adult haven't provided much more information that would help you decide if you were interested in reaching out to me:

Business Partner/Sales Manager, IBM Lotus
Director of Corporate Affiliates, Up with People
Founder and President, Leader's Challenge
CEO and President, Up with People
Founder and President, the National Leadership Academy
President, Spaulding Companies LLC

Tens of thousands of relationships begin each year with one person handing another person a business card. And what are they exchanging? Name. Title. Organization. Contact information. It doesn't get more basic than that.

In Western cultures, cards are the currency of networking in business. But they serve a limited purpose. They give you something to enter into your contact file. You slip the card into your pocket or wallet or purse, intending to dig it out later so you can add the information to your computerized collection of names, numbers, and e-mail addresses. Or, more likely, you intend to, but end up throwing it out or tossing it into the bottom of a drawer, having already forgotten the person's face and distinguishing characteristics.

In Eastern cultures, a business card typically carries more significance. In Japan, for instance, where it's called a *meishi,* it's more than the currency of networking—it's the face of the person. There's a ritual for exchanging the cards. Whether giving or receiving a *meishi*, you hold the card with two hands, never allowing your fingers to cover the name or contact information. After the exchange, you both bow. But if the other person is considered more important than you, you bow lower. After taking the card, you study it. The longer you look at it, the more respect you show the other person. You do not put it in your wallet or your pocket in front of the other person. If you're in a meeting, you put it on the table before you until the meeting ends. If you're at an event, you hold it until the person leaves. And you never write on the card. It would be like writing on the person's face.

At the end of the day, of course, the ho-hum approach of Americans (and Europeans) and the cherished rituals of Easterners leave you with exactly the same thing: basic information.

If you want to build a genuine relationship, you need much, much more.

Turn over the typical business card—in the East or the West—and here's what you'll find: nothing.

I like to think of the back of the business card, however, as the most important part. It represents everything of real value that you know about the other person (nothing), and, therefore, how much you need to learn (everything). When I meet someone new, I immediately start working to fill in the metaphorical back of the business card—whether they have an actual card or not—with all the things that really matter.

Some of this information comes from research (see chapter 7), but much of it comes from observation and questions.

You can learn a lot of information about someone without ever saying a word, just by paying attention to the things on her bookshelves, on her desk, or on her walls, or to the things she's wearing. Even our cars tell a piece of our story. A friend of mine used to play a game with his kids while driving them to school. They would look at the car in front of them and try to guess as much as they could about the driver based on the license plate, the bumper stickers, the make and model and accessories, and any other outward appearances. *That person's a Democrat who enjoys skiing, had some experience that involved a drunk driver hurting someone she loves, and is proud of her honor student child.*

Think about your home or office. How much could someone learn about who you are simply by walking through for ten minutes and paying attention to the things they saw? Will they know where you went to school? How many kids you have, and what their interests are? What will the state of your workspace tell them?

What we don't learn from homework or by observation, we learn by asking and listening. And the more homework and observation we've done, the better the questions we ask. Before long, you'll have moved beyond the surface level of a relationship into what's really important in their life—their passions, their dreams, their challenges, their goals, the people in their lives that they care about, the things that bring them joy and fulfillment.

When I think of the people I know, I seldom think of their business card; I think of their back-of-the-business-card information.

Mariner Kemper's business card might tell me he's the chairman of UMB Bank in Denver, but the back of his card tells me about his devotion to the arts.

Business guru Ken Blanchard's business card might tell me he's an author and founder of one of the top management training companies, but the back of his card tells me he's passionate about golf, helping others, and studying the leadership lessons of Jesus.

Noel Cunningham is a restaurant owner and renowned chef; but he's passionate about creating solutions to end hunger in Ethiopia.

Jerry Middel, a retired founder of a corporate insurance and benefits company, loves fly fishing and mentoring at-risk kids.

Chris Mygatt, the president and COO of Coldwell Banker in Colorado, loves flying airplanes.

Steve Farber, a leadership guru, consultant, and speaker, is passionate about playing the electric guitar.

Thomas Spaulding Sr., my father and a former English teacher, loves his children and playing the piano.

My business card might tell you that I'm a public speaker, a business consultant, a life coach, and a social entrepreneur. But on the back of that card, those who know me know that I love to travel, especially with my wife; that I love to volunteer; that I'm a huge Yankees fan; that I have three kids; that I'm dyslexic, and that my struggles to read helped turn me into a serious movie buff; that I love Broadway shows, concerts, U.S. history, and staring for hours at world maps.

When you think of the people you are getting to know, take out a piece of paper and write down the back-of-the-business-card information. That's what really helps you develop the relationship.

For instance, if you wanted to send me a gift for my birthday, think how much more meaningful that would be if you picked out something connected with the back of my business card—a historic map of Denver, or a baseball signed by one of the Yankees starters, for instance.

Even when you only have a few minutes, take the time to ask at least one probing question that you can put on the back of his business card. And by focusing on the person and not on his position, you gain the kinds of insights that will lead to a deeper, more meaningful relationship.

Relation*Shifter*

New relationships start with basics, but you advance them by focusing on the less obvious and more personal information that's not found on a business card. Examine your relationships. What don't you know? Now go about the enjoyable work of finding out the hopes, dreams, and interests of the people in your life.

Chapter 10

Leveraging Philanthropy

Buying a ticket to a charity fund-raiser in a banquet hall full of people I had never met seemed like a perfectly good idea the first three or four times I tried it.

Many of my life experiences, but especially my work with Up with People, had fed my strong desire for volunteering with nonprofits that served the greater good of a community. When I decided to call Denver home, I saw volunteering and attending charity fund-raisers as an important relationship-building strategy. It allowed me to engage in the community, as well as meet influential leaders.

Denver, like most cities, has a strong philanthropic culture. The United Way movement began in Denver more than 120 years ago. There are now more than twenty thousand public charities and private foundations in Colorado. CEOs and other top executives typically serve on multiple boards, and charity events draw leaders from business, nonprofits, politics, and entertainment.

Traditional networking events are highly transactional—you do this for me and I'll do that for you. Everyone has something to sell; everyone is looking for something else in return. People hand out business cards the way blackjack dealers toss out playing cards. But building genuine relationships requires an understanding of people's hearts. And the people who get involved in philanthropic efforts usually do so because the cause is near and dear to their hearts. I saw volunteering and attending charity fund-raisers as smart ways to engage in the community, while establishing relationships that had a shared vision for helping others.

Volunteering proved to be a great way to meet my peers. I sought out organizations that appealed to my passions, gave them a call, and never tried to hide my motives. "I'm new in town," I would tell the volunteer coordinator. "Do you have any volunteer opportunities that would allow me to help and also meet other people my age?" I can't remember any group telling me no, and I soon found myself working shoulder-to-shoulder with my peers in food banks, for homeless shelters, and on Habitat for Humanity construction projects. It was easy to talk with people and get to know them while we worked around a common cause.

Some of the city's most influential leaders volunteered for such projects, and I met a few of them that way. But I knew the better place to meet the people I needed to meet was at charity fund-raiser events.

The problem was that most people go to fund-raisers with friends or spouses or co-workers. They're already connected. If you go alone, you end up at the single-ticket table, seated at the back of the room. Most of us were on the lower rungs of the ladder of community influence.

I could get to know the people at my table, but those were mostly random relationships. Each one had potential, but the room was filled with people who I *knew* I needed to meet to further my nonprofit ambitions.

Moving beyond that table was a huge challenge, even for an

extrovert like me. I'd feel a knot form in my stomach as I looked at the intimidating mass of people across the room and wondered how I could break into this community.

Still, my strategy was sound. To meet key community leaders, I had to go to the places where such leaders gathered. I couldn't get through the gates of golf courses and country clubs, and it's rude to interrupt someone during lunch or dinner at a restaurant. But anyone with a ticket can attend a charity fundraiser.

However, getting in the same room with the people you want to meet isn't enough. They tend to mix with people in their own groups. I found myself on the outside looking in. Leveraging my interest in philanthropy to launch strategic new relationships hit the wall of reality.

Then Barry Hirschfeld introduced me to Michael Smith.

Every community has its influencers. Most communities have dozens of them; major cities like Denver have hundreds. The key to meeting and building relationships with the people who can ultimately shape your future starts by building a relationship with just one of them.

For me, that person was Michael Smith. Michael unlocked the door for me in terms of leveraging philanthropy. And I met Michael thanks to Barry Hirschfeld.

Barry ran a printing company founded more than a hundred years ago by his grandfather. As the third-generation owner of what became a mega-successful family business—at one time among the largest printing companies in the West—Barry carries enormous influence in Denver.

Barry was on the international board of directors for Up with People during my year as director of corporate affiliates. When I left, he was kind enough to invite me to be a guest in his skybox for a Denver Broncos football game. Michael Smith was also his guest at that game. Michael's daughter Tara, a talented high school singer (who later worked as an actress and is now a producer in New York), performed the national anthem before kickoff. As we talked about what a great job she did singing that day, Michael told me that she had been "coached" by some of the staff at Up with People.

That common ground launched our relationship, and led to a meeting at which Michael agreed to support my efforts to start Leader's Challenge. He not only gave me a generous donation, but also became a trusted mentor to me. And one of the first things he did was to invite me to a charity fund-raiser.

When Michael and I met to talk about Leader's Challenge, I didn't merely ask him for money. I explained that I was still new to the community, and that I'd appreciate any help he could give me in meeting other community leaders.

In other words, I asked him for help. I was straightforward, sincere, and as it turned out, that was the kind of person Michael Smith could relate to.

For his part, Michael was interested enough in me and my mission to help me meet his circle of upper-echelon community leaders. He recognized that the best way to do that was to invite me to a fund-raiser for National Jewish Health, one of the top hospitals in the country and one of his favorite charities.

That's when I realized what was missing in my attempts to reach out to others by leveraging philanthropy. I needed an advocate, someone the community leaders knew and trusted.

Within the first half hour at this event, I met the governor of Colorado, the mayor of Denver, and the managing partner of one of the biggest law firms in the state. I met more people that night than I had met at all the previous fund-raisers I had attended, combined.

At future fund-raisers, those people remembered me as Michael's friend. I had newfound credibility, as well as new opportunities to extend those relationships into something more. In addition, in what I think of as the Snowball Effect, each new relationship led to additional contacts, opportunities, and relationships.

I stopped going to fund-raising events alone, and started going as someone's guest. This gave me a better way to meet new people of influence, but it also allowed me to go to more events than I ever could have afforded to go to on my own.

Over the next five years—until I got married—I attended a fund-raiser of one sort or another nearly five nights a week, sometimes even hitting several events on the same night. I made a list of the "top fifty" Denver charity events, and made it a point to attend each of them. I went to just about every charity event I could—the Children's Hospital Gala, the Boy Scouts Breakfast, the Children's Diabetes Foundation's High Hopes Tribute Dinner, the Boys and Girls Club Gala, the Red Cross Breakfast for Champions, the Volunteers of America Western Fantasy Gala . . .

Sometimes I paid for my ticket. Other times I'd just go to the reception (where they usually didn't ask to see a ticket). But most often I went as the guest of someone I had met at a previous fund-raiser.

Keep in mind, this was a time when I didn't have much money. In the early days, I was the president of a new and not-yet-funded nonprofit, and my savings had dried up. Donations weren't coming in early on, because Leader's Challenge hadn't attained its tax-exempt status. I sublet my loft, parked my car because I couldn't afford car insurance, and slept on a cot in a room above my office (until we were evicted from the office). Things eventually got better financially, but the first couple of years were extremely tight—and exciting.

When I shared my vision of Leader's Challenge with potential donors, many wanted to take a wait-and-see approach before writing a check. So I told them there were other ways they could help—not the least of which was by taking me as their guest to a fund-raiser.

Charity events usually sell blocks of tickets to major sponsors, and those organizations often have a hard time filling the seats. They buy a table for ten, but they may have only eight people who can go. So giving me a ticket helped me and helped them fill the seats at their table.

Each event helped me strengthen or reaffirm relationships with people I had met previously, while leading to new relationships and opportunities.

Regardless of who I met, I always tried to be myself. I never was starstruck at some of the influential, wealthy, or famous people I was introduced to, and I never tried to be something I wasn't. I tried to focus our conversation around our mutual passions. And I never asked the people I met for anything. Ever. My goal was to meet them, not sell to them.

This is particularly important if you work in a for-profit environment. My advantage in working for a nonprofit was that my intentions revolved around a good cause. By their very nature, my efforts were not about self-promotion. The point of this strategy is to meet people and launch relationships, not to close a deal. If you create a genuine relationship, the business will follow.

I usually made ten or twenty new contacts at each event. And I always followed up with at least a handwritten note telling them how nice it was to meet them. The next time I'd see them (often at the next event), they'd thank me for the note, which gave me a natural way to restart a conversation.

By leveraging philanthropy, I built a reputation as someone actively involved in the community. And the more involved I became—not just by going to fund-raisers, but by volunteering my time and energy—the more I got to know the people who were active leaders. Before I knew it, I was sitting on five or six boards, and had a peer-to-peer relationship with many of the influential leaders in the community.

The result was that I engaged my community in ways that helped others and I eventually built momentum for building dozens of key relationships.

Leveraging philanthropy, however, isn't just about one person expanding his network. It can become the focus of entire organizations. The old-school corporate model for engaging community nonprofits was pretty much limited to a company purchasing a table's worth of tickets to a charity fund-raiser and encouraging top executives to serve on boards. Today the most innovative and creative organizations encourage their entire workforce to engage in community service and philanthropy.

The best organizations today give employees a certain number of paid days off to volunteer. They encourage employees to get involved at leadership levels of nonprofit organizations. Jim in customer service may be on the board for the Boys and Girls Club, where he coaches his nephew's basketball team. John in accounting may head up a Watch Dog Dad program for his daughter's school district. Jenny in HR reads stories to children once a month as part of a literacy program at the library; it reminds her of going to the library with her grandmother when she was a child. Mary, a custodian, is on an advisory committee for the county's food bank—the same food bank that provided her with assistance when she was going through a tough time.

Preston in sales may be on the board for the battered women's shelter that helped his sister get free of an abusive relationship.

You don't need an organizational initiative to get involved, of course, but companies that take this opportunity are building relational capital with their employees and with their community. That's leveraging philanthropy.

Most of the benefits are obvious. But sometimes such a benefit can come in an unexpected form. It isn't part of some grand plan. It arrives like an unexpected gift in the mail. And you open it up and it totally transforms your life.

For instance, none of the relationships I've built were more pivotal to my future than the one that started in December 2003 at a fund-raiser for The Gathering Place, a day shelter for homeless women and children. I had volunteered to emcee their event. One of the first people I met that night was a volunteer at the front check-in desk. That volunteer—Jill—eventually became my wife.

Relation*Shifter*

Engaging in your community by volunteering and by attending charity fund-raisers provides opportunities to strategically meet people you need to know and lay a foundation for a long-term, meaningful relationship.

Chapter 11

Never Kiss on the First Date

I'd love to tell you that my wife looked into my eyes the first time we met and instantly knew that I was *the one*. But it didn't go down that way. In fact, it took me so many attempts to persuade her to go on a date with me that I started to worry that she might get a restraining order to keep me away! I must have asked her out twenty times before she finally agreed to meet me for coffee.

At the time, Jill was the single mother of a three-year-old boy. She'd been divorced less than a year, and she was taking a cautious approach to dating. For me, it was love at first sight. That made me all the more nervous as I drove to meet her at the coffeehouse. I felt this was my only shot to get a second date, and I didn't want to mess it up.

On the way there, I rehearsed all the things I wanted to tell her about myself. I wanted her to know everything positive about me that I could think of. I wanted to "sell" myself. In fact, I distinctly remember actually praying about it as I drove to meet her.

Then I realized that if I wanted to build a relationship with Jill, our first meaningful conversation didn't have to revolve around me.

When we sat down for coffee, the first thing I asked about was her life: "I understand you have a three-year-old son. Tell me about Anthony."

In the blink of an eye, our fifty-minute date lasted three hours. And it all began with me asking Jill about her life. And when we got up to leave, she was almost apologetic.

"All we've done is talk about me. Tell me more about yourself," she said.

"I've got to run," I said. "Let's save that for the next time."

There turned out to be many more "next" times, but I deliberately took things slowly. For the first time in my life, I was dating someone just to get to know her. I never knew what I'd been missing before.

Except, in a way, I knew exactly what I had been missing. Because that was exactly how I'd always approached my professional and other personal relationships. Dating had been the one area where I'd tried to move too fast or had taken the relationship too casually.

In all my other relationships, I instinctively understood not to, as one might put it, kiss on the first date.

Dale Carnegie hit on this when he talked about "six ways to make people like you." I don't think you can "make people like you," at least not over the long haul. But his principles on this topic are golden when it comes to getting a relationship off to a good start.

He said things like, "Be a good listener," "Encourage others to talk about themselves," and "Talk in terms of the other person's interests."

He also talked about being "sincere" and "genuine," which are key to the strength of any relationship. If you're not interested enough to listen to what someone else has to say, you don't deserve to earn a relationship with that person—or his business.

What Dale Carnegie was really saying, when you combine his six principles, was that it's bad form to "kiss" on the first date. If you rush forward with something, it might provide you with immediate gratification, but you'll likely push the other person away rather than draw him or her to you. The better approach is to listen—genuinely and sincerely.

Focusing on the other person is something I've done naturally as long as I can remember. I didn't even know it was a smart thing to do—I am just naturally interested in other people.

When I graduated from business school and went looking for a job in corporate America, I set my sights on a high-paying job with a high-profile organization. Several well-connected people were able to get my foot in the door of a few Fortune 500 companies. So I had six or seven meetings with top corporate executives.

I went into all of those meetings trying to learn as much as I could about the person on the other side of the desk. I didn't talk about myself at all. I had done as much research as possible about the executive and his company, and, armed with that research, I asked a ton of questions.

Toward the end of every meeting, the executive inevitably would realize that he had done most of the talking. And then he'd ask about me. I didn't have to sell myself—he or she *invited* me to share my story.

Each of those meetings led to formal job interviews within the company. "Find a place for this young man," the executive would say, and, with his blessing and support, they always did.

I was fortunate to have such doors opened for me, but I also knew that I had to make something of those opportunities. And I still had to interview at the department level. I didn't want them to go back to their boss and say, "We'll hire him if you make us, but he's not a good fit." The people doing the hiring were always more focused than the higher-level executive on asking me questions about my background, skills, and experiences, and so I answered them. But I also asked plenty of questions about them, as well, and I didn't push myself on them.

I wanted to show that, first, I had done my research about the company and, second, that I was interested in them as people. I instinctively knew they would remember me as much for the questions I asked as for the answers I gave. It wasn't about me chasing a first kiss—or a first job. It was about winning hearts and minds.

Was it effective?

I got a job offer at every single company.

Relation*Shifter*

Building a relationship begins by focusing your genuine, sincere attention on the other person. It's not about you. Take your time. Get to know the other person. Don't push for the things you might want; figure out what they need.

Chapter 12

Don't Be a
Chirping Bird

Working on the top floor in the 1996 presidential campaign headquarters of Senator Bob Dole, I met some of the most famous and influential people in the country. It's also where I put into practice some of the best advice anyone's ever given me about building relationships.

I had returned from teaching English in Japan, but I had six months before I would leave for Australia to work on my MBA. So I moved to Washington, D.C., where my friend Carolyn Gay helped me land a job on the Dole campaign. Carolyn, you might recall, had encouraged me to apply for the Rotary Ambassadorial Scholarship. She told me that if I worked my way up the ladder I'd likely come in contact with influential political figures, high-ranking officials, and all sorts of wealthy donors. "Don't ask for autographs and don't ask to have your picture taken with them. They'll look at you differently. You want them to look at you as a professional, not as a tourist."

Over the years, that advice has cost me all sorts of memorabilia. But it's also helped me launch some of the most incredible relationships I've ever had.

One of the most common mistakes we make when first meeting someone who we know can be influential in our life or career is to be overly aggressive. It's a short-term approach that can defeat our long-term goals.

We all enter some relationships with little or no expectations of what they can do for us. But some relationships are more strategic. We are well aware of their potential to help us advance our personal or professional goals. As a result, consciously building the relationship becomes an intentional part of our plans. There's nothing wrong with reaching out to people who can help you. Whether we're building a career or trying to grow in our personal lives, certain people are in better positions than others to help move us along. We're foolish not to seek them out.

So while we all leverage existing relationships—to make a sale, to forge a business partnership, to make new relationships possible—it is how we go about that process that makes or breaks our success with relationships. And in my experience, a key to leveraging relationships without abusing them is this: Don't be a chirping bird.

When a mother bird returns to her nest, what greets her? A nest full of chirping birds, each hungry and calling out for what it needs without regard for anything else. The birds eventually learn to fend for themselves. Some people, on the other hand, leave the nest but never stop chirping for more. Their needs are so great, and so insatiable, that their attention is always, first and foremost, on what others can do for them. Chirp. Chirp. Chirp.

Let me give you an example from the insurance industry. The insurance salesmen I count among my closest friends have one thing in common: they aren't chirping birds. They never ask me to introduce them to someone so that they can make a sale or ask for that person's business. These are good friends, and I'd be fine if they did ask. But they don't, because that isn't why we're friends. Nonetheless, I recommend them whole-heartedly anytime the subject comes up.

Others just want a referral so they can chase a sale.

One salesman I know once took a Leader's Challenge annual report, turned it over to the back where we had printed a list of donors, and circled the names of a number of people. They were people he didn't already know.

"Tommy," he said, "any chance you can introduce me to any of these people?"

Wow. Was he asking for my help in building lasting relationships? No. Did he plan to leverage those relationships to give back to the community? No. He was attempting to trade on our acquaintance to get referrals he could mine to chase sales and make money.

When I introduce two people, I do so because I believe they can mutually help each other; I'm delighted to facilitate such an introduction. My goal is to add value to their lives, and to the world at large. So I love introducing good people to other good people.

But introducing a chirping bird—a vulture or other predatory bird—to someone I know can hurt my friend and undermine my own relationship as well. They're likely to ask themselves, "What is it that drew Tommy to this person? What is it about this person that made Tommy think of me? Why does Tommy think we should know each other?" And if they can't answer that to their satisfaction, then I have failed.

I deeply value the trust they put in me. And the last thing I ever want to do is diminish that trust by introducing them to someone who only wants to use them. Their trust in me leads them to look for positive answers to those questions. If, in the short term or the long term, someone's behavior makes that relationship a negative experience, then the other person's trust in me diminishes and the opportunity for building our relationship to a higher level takes a hit.

If I learn that you've been a chirping bird, that you've abused the relationship instead of adding value to it, do you think I'm going to continue giving you a hand up into further value-driven relationships? Absolutely not.

My point? Never abuse an introduction that someone makes on your behalf. Honor your relationships. That is how you develop and maintain them.

If someone asks you for an introduction, be sure of the motives of the other person involved. Follow your gut on this—allow others to use your good name as an introduction only when they have the other person's best interests at heart. If you have doubts, don't make the introduction. And if you're not sure of your instincts, hold off, and get to know the other person better.

Now, there's nothing wrong with making an introduction purely for the purpose of enhancing business. If I know a friend or professional acquaintance has a particular need, like insurance, I'll gladly introduce him to someone I know and trust who can help him out—someone whose first priority will be building a new relationship. And they'll go into the relationship with an understanding that, professionally speaking, they have a skill or expertise the other person needs.

After all, leveraging my existing relationships to make new ones is a big part of how I've built such an extensive network.

Everyone has an inner circle—a "Fifth Floor Team"—and I've always made a point of learning who is in the inner circle of the people I want to meet. I don't believe in cold calls. They don't work very often. When someone approaches me from out of the blue, they have little credibility. And the busier and more influential the other person is, the less likely they are to be receptive to a cold call; they just don't have the time, and it's one of the easiest things to filter out. On the other hand, if someone on my Fifth Floor Team suggests that I meet someone new, I always agree to it. Always. In the same way, I know that if I want to meet a particular person, the best way to do it is to get an introduction from a mutual friend—someone I know who is in the other person's inner circle.

But I've always made one thing clear: I won't become a chirping bird. I won't overaggressively chase what I want or need. In other words, I will build the new relationship before asking something from it. I won't charge in asking for favors or business deals. I will build trust and give to the relationship before worrying about what, if anything, I will get.

People who are in a position of influence—in politics, church, business, sports, entertainment, or whatever—become very used to people calling because they want something. Everywhere they go, they find another nest filled with chirping birds. So when they meet people for the first time, they naturally become guarded.

The owner of the Colorado Rockies and the club's president are both good friends of mine. But I never ask them for tickets unless it's to give them to charity. I have another friend who owns one of the largest auto dealerships in Arizona. But I've never asked him for a deal on a car. I have a friend who is a well-known recording artist. But I never ask him for free tickets to his concerts.

My no-chirp approach to relationships has paid off.many times in many ways, not the least of which has been through my friendship with Jennifer Holtz. Jennifer is married to Skip Holtz, the former head football coach at East Carolina University and the son of coaching legend Lou Holtz.

I graduated from East Carolina University, and I've been

involved for years as an alumnus. In 2008, when I took the consulting job as ECU's leader in residence, part of my role was to meet with community and school leaders. None of that opened the doors of the head football coach's office. But I did have a relationship with Lynda Spofford. She is Jennifer Holtz's best friend from their days as coeds at Florida State. And Jennifer is married to Skip.

When I was president of Up with People, we sent a cast on a tour through the South. I approached the late Millard Fuller, a mentor of mine and the founder of Habitat for Humanity, about a sponsorship. His new organization, the Fuller Center for Housing, supported our tour, and our cast members volunteered on projects in the cities they visited. As the Center's vice president for communications and development, Lynda was our point person, so we got to know and respect each other. And a few years later when she learned I was going to spend a week each month at ECU, she suggested that I get to know her friend Jennifer.

Jennifer and I had lunch the next time I visited Greenville, and we became fast friends. But my relationship with Jen was never about getting to know her husband or her father-in-law (although my father-in-law is a huge Lou Holtz fan). While I like, admire, and respect Skip and Lou, my relationship with Jennifer has never been about anything other than building a friendship with her and her family.

Chirping birds always want something—tickets, autographs, influence, favors—and they will sacrifice the relationship to get whatever they want. Focusing on the relationship first means taking the risk that you might never get some of the things you want. But whether those "things" eventually come or not, you win because you have a relationship that's grounded on mutual interests and respect. And those relationships always pay off.

Relation*Shifter*

Chirping birds are out for their own self-interest. It prevents them from building meaningful relationships based on a position of authenticity and trust. Don't be a chirping bird. Life as a chirping bird might produce short-term results, but it ultimately will damage your relationships and divert your path from real success.

Chapter 13

Pardon Me While I Talk to Your Wife

Jill and I go to dinner four or five times a month with someone I'm getting to know on a professional basis. Sometimes the other person invites me to dinner, and sometimes I do the asking. I always ask Jill to come along. And if the other person is married or in a special relationship, I invite that person as well.

Jill and I keep busy schedules, so I love having her on these business meetings partly because I want to spend time with her. But we also go out with friends quite a bit, and we attend a lot of charity fund-raisers. So our relationship could survive if she didn't come with me on every business dinner. There's another reason, however, why I like to have her there: Jill is the most important person in my life, so how someone else receives her is a huge indicator of where my relationship with the other person might go.

The people who respect Jill and who value her opinions and ideas earn a lot of relationship capital with me. And I've discovered over the years that most people miss that opportunity—not just to win favor with me but, more important, to get to know the best part of me.

If you want to get to know Jill, ask her what it's like raising three young kids. Or if she misses her career as an elementary school teacher, now that she has a career as a stay-at-home mom. Or what she enjoys—and finds most challenging—about volunteering with so many different organizations. Ask her about her dreams or her daily challenges. Ask her about her world.

Most people, however, hover around the news, sports, and weather questions with Jill and ask me the more penetrating questions. Why? Because they see me as the decision maker. They think I'm the one they need to impress to get the business or establish the professional relationship.

But what happens when dinner ends and we close the car doors for the ride home?

I almost always ask Jill for her impressions of the person we went out with. Jill is a great judge of character and people. If the person invested time in learning something about my wife, wasn't self-focused, and engaged her in a meaningful dialogue, that speaks volumes. She's not one to speak poorly of other people, but it's not hard for me to tell if she felt ignored and passed over by the other person at the table.

I also recognize that my spouse is a reflection on me. When people meet Jill, I know my stock goes up. They think, "Tommy must be special if he can marry someone as genuine and smart, as sweet and sincere as Jill. He must be doing something right."

Similarly, when I'm building a relationship with another person, I want to identify what is important to him or to her. If they are married, that's often their spouse. But it might be some other family member, or a supervisor at work, a mentor or a friend, an administrative assistant, or even a cause.

If they don't seem to respect their spouse or administrative assistant or co-workers, that, too, is telling. It usually means our relationship will stay on the lower floors or won't get off the ground at all. If their true love is making money to the exclusion of other things, that tells me something. If they devote time to helping the homeless, that tells me something as well. Whatever their interests and personality, it will show itself in how they treat others. If you want an inside view of someone's character, watch the way they treat the doorman, the waitress, the flight attendant, the receptionist, the taxi driver—anyone they interact with who doesn't hold a position of influence. It they don't treat them with respect, a red flag should immediately go up.

But if building a relationship with a person is important to me, then what he or she finds important instantly takes on a new level of importance for me, as well. Said more simply: if it's important to the other person, it's important to me.

When we're at dinner or in some other social setting with someone I'm trying to build a relationship with, I almost always give more attention to his or her spouse. What's his career like? How does she spend her time? What's important to him? What are her dreams, her challenges? What does she see as her greatest accomplishments?

One of the best compliments I've ever received was from a friend who told me why he enjoys hanging out with Jill and me: "You make my wife feel so good," he said. "You ask her questions no one's ever asked before. Most of the time when we go out, people just ask about me."

Relationships seldom involve just two people. The best relationships are more complex, more robust. So if you care about someone, invest in the people *they* care about. Pick any ten relationships that you have right now. Think of several that you'd like to improve. Next, ask yourself who are the most significant people in their lives. What can you do to honor not just the person you have a relationship with, but the people who are important to them?

I see this idea lived out among the board members of a

nonprofit I support. When I was asked to join the board, I found myself among some nationally respected heavy hitters in their respective fields. And yet this board intentionally includes the spouses of board members in all their events and all their meetings. They want the spouses engaged in their mission. They want to honor the people who are most important in the lives of their fellow board members. It's a remarkable vision, and an example worth following—in business and in life.

Relation*Shifter*

If you're building a relationship with someone, you're also building a relationship with the people who are important to that person. What they think of you matters. It can go a long way in the shaping of your relationship. How you treat other people says a lot about who you are.

Chapter 14

Relentless Communication

Brad Billingsly works for Lockton, the world's largest privately owned independent insurance broker.

Brad epitomizes what I call "relentless communication" in relationships—the idea that if we want to create, build, and sustain relationships that matter, we have to consistently and persistently reach out to people in creative, personal ways.

Brad heard me speak a few years ago during a Leader's Challenge fund-raising breakfast, and something I said must have touched his heart. A few days later I received a handwritten letter from Brad, telling me how moved he was by my vision for helping young people and for volunteering in general. My talk had inspired him, he said, to get more involved. He wrote me the letter to encourage me and to thank me.

Brad's simple but sincere one-page letter touched me so deeply that I shared it with my wife. I put it in a folder I use for the cards and letters that I have treasured the most over the years. And when I was asked to give a speech to Lockton's Denver-based employees on creating a culture that values authentic relationships, I took the letter with me and I read it to the audience.

"As you can see, you already have someone on your team who understands the value of authentic relationships," I told the group. And then I explained the impact the letter had in launching my relationship with Brad.

Brad had ended the letter with the suggestion that we get together for a cup of coffee.

So we did. I knew from the letter that Brad was someone who cared about people not just on a surface level but in the ways that really mattered. He was transparent about his own shortcomings—he felt he didn't spend enough time serving others—and he cared enough to take the time to handwrite me a letter. He was my kind of person. His letter was the spark that ignited one of the closest friendships in my life.

It was the first of many cards, letters, phone calls, and meetings between us.

In an age when so many people see social networking through the pixels on a computer or cell-phone screen, Brad continues to handwrite letters and put them in a mailbox. A talented artist, many of Brad's missives include pencil-drawn sketches.

If you want to relentlessly communicate, there's nothing wrong with cell phones and e-mails. I send and receive more than a hundred text messages and e-mails every day. I'm the poster boy for "Crackberry" addiction. But sometimes it's the personal touches that set you apart from others and create the greatest opportunities for lasting relationships.

We get flooded every day by text messages and e-mails; meanwhile our mailboxes are filled with bills, advertisements, and solicitations. And that's exactly why handwritten letters and notes are so special—they are the rare personal note amid a sea of impersonal statements and bills. Just seeing my name handwritten on the outside of the envelope brings a smile to my face. It hardly matters how long the letter is or what it actually says. Though a cliché, it really is true that it's the thought that counts, because we remember the fact of the letter long after we've forgotten the actual words.

When I think through my contact list, I can tell you who among them communicate with handwritten letters. I get a handwritten note after any time I spend time with my friend Wil Armstrong. Susan Stanton, my wife's sister, is my ultimate role model in keeping this endangered species alive. If I do something for Susan, no matter how small or routine it might seem to me, she sends me a handwritten thank-you note. I must get a dozen or more a year from her. If anything significant happens in my life—from Anthony's hockey team winning a game, to my landing a new business deal—she knows about it and sends a note of congratulations or encouragement.

Handwritten notes, of course, are just one form of relentless communication. I have a friend in Minnesota who puts American flags in the yards of his clients every year on the Fourth of July. Another friend gives pumpkins to his clients each Halloween. They call and stop by as well, but these things in particular set them apart. They give people in the community a reason to think of them and smile.

Brad distinguishes himself through his sketches. Once Jill and I planned a vacation in Cabo San Lucas, Mexico, and we invited Brad and his wife, Amy, to stay with us. When we returned, Brad gave us a framed, hand-drawn sketch of the beach where we'd stayed. Other than my sister, who is a professional artist, no one else has ever given me a drawing representing a significant time in our lives. What a message!

What can you do to distinguish yourself from the crowd?

How can you practice relentless communication? What can you do when starting new relationships—the type of thing I displayed when sending thank-you notes to everyone who invited me to a charity fund-raiser during my early years in Denver? What can you do to keep your existing relationships healthy? I call my closest friends on their birthdays and sing "Happy Birthday" to them (sometimes to their embarrassment!), or drop them a handwritten note to let them know they were on my mind.

My friend Scot Wetzel, a prominent banker, often gives flowers to clients on special occasions. I'll never forget the flowers he sent Jill and me when Caroline was born.

What are you doing for your co-workers? Your clients? Your customers? Your donors?

My work now involves running for-profit and nonprofit ventures. On the nonprofit side, I make sure we send things like tax receipts, newsletters, and thank-you letters to all of our supporters. But to build deeper, stronger relationships with these donors, I go beyond those mandatory obligations. The same holds true for customers, clients, vendors, employees, and any other stakeholders in your professional world. Fund-raisers suggest that nonprofits need to find at least seven opportunities to thank a donor for every one time that you ask for a donation. I believe the same standard applies in business and in our personal lives. A thank-you on an invoice or a card at Christmas simply isn't enough.

Relentless communication is an intentional practice. It's playing offense, not just sitting back and playing defense. It's not something that just happens—you have to *make* it happen. I break it down in terms of the Scheduled, the Spontaneous, and the Super Routine.

The Scheduled

When I meet someone, I don't just enter their phone number and e-mail address in my contacts file. I also enter birthdays and anniversaries. But I don't stop there. I enter just about any piece of information I can think of—the names of their spouses, where they went to school, activities I know they enjoy. And if it's possible to put it on the calendar, I put it on the calendar.

If the child of one of my friends or significant contacts is graduating from high school or college or is scheduled to perform in a musical or play in a big game, I try to know about it and send them a gift, drop them a note or e-mail, or give them a call. When I was in sales with IBM Lotus, I often attended the youth soccer games and junior-high band concerts just to let my clients know I was interested in who they were, rather than just in the things they could do for me or buy from me.

How much do you know about the daily lives of your clients, co-workers, customers, and other key relationships? What can you do to encourage them, thank them, and support them in their lives?

The Spontaneous

Of course, not all communication fits on a calendar. Spontaneously reaching out can be meaningful. But even with spontaneity, you have to be intentional about keeping up with people's lives. It doesn't happen magically. You have to intentionally stay in tune with the world around you, or you'll miss some of the greatest opportunities to spontaneously communicate with the people you care about or would like to know.

One easy way to do this is to read the newspaper. Cut out any articles and highlight any information those you know (or want to know) might appreciate. Send it to them with a note. That's a good start.

But if you really know the things that matter most to your friends, you'll find other reasons to send them a note or give them a call. Maybe you know that a friend has had his eye on a new golf club, and you just happened to see it on sale. You can tell him the next time you see him—or you can pick up the phone right then and call.

I've written hundreds of letters to people I don't know, simply to say thanks for something they did or to encourage them. When I read a good book, I'll write the author. When I see that someone has won an award, I'll drop her a note saying congratulations—sometimes even if I don't know her. Many times, such a letter or note has been the starting point of a relationship.

The Super Routine

I make communication "super routine." It isn't just something I schedule. It is a part of my lifestyle. It's like brushing my teeth—once someone had to teach me to do it, but it's now a regular part of how I go about my daily life.

Let me share a few of those routines that I've developed, in case you want to adopt a few for yourself.

First, I routinely make a list of everyone I meet with during the week. Then I send at least twenty personal notes from that list. People I haven't met with during the week inevitably pop to mind, and I'll include notes to some of them, as well. Some people might see that as networking, or relationship maintenance. But I really don't think of it in those terms. I just see it as a good thing to do for people I care about. I address and stamp the envelopes, then put them in a folder in my briefcase with blank notes. Each day I carve out ten to fifteen minutes to write the notes. I never ask an assistant to address them or send them. I do it myself.

I have stationery with my name it. I never send personal notes on company letterhead or blank paper. At Christmas, my wife and I send hundreds of Christmas cards. We don't handwrite all the cards, but we handwrite all of the envelopes. And we make a point of *thinking about* each person or family to whom we send a card.

I also enjoy giving gifts that show I'm thinking about the other person—gifts that show I'm thinking about their interests and lives. Alan Holman and I were playing golf one day when he commented on how much he liked a watch I was wearing. It was a Calloway watch that I'd received as a gift for playing in a charity golf tournament. A month or so later, I invited Alan to a fund-raiser for Anthony's hockey team. Alan was battling an illness and was going through a divorce, and I wanted to do something that would lift his spirits. So I put the watch in front of him at his table and said, "I've been wanting to give you this for some time." It wasn't an expensive watch. But it let him know I had remembered how much he liked the watch and that I had been thinking about him.

Books make for great relationship-building gifts. My wife and I read the bestseller *Same Kind of Different as Me* by Ron Hall and Denver Moore (Thomas Nelson, 2008), and we liked it so much that we've given more than a hundred copies away as personal gifts to friends. And I give books to people I have professional relationships with all the time. In fact, I keep several boxes of books in my office that I can give to people facing different kinds of challenges. I always have copies of *Good to Great* by Jim Collins (Harper Business, 2005), *The Five Dysfunctions of a Team* by Patrick Lencioni (Jossey-Bass, 2002), *The Fred Factor* by Mark Sanborn (Random House, 2005), *Radical Leap* by Steve Farber (Kaplan, 2009), and *The One-Minute Manager*, the classic by Ken Blanchard (William Morrow, 1982). I probably hand out several hundred books a year.

These types of gifts send a message that I'm paying attention to personal and/or professional needs of others and that I care enough to act on what I know. The only gift I've ever regretted is the one I didn't give.

My point: Find ways to move the relationship forward.

When I have a conversation with someone, I'm always looking for at least one opportunity in which I can follow up with an e-mail, a call, a card, or a follow-up meeting. Sometimes I e-mail or call someone with a restaurant recommendation. It lets them know I'm thinking about them. If I write someone a note or letter after meeting them at a dinner party, they'll know I care enough to follow up immediately. They'll realize they made a positive impression and that I meant what I said when I told them I enjoyed meeting them. If I drop by someone's office with a basket of their favorite fruit and a thank-you note, they'll know I remembered their love of fresh Colorado peaches and that I valued them so much that I went out of my way to say thanks.

I think of communication in terms of its impact. There is a hierarchy. A text is nice, but an e-mail is better. And a phone call is better still. Sometimes, however, a handwritten note is even better. A gift with a handwritten note is special. But hand-delivering a note along with a gift is the best.

All of these things—all of this relentless communication—shows that you care, that you want to continue to build and grow the relationship. In most cases it leads to the thing you want next—face-to-face time with the person you want or need to know.

Sitting down with someone after an initial meeting is critical when trying to launch a professional or personal relationship beyond the First or Second floor. People are busy. You have to expect that it will be up to you to make a relationship blossom. You can't do that by e-mail. Find a reason to get together again—for coffee or lunch, or for a more formal meeting, if that's what your business requires.

When I was pitching my vision for Leader's Challenge, there were times when I'd drive prospective donors to the airport just to get some face time with them. I wasn't shy about it. If we were having a hard time scheduling a meeting, it often was because they traveled so much. So I'd volunteer to drive them to the airport so we could talk. (I usually suggested this in a handwritten note.) Not only did I get time with them to cultivate the relationship, but I think they appreciated my tenacity and my creativity.

Yes, I'm a bit zealous when it comes to these things. But that's why I call it "relentless communication." It takes time and energy, and sometimes a few bucks. The cards and books and gifts add up, to be sure. As does postage. But it's an investment that to me is well worth the cost.

If you want to create and nurture relationships in your life, make an investment in relentless communication. You don't have to send twenty handwritten notes a week, but why not send five? Or find other ways to uniquely express your thanks to the people you know—a flag on the Fourth of July, a yellow rose as a birthday gift. Make this a part of your life, something that you can make part of your relational DNA. When you do it, people will think of you and smile. And they'll want to know you better. And that's the heart of any relationship.

Relation*Shifter*

Whether you're trying to create a new relationship or building an existing one, stay in touch with the other person. Find unique, consistent ways to stay connected to their lives. When they hear from you, especially in personal ways, they'll know you care. And they'll want to know you better.

Chapter 15

Play Chess, Not Monopoly

My father taught me to play chess when I was in elementary school. My learning disability made it hard for me to read, but for some reason I was able to visualize the chessboard and the moves each player could make and how all the pieces worked together—for me and for my opponent.

My dad and I played all the time; it became one of the defining activities of our relationship. I still play whenever I can, and I look forward to teaching my children. And although I'm no Bobby Fischer, I typically enjoy the upper hand.

The thing I love about chess is that it teaches me to think strategically and challenges me to anticipate the future. The great chess masters always are thinking and anticipating the multiple scenarios to which they will have to react, based on the likely moves—and sometimes the unlikely moves—of their opponents. Good chess isn't reaction-driven. You don't base your next move solely on the last move of your opponent. You make moves to set up future moves; you make moves that anticipate your opponent's strategy. You try to see the big picture and act accordingly.

The lessons of chess can apply to our relationships, as well.

You can look at each relationship you have and see how it connects to all the other relationships, and anticipate how those relationships can help each other based on whatever actions you take or the other person takes.

Call it relationship chess. But instead of capturing a pawn or trapping a king, we're connecting people from multiple relationships in ways that benefit everyone involved. Making this work requires that we pay close attention to the needs and interests of the people around us. As with chess, we have to know what each person can offer the other—and we have to know how people can help or enhance each other's community of friends. It requires that we anticipate—five or six moves ahead—how the interests and needs of the people we know might fit together with our help.

I can give you dozens of examples of this. One connection leads to the next one, like eating popcorn out of a huge bowl in front of the TV.

Let's start with an example of an editor I know.

He and I were working on a project, and I wanted to find a way to express my appreciation. I began scanning the chessboard, looking for a way to let him know how much I appreciated his input.

One day we were on the phone and he mentioned he'd be out of the office one week the next month on a family vacation on Hilton Head Island, South Carolina. I asked where he was staying, and he said he was still trying to settle on a hotel. I saw an opportunity.

The nicest hotel I know of on Hilton Head Island is the Westin. I happen to know Mike Hanson, the president of Westin and a partner in the company that owns it. Mike also owns the Westin La Paloma in Tucson, Arizona; when I was CEO and president of Up with People, we held reunions in Tucson and would book the entire resort. Mike lives in Tucson, and we've become good friends over the years.

I know Mike well enough, in fact, that I could call and ask for a favor. He knows me well enough to know that I'm not a chirping bird—I don't ask often. I told him about the editor, the project we were working on together, and how I wanted to do something for him to help out during his vacation.

"Would you help me take care of my friend?" I asked.

Mike agreed to give him a complimentary room during his stay. Next, I sent the editor an e-mail: "The other day you said you were going to Hilton Head. What were those dates?" He responded with the dates and a question: "Why?" After confirming with Mike, I sent another e-mail: "A friend of mine is the president of the Westin, which owns the nicest hotel on Hilton Head. I made a phone call, and you're all taken care of. Here's your confirmation number."

The editor, of course, called to thank me, both before and after the trip. But I didn't do it for his thanks. In fact, I wanted to thank *him*.

Too often, people do a favor in the expectation of basking in the other person's praise and gratitude. To me, a good deed loses a little of its luster when the focus shifts to the giver.

Finding ways to do something nice for someone important in your life is a good enough lesson on its own. But relationship chess requires more. It requires thinking several moves ahead.

I wanted to thank Mike Hanson as well. I knew Mike enjoyed playing golf and watching football, and that he had a son attending the University of Colorado.

So when I called Mike back to thank him for providing the room, I asked him about his son. "When you come to visit him this fall, why don't you pick a weekend when the Broncos are playing at home, and we'll all go to the game," I said.

Mike took me up on the offer and picked a weekend when the Broncos were playing the Dallas Cowboys. Next I asked him if he wanted to play golf while he was in town and if he planned to stay in Boulder with his son, or if he wanted a hotel in Denver. He said his son's place was small, so, yes, a room in Denver would be nice. And, yes, he'd love to play a round of golf.

So I called my friends Mark Urich and Marcel Pitton.

I had introduced Mark and Mike Hanson during a visit to Arizona for Major League Baseball spring training earlier that year. I was sure that the more they got to know each other, the more they'd like each other. I also suspected Mike could well end up a client of Mark's insurance services. So I asked Mark if he would be interested in taking Mike out for a round of golf. I knew Mark would not put a heavy "sales" pitch on my friend. Mark would focus on Mike, and their relationship and a fun round of golf, regardless of whether it led to more business.

My other call was to Marcel, the general manager of the Brown Palace, a historic four-star hotel in downtown Denver. I told him a friend was coming to town and we were going to the Broncos game. Would he like to join us? And could he possibly provide Mike with a complimentary room during his stay?

I have several friends in the hotel business in Denver; most would have gladly done me that favor. But I called Marcel for a particular reason; I felt he needed to know Mike Hanson.

Marcel and his wife, you see, own a home on Hilton Head Island. They plan to retire there eventually. For now, they rent it out. When they travel to Hilton Head each year to check on the property, they have to stay at a hotel. To me, it made sense that Marcel should stay at the Westin when he visited Hilton Head, and that Mike should stay at the Brown Palace when he visited Denver. This type of trade-out is common in the hotel industry. All Mike and Marcel needed was an introduction.

By thanking the editor I was working with, I also was able to help nurture the relationship between Mike Hanson and Mark Urich, and help to start a relationship between Mike Hanson and Marcel Pitton—with mutual benefits for all involved. And I got to meet Mike's son, Greg, at the football game. He's a terrific young man who dreams of studying abroad in New Zealand. Greg and I are staying in touch while he's in school, and I've helped connect him with the largest company in the world that specializes in study-abroad programs in New Zealand. The company happens to be based in Denver.

So, at the end of the day, what was in all of this relationship chess for me? Did I "win" the game? Of course I won! My winnings, however, aren't easy to quantify. They came in the form of relationship capital. In fact, had I been seeking anything else, I would have lost.

Let's consider another board game: Monopoly. You need a strategy when playing Monopoly, but the game is much more reactive than chess. You react to the roll of the dice and to the cards you draw or the spaces you land on. You take each turn as it comes, and you go about the business of trying to rule the world—buy all the property, win all the money, own all the houses, hotels, railroads, and utilities.

When you approach relationship building focused only on your own benefit, with your own self-serving agenda, and with ulterior motives, everyone around you can see it for what it is. It's like playing Monopoly; even if you buy all the properties and fill them with hotels, you will never build meaningful, long-term relationships. Your relationships will be as bankrupt as the opponents you defeated in the game.

My goal with relationship chess is simple: to help and serve people. When people who know me do a BlackBerry Scroll and come across my name, I want them to mark me down as a Giver, not a Taker. That only happens if my intentions are pure. When they are, there's no way I can lose. It all comes back in good ways—although they are ways I may not be able to foresee or plan around. When I play chess or Monopoly, I play to win. But when I build personal relationships, I play to give. I play to serve. I don't want to finish with all the property and all the cash, nor do I want to capture the other person's king. I just want to help make their world a little better.

Relation*Shifter*

Building value-driven relationships requires forward-thinking strategies that lead to creative ways of helping others, connecting them with the people who can meet their needs and be a positive influence in their lives. Review your relationships with an eye not just to how you can help each other, but to how all of the people you know can help one another. Be a facilitator—help to make that happen.

Chapter 16

Seek Advice, Not Business

The most valuable questions I've ever asked another person had little to do with what they could *do* for me or my organizations, and everything to do with what they *thought* about something.

It was just such questions that led me to stay in Colorado rather than move back to New York. As I mapped out ideas for launching Leader's Challenge, I sought the advice of friends and mentors, who helped me tweak my business model, but also suggested that I start it in Denver.

I learned a similar lesson about building relationships ten years later, when Leader's Challenge closed its doors.

The principle is simple: ask others what they think instead of what they can do.

This works in every sector of the economy—corporate, nonprofit, and public. And it will help you strengthen relationships at every level. Those relationships blossom into creative partnerships and collaborations that take off in ways you never would have expected. Within an organization, they lead to better, more effective teams. Between organizations, they lead to deals that help both sides prosper. Whether you deal in products, services, or ideas, your chances of advancing them go up dramatically with relationships built on a shared vision.

We all want to be valued for our opinions, so we all appreciate it when someone asks us what we think. But asking what someone thinks isn't a tactic to stroke someone else's ego to get them to like you. Getting their opinions is important for much bigger reasons: first, it shows that you value and respect their opinions and viewpoints; second, you need the help; and, third, you need the buy in.

If you think you have all the answers on your own, well, you're kidding yourself. No matter what challenges you face, you can always benefit from the input of others. You might need their technical expertise or their detached point of view. There are always people who can add to your knowledge and expertise.

Feedback is also invaluable in creating support for your work. Leader's Challenge didn't launch with a *program* for teaching leadership to youth, but with a *mission* for teaching leadership to youth. The program came almost a year later, after I had spent countless hours visiting principals, teachers, superintendents, donors, and other leaders to get their input on what was needed, and on what would and wouldn't work. The fingerprints of hundreds of people covered the pages of the Leader's Challenge business plan, giving all of those people a sense of ownership in the program we eventually delivered.

One of those people was K. C. Gallagher, the managing director of Gallagher Enterprises. We met in August 2000. When I told him we wanted to put together a summer academy and bring in students from all around the state, he said, "Wouldn't it be incredible if you took an inner-city kid and had him room with some kid from the suburbs? You could put them in rooms with other kids of different races and backgrounds and socioeconomic conditions."

That was the exact opposite of my plan. I had intended to

group the students by school. But K.C. had a bigger and better vision, one that allowed the students to build bridges of understanding while sharing ideas.

When I visited with K.C. the next year, I told him that we had taken his advice and that it had worked out wonderfully. My vision and his vision had become a shared vision—along with more than a dozen others who helped shape the program. Do you think K.C. supported the program financially? Yes. He gave money every year for ten years. When you create a shared vision, you create a shared investment.

Even if you don't use all the advice you get—and you won't—you'll still have taken an important step toward getting support from people who matter.

When you focus on the relationship and not the business, the business thrives—even when the suggestion is the last thing you think you want to do. If you have a self-interest at stake—a sale to make, a business idea or nonprofit that needs funding— you have plenty of motivation for building relationships and seeking the opinions of others. But sometimes you need to "hear people out" just because it's the right thing to do. And that's never more difficult than when people are unhappy with something your organization has done.

I experienced this in 2009 when the board of directors of Leader's Challenge voted to close down the ten-year-old organization that I had founded. When I left Leader's Challenge to become president and CEO of Up with People, it was the largest student leadership program in the state. Unfortunately, within a few years it began experiencing management problems, and the tough economic times only made matters worse.

About a year after I left Up with People to start the Spaulding Companies, the Leader's Challenge board asked me to return, first as a consultant and then as interim part-time executive director. But our attempts to revive the organization came up short. In the fall of 2009 the board, over my objections, made the hard decision of shutting it down. They did so in the typical business-world manner. Once the decision was made, they ceased operations. They didn't look back, and they offered very little explanation about the closing. They simply closed it down and moved on to the next thing.

The decision was beyond my control, but obviously I had a tremendous emotional connection to the organization and the people involved with it. I had never lost my passion for its mission. Seeing it close was one of the toughest things I've ever dealt with. While the board did everything by the book during the closing, I felt a deep obligation to the people—not just the staff but the volunteers, students, parents, alumni, creditors, donors, and school officials.

So I went to talk to them. I made a list of more than one hundred people, and I made it a point to visit with every one of them, no matter how upset they were over the closing. I went to look them in the eyes and thank them for all they had done to support the vision. I wasn't asking for anything.

In doing this, several things happened.

First, many people on my list were still upset, but they were grateful that I cared enough to meet with them.

Second, the parents, students, and volunteers showed an amazing resolve to keep the program alive for the remainder of that school year. I spent six months putting together and leading a volunteer committee of parents, teachers, and principals and helping them self-direct a leadership program. That committee, ironically, came up with improvements that made the program better than ever. The lesson was clear: when you do the right thing in terms of your relationships—not just what's right "by the book"—extraordinary things can happen.

Third, a number of relationships were salvaged just before they fell into the basement. Avoiding confrontation is easy, but it comes at a high price. It was hard for me to talk to the Leader's Challenge creditors and donors, but it would have been worse to lose their respect.

A fourth thing happened. I heard a consistent message from all of the people I met with, saying, "Your work is not done." Through grace and prayer and the heartfelt advice and opinions of all the people I talked to on that list, I realized that sometimes when things die, new things are born.

Leader's Challenge lost its way. But there's still a need for teaching servant leadership, volunteerism, and citizenship to our youth. That need never goes away. What arose from the ashes of Leader's Challenge was the birth of a new initiative called the National Leadership Academy—a bigger, better version of the original vision.

Leader's Challenge was born because I had a vision and went about building relationships centered on the advice people offered for making it a reality. The National Leadership Academy was born because I sought to repair relationships, and I went where those relationships naturally took us. In both cases, seeking the advice—and forgiveness—made all the difference in creating the relationships, and building the business.

Relation*Shifter*

If you want to build relationships that matter, honor the other person. Listen to his advice—or his complaints. Find out what that person thinks, rather than telling her what you want. And if the situation requires it, seek forgiveness.

Chapter 17

He's Just Not That into Me

Life isn't perfect, and neither are relationships. There are times when the relationships we covet—whether for personal reasons, professional reasons, or both—simply don't pan out.

Some never get off the ground. No matter what we do, we can't get them off the First or Second floors. There are people out there who don't return my calls or respond to my letters. Other relationships find themselves buried *below* the First Floor, down in the dark, dingy basement. And other relationships get off to a good start, but later crash and burn. We've all had former co-workers who have betrayed us, left knife wounds in our backs, or failed to deliver on their promises. I've had mentors—people I completely trusted—turn against me. I've been hurt, misunderstood, and disappointed. And, unfortunately, I'm sure I've done the same to other people.

I've learned to deal with those hurts and disappointments by respecting **the Law of Mother Teresa**: results, while important, are secondary to doing the right thing the right way.

Mother Teresa lived with and served the most desperate souls in Calcutta, India, for forty-five years. Few of us are called to her lifestyle or mission, but I believe all of us can benefit by adopting her attitude and passion for putting the love of others over the results of that love.

I can't prevent a trusted mentor or friend or family member from letting me down, but I can control my attitude about that person. I can't force customers, co-workers, and vendors into a Second, Third, Fourth or Fifth Floor relationship, but I can give them every opportunity and reason to make that ascent with me. And I can find joy in the relationship no matter what the level.

It's easier to say that, of course, than to live it, and I struggle as much as anyone does (and sometimes more). We all want to be liked. None of us enjoys rejection. But when you find yourself trying to launch a relationship with someone who shows little interest, there are things you can do to limit or ease the potential for disappointment. In some cases they will even lay a foundation for getting the relationship on track.

First, exercise patience. This isn't always easy for me. I'm the sort of guy who wants to see my ideas implemented yesterday. I tend to move at full speed, and at times I trip over my own feet or step on people's toes. But patience is a key when building relationships. If you push too hard or too fast, you can offend others and cause them to withdraw. You want to be persistent, but without being a stalker or a nag. You have to recognize when it's time to simply move on. I had to ask Jill out about twenty times before she said yes. But I knew she was the love of my life. In business, if I see the relationship is going nowhere after a number of attempts, I'll move on—although always with a willingness to circle back if an opportunity presents itself.

You can't take rejection personally. Sure, there are times when you make mistakes in building a relationship. If your attempt to make a contact meets with rejection, do a quick self-assessment of your outreach. Try to learn from your mistakes.

But there also are times when it has absolutely nothing at all to do with you.

There are all sorts of reasons why someone might not be receptive to building a relationship with you. It might be that your personalities or interests are just too different. There's a reason you can usually find a burger joint, a pizza place, and a Chinese restaurant all within three or four blocks of each other. People have different tastes.

There may be something happening in another person's life—outside your control—that's preventing him or her from investing in a relationship at this time. The marketing vice president on your "need to know" list might be distracted by a troubled teenage daughter. The contractor you want to meet might be overwhelmed by the impact of falling sales, or by the collapse of his IRA. The CEO who promises to meet you for lunch but never puts it on his calendar might be under extreme pressure from the board, or battling a hostile takeover attempt.

When I keep running into a brick wall in my attempts to connect with someone, sometimes I'll send a note saying something like, "Sorry we haven't been able to get together. I realize you have a lot going on right now. When the dust settles, maybe we can reconnect." Then I move on. More often than not, I discover that it simply wasn't the right time.

The other thing to remember is that some people aren't naturally inclined to create new relationships. Yes, they could be better at it, but you can't force someone to connect with others. In some relationships, you're going to have to be the one who initiates most of your encounters.

I have friends I call all the time and who I know love me unconditionally, but who almost never call me. In fact, my father is like that.

My dad is my hero. He defines unconditional love. He's a mentor and my best friend. But I can count on two hands how many times he's picked up the phone and called me, or how many times he's written me a letter when it didn't involve my birthday or Christmas.

When I call him, however, I know from the excitement in his voice that he's glad to hear from me. We talk two or three times a week, and he'll stay on the phone with me for as long as I want to talk. Should I take offense because he seldom dials my number? Should I go a month without calling him just to make a point, to punish him? Of course not! I know my dad's heart. But I also know his personality. He's genuine, authentic, and humble, but he's also a bit introverted.

Not everyone can be the person who invites people over, or initiates phone calls, or is the life of the party. You can't put expectations on others to be like you, nor can you give in to undue pressure to become like someone else. It's a lesson I've learned the hard way over the years. I have certainly had unfair and unrealistic expectations of people at times. I wanted people to treat me the way I treated them. When they didn't, it left me hurt and disappointed. But it wasn't their fault—it was mine.

Living with unfair expectations—of ourselves and of others—can lead to relationship paralysis. We think other people don't like us or that they aren't doing enough to nurture a relationship with us, so we simply stop trying. And that guarantees one thing: relationship failure. As the hockey legend Wayne Gretzky once said, "You miss one hundred percent of the shots you don't take." When it comes to building relationships, we miss with some shots, and some get deflected or rejected. But we never score with the shots we don't take.

Relation*Shifter*

When a relationship just doesn't work out, move on. All you can do is to reach out in the right way and let what happens happen. Exercise patience. Don't take rejection personally—you might not know what's going on in the other person's life.

The Power of Net*giving*

Chapter 18

Making Business Personal

One of the hardest things about writing a book about building relationships, I quickly discovered, is the tendency to turn it into another book about "networking." When I told people I was working on a book, some well-meaning friends and colleagues said things like, "Tommy, you're one of the most networked guys I've ever met. I don't know anyone who knows more people than you know. You could write a killer book on networking."

And while I'm not exactly sure how you'd score such a thing, I wouldn't argue their point. I can touch down in just about any major American city, as well as many foreign countries, and find contacts that I've developed over the years, people who know me and would welcome me without any advance notice— people, you could say, who are part of the "Tommy Spaulding network."

So I *could* write a book just on developing networks. And I *could* develop a business just around helping others develop their networking skills. As one friend put it, "Tommy, you can get rich teaching people how to make people like them."

The idea of writing a book about networking, however, appealed to me about as much as a long bath in boiling oil. That's because although I'm extremely well connected and extremely good at networking, I absolutely detest the modern understanding of what networking means.

Here's the problem: networking is shallow.

If you see it as *just* a strategy, it's shallow. And when you pull out the tactics that make it work, they are shallow too. Networking, in the popular business sense, has become all about First and Second Floor transactional relationships. Put simply, that's not me.

I set out to write a book about something *more* when it comes to creating personal and professional relationships. But I struggled whenever I started writing about the practical or "how to" parts of relationship building. And after a sleepless night during a business trip to North Carolina, I realized why. I kept hearing the message my friend told me when I first talked about writing a book: "You can get rich teaching people how to make people like them."

What's wrong with that?

Two things. First, I'm not writing a book to help others "get rich." To be more successful, yes. But to make more money— that has never been the thing that has motivated me. And, second, and even more important, I have no desire to teach others how to "make" people like them.

Plenty of books offer lists of tactics that teach you to "get" friends so you can make more money. I want to offer something more—something better. Something that will change your career, change your business, and change your life.

You can (and should) make money along the way. I'm certainly not anti-wealth. We all have to provide for our families, and the more we make, the more we can give. I just believe that if "getting" is your primary goal, then you're missing something much, much bigger.

The truth is, you can't make people like you.

You can tie a bone around your neck and get the dogs to play with you. And you can come up with similar tactics with people. You'll win some Second Floor and maybe even a few Third Floor friends and customers, your business may grow, you'll most likely make more money, and you'll be able to tell people that you're incredibly "networked." It will all seem great at first, until you wake up one night (as I did years ago) and realize how little it all really means.

In itself, networking isn't bad. It's just not enough. With a paintbrush and a can of paint, you can create chaos or beauty; it all depends upon what's in your heart. The same is true of networking. When a heart centered on others drives your actions, networking is replaced by something far, far more powerful—Net*giving*.

Networking is all about *you*. Netgiving is all about *others*. Networking is all about collecting contacts and using those contacts for *personal* gain. Netgiving is all about building relationships that help *others* around you succeed. Networking is about winning friends and influencing people for personal gain. Netgiving is about influencing friends to make a difference. Networking is about business in a world in which business isn't personal. Netgiving is about intentionally making business personal.

Netgiving, to put it boldly, is about love. That's the most important ingredient in developing relationships that make life and business something greater than just *who* we know.

Without love, you'll never take a relationship to the Fourth Floor or the Fifth Floor. All of your relationships will feel empty. The business cards you collect at the typical conference or networking event will never become anything more than a mess of three-and-a-half-inch by two-inch pieces of paper.

This is the message the business world so often can't seem to embrace. In individual relationships, we're all for love. It's a great idea for do-gooder nonprofits and starry-eyed newly-weds. But it has no place in business.

When Tina Turner won a Grammy in 1985 for "What's Love Got to Do with It?" she probably didn't realize she'd recorded the theme song for the modern hard-line business world. Yet, many of the most financially successful business leaders in the world will say just that when it comes to business: What's love got to do with it?

As Donald Trump puts it: "Business is about making money. It's about the bottom line. The sooner you realize that it's not personal, it's business, the sooner you'll make it to the top in the business world. I'm often surprised by people who think business is something else. They come in with lofty ideas and philanthropic purposes that have absolutely no place in a business meeting. It's a waste of everyone's time."*

If all you're interested in is making money, then Trump's advice makes perfect sense. You can take all the tips, tactics, and strategies I offered in the earlier chapters and run with them. But leaders like Trump miss a huge point when it comes to the human side of business. They see the "personal" as a roadblock to success, because the "personal" can cloud a leader's decision-making process. The irony is that the leaders who let the "personal" cloud their business decisions usually are "loving" too little, not too much.

What many leaders have is a faulty understanding of what it means to "love" someone forward. When we really love someone, we're committed to that person's best interests. That is

---

* Inside Trump Tower, Issue 14: http://www.trumpuniversity.com/ mynetwork/inside-trump-tower/issue14.cfm

true of our employees, co-workers, vendors, clients—all of our contacts, even the ones we hardly know.

What's this look like?

Let's say your spouse comes to you and says Cousin Jimmy needs a job. Cousin Jimmy isn't qualified for any of the job openings in your company, but you love your spouse and you want to keep the peace in the family. Donald Trump would say not to give him a job because it's bad for business. You can tell Jimmy and your spouse the same thing: "It's not personal, it's business." I would say something slightly different. I would say don't give him a job, because it's not in his best interest to be in a job he won't enjoy and for which he isn't qualified. You love him too much to allow that. Instead, help him find the *right* job somewhere else. It's business, and yet it's totally personal.

Chapter 19

Beyond Networking

The real answer to Tina Turner's question—What's love got to do with it?—is quite simple: everything.

Most of us are OK with the idea that we love our family and friends. Yet we spend at least as much time at work as we do with family and friends. Why wouldn't we love the people in that circle of our lives as well? Why would we segment the most powerful emotion in the universe out of the part of our lives where we commit so much of our time, resources, and energy?

So if business is personal and love is the most important part of building meaningful relationships in business, then what does it take *within* us to make business personal? What does it take to make *love* part of who we are professionally? What does it take to embrace netgiving, and make networking a by-product of who we are, not a function of what we do? What does it take to move beyond transactional relationships? What does it take to put others first and trust that our needs won't go unmet? What does it take to become selfless rather than selfish?

What does it take to give relationships significance on the First, Second, and Third floors, and to move them to the Fourth Floor or all the way to the Penthouse?

To answer those critical questions, we have to go beyond net-working, because networking, by itself, involves nothing more than self-serving manipulative skills and techniques to get people to like us. The good news is that going beyond networking is something anyone can learn. It's not just for the select few extroverts who are born with certain qualities or gifts.

But here's the rub: It's a choice.

Before any of us can really advance when it comes to building deep, meaningful relationships, we first must make a choice to love others—in business as well as in our personal lives. That means we put the needs of others ahead of our own. It means we're willing to sacrifice. It means our decision-making process starts with "How can I help?" not "What can I get?" It means our litmus test must be to strive for significance, not just success.

If we don't first make that choice, then everything we do when it comes to building relationships ultimately will fail.

Simply stated, we have to be authentic.

Authenticity is the one of the keys to successfully building genuine relationships. The other keys are humility, empathy, confidentiality, vulnerability, curiosity, generosity, humor, and gratitude. These are the traits that touch upon "who you are," and they are the things that give meaning and purpose to what you do. They will give meaning and power to all of your relationships. In fact, you can't take a relationship to the Penthouse without them.

Focusing on who we are requires a certain level of self-awareness. For instance, I'm a hugger. When I meet people, even people I haven't known very long, I often give them a hug. It's who I am. Many people aren't huggers. If you aren't a hugger, don't fake it. In other words, know yourself. Be authentic.

I believe, however, that we all can develop minimal levels of competency in all of these essential areas. You can't fake authenticity, humility, empathy, or gratitude, and you can't compromise on confidentiality. But you can grow in vulnerability, curiosity, generosity, and humor. You can make a commitment to make and keep all of those areas a priority in your life.

You might never tell jokes like Jerry Seinfeld or Jimmy Fallon, but you can learn to see the lighter side of life and develop your own unique sense of humor. You don't have to act and think like Ebenezer Scrooge. Do you find it hard to open up about yourself? I'm not suggesting that you force yourself to tell everyone your darkest secrets. But anyone can be open and vulnerable with the right people in the right circumstances; doing so will deepen your relationships and make a positive change in your life.

So let's look a little closer at those nine traits.

Chapter 20

Authenticity: Making Relationships Real

Authenticity is often the first hurdle in developing a meaningful relationship. The idea that you genuinely care about others has to be real and pure, and others have to see it and believe it.

Unfortunately, that kind of selflessness has become such a rarity in our culture that many people don't believe it when they see it. We've become cynical, jaded, and suspicious. We see people who appear to give, give, give, and our reaction isn't "Wow, what a special person!" Instead we think, "What's the catch? What's the hidden agenda? What's in it for him?"

Mark Urich, the executive vice president of a large insurance company whom I introduced you to earlier, is one of the most genuine and authentic people I know. He doesn't pretend to be something or someone he's not. He's comfortable in his own skin, as the saying goes. So he naturally seeks out relationships with other people who are authentic, and sometimes it takes time to know who is real and who is faking it.

In fact, Mark had questions about my motives when he and I first met. And he's not alone. It doesn't bother me; I know how often people—including me—have been burned by people pretending to be something they're not. We've all fallen for too-good-to-be-true relationships.

I met Mark in 2008 through Leader's Challenge. It wasn't long before he and his wife, Kate, invited Jill and me out for dinner. On the way to the restaurant, he turned to his wife and said, "I can't wait for you to meet Tommy. I really want to get your opinion of him. He's either the most genuine person I've ever met or the biggest phony on the planet."

Without my knowing it, dinner had become something of a test of my authenticity.

As the evening progressed, I asked them dozens of questions. Both Mark and Kate later confessed that they learned things about each other that they hadn't known.

I also ended up having a wonderful one-on-one conversation with Kate about the things that were going on in her life. I told her tidbits from my life, especially those that related to her situation.

She told me about a stressful upcoming event—a visit from a difficult relative with whom she didn't have a great relationship. The very idea of the visit had her twisted in knots.

A week later, on the day the relative was scheduled to arrive, I called Kate and left her a message. I told her I was thinking about her and that I'd been praying all week that the visit would go smoothly and peacefully.

I didn't do any of this to score points with her or with Mark. I simply called because I cared about her. I wanted her to know that our conversation over dinner had made an impact on me. Sometimes it makes a big difference just knowing that someone else out there knows about your struggles and cares about you. I tend to make dozens of calls like that during the week. None of them are designed to "make people like me." I call them because I care, and I've found that eventually people see that.

Mark said as much the next time we talked. "When you took the time to call my wife," he said, "I knew you were the real deal."

Authenticity isn't something we establish or prove with a one-time act of kindness, however. It's something people see *in* us when they are around us. And whether they see it or not really isn't the point. The point is this: we need to live it. If we really care about others and we live it out, that's enough. But if we fake it, people will most certainly see through the façade, and whatever relationships we build on that foundation will eventually fall apart.

Chapter 21

Empathy: Setting a Cornerstone for Trust

Y ou can't lead with greatness without genuinely caring about others, and you can't care about others until you can learn to empathize with them. It's not something you can fake.

Showing empathy for others makes it clear that you care. It creates trust. And trust is a critical step in building effective teams and creating transformational relationships.

Empathy allows us to understand the people we work for, the people who work for us, our clients, our customers, our vendors—everyone with whom we come into contact. That allows for two important outcomes: first, we earn a level of trust and respect that allows us to tell someone the truth, candidly, even when it's difficult; second, it permits us to see the bigger picture, which is especially important in business.

Much of the time, empathy is good for the bottom line. If you're a retailer who is empathetic toward your elderly customers, you'll stock the items they most want to buy on the lower shelves so they can reach them more easily. You do this because you care. But guess what? Your sales will go up as well.

Empathy sometimes leads us to make a decision that goes against the bottom-line recommendations of a dry cost-analysis report. In the 1970s, for instance, the Ford Motor Company's recall director evaluated what some saw as a flaw in the design of their subcompact car, the Pinto, and he came to some clear conclusions: first, that a rear-end collision at thirty miles an hour or higher would cause the fuel tank to rupture; second, that a ruptured tank would likely lead to significant injuries or death to the driver and passengers; third, that the flaw could be fixed for about eleven dollars per vehicle; and, fourth, that the overall cost of such a recall would be more than the anticipated cost of paying claims from lawsuits that might result from the accidents.

Follow the hard-line idea that making business personal is a "waste of everybody's time," and the choice is clear: don't recall the Pinto. But if you have empathy for your customers—if you can visualize your best friend driving around in a faulty Pinto—then the choice is equally obvious: fix the problem. (Ford eventually issued a recall on the Pinto, but only after considerable pressure from the National Highway Traffic Safety Administration.)

When empathy suggests that we go against what appears best for the bottom line, it creates a dilemma that many hard-line business leaders don't want to face: if you can't do the right thing and still make a profit, then the answer isn't to do the wrong thing; the answer is to find a new business.

No business will survive long if it can't make a profit; but no business deserves to survive at all if it can't make a positive difference in the lives of its employees, customers, clients, and community.

Chapter 22

Vulnerability: Opening a Window into Your Inner World

Humberto Lopez lives in Tucson, Arizona, where he owns and runs HSL Properties. HSL's holdings own apartment complexes, office buildings, and hotels in six states. They're the single largest apartment owner in southern Arizona. In other words, Humberto has done very well financially; he's accustomed to people asking him to invest in their startup company or to give to their charity.

When Humberto and I first met, we both knew that I was seeking his support for Up with People. Jim Click, a mutual friend, had introduced us. We met a couple of times with the express purpose of my sharing Up with People's vision with him so he could decide if and how he might get involved.

In general, Humberto is a friendly but "guarded" person. That quickly became pretty clear in our first few business meetings. He kept his personal life close to the vest.

So I found myself at a crossroads in my relationship with Humberto. On the one hand, I felt confident that we connected and that he believed in Up with People enough that he would support it. We'd have dinner and play golf once or twice a year.

Our relationship would find a comfortable home on the Third Floor.

On the other hand, I sensed that Humberto might be interested in being much, much more than a donor. I sensed that he needed real friendship in his life, not another cause. I thought our relationship had the potential to move beyond news, sports, and weather—and even business.

So I never asked Humberto for a donation. Instead, I opened up to him and sought his counsel.

My biggest struggles at that time revolved around my travel schedule. My job with Up with People kept me on the road constantly, which meant it kept me away from my wife and young children. I never thought I'd love anything more than working and traveling, but I'd moved into a new stage of life. I missed Jill, Anthony, Caroline, and Tate, and longed to spend more time with them.

I shared this with Humberto. In fact, he was one of the first people I told that I was thinking of leaving Up with People and that the travel demands were a big part of the reason why.

At that point, Humberto had to decide how to react to my openness and vulnerability. Not only did he listen empathically to my challenges and offer encouragement, but this very private man opened up to me about some of his personal challenges. Because he was a business leader of some note, some of the personal problems in his marriage had become public. His willingness to share the more private aspects of that struggle helped to take our relationship to the Fifth Floor.

Our conversations went from NSW to NBS—No Bullshit. I'm not sure I have another friend who speaks more candidly to me about what I'm doing or not doing, or who allows me to speak more candidly to him.

Many people—men in particular—struggle with the notion

of vulnerability. But in my experience, even the most private of individuals can let themselves be extremely vulnerable when they find themselves in a safe, trusting environment. Our earlier meetings turned out to be the foundation for creating that environment.

Not long ago, Humberto sent me a series of text messages. In one, he said I was one of the few friends he had who never judged him. I know what it's like to feel judged. We all do. That compliment was one of the nicest, most affirming things anyone could say to me.

We're most vulnerable with those who don't judge us—or, to put it another way, with those who extend to us their grace. When we offer it—and when we find it from others—we're able to let go of our pride and take some risks when it comes to letting other people see us for who we really are—not just the parts we'd like for them to see.

This type of vulnerability isn't easy—and it's another thing that can't be faked. But it's essential in establishing deep, meaningful relationships.

Moving from a transactional to a transformational relationship is impossible without vulnerability. We have to be willing to open up—to go beyond news, sports, and weather—and share what's really important, even painful, in our lives.

If we only present an "everything is perfect" mentality, people won't trust us and follow us. Why? Because they know everything *isn't* perfect. The way to earn trust is to show our less flattering sides, our pain as well as our progress—sometimes even our "shadow" side. It's essential to listen to others, but also to share from the heart in the spirit of humility. The deeper the level of vulnerability between two people, the deeper the relationship grows and the better chance you have to reach the Fifth Floor.

Chapter 23

Confidentiality: Living the Law of the Vault

Information is power. When friends, clients, co-workers, or customers trust us with delicate and confidential information, they're taking a leap of faith—faith in our commitment to living out what I call the "responsibility of vulnerability" or **the Law of the Vault**. The Law of the Vault says that in Fourth and Fifth Floor relationships, you guard sensitive and private information about others like the gold at Fort Knox.

This is true not only with personal relationships, but with professional relationships with clients, customers, vendors, and co-workers. We can strengthen those relationships by trusting each other with sensitive information. But the relationship is only as secure as the vault that keeps that information locked up.

It's hard to underestimate the value of vulnerability and confidentiality when building relationships with the leader of an organization. That's why these traits became such a big part of my relationship with Steve Ballard, the chancellor of East Carolina University.

Chancellor Ballard and I met in 2007 when I was given ECU's Most Outstanding Alumni Award. Jill and I flew to North Carolina with my father and his wife, Angie. I accepted the award during a banquet hosted by the ECU Alumni

Association and gave a short thank-you speech to the university's trustees, faculty, and staff. Steve enjoyed my speech enough to invite me back the following year as the commencement speaker for the school's centennial graduation ceremony.

During my trip for the commencement address, Steve and I got a chance to sit down and really talk. I got to hear about his vision for East Carolina. He lives and breathes the type of leadership I admire and long to live out myself. He told me he wanted East Carolina to become the nation's finest "leadership university"—where every one of the nearly 28,000 students graduates with experience in leadership development. We connected almost immediately and spent hours talking about our ideas and dreams.

Later, when I accepted the position as leader-in-residence at ECU, I began traveling to the campus a week each month to help Steve's senior team develop the school's leadership institute. And every time I came to town, Steve and I would have lunch or dinner together.

We soon developed a relationship that allowed us to share information we couldn't share with others. Life as the CEO of a large organization is at times a very lonely job, and a university chancellor lives that reality. The fears and challenges a chancellor faces can weigh heavily, especially when there are very few people he can confide in. When Steve opened up to me, it was an opportunity for our relationship to grow.

During that time, Steve interviewed for the top position at Kansas State University. Because very few people knew Kansas State was courting Steve, I called him almost every day to make sure he knew he had a trusted friend he could talk with while weighing that decision. On his way to the interview, he called to tell me how much he loved ECU, and that he felt he had unfinished work there, especially with the leadership institute.

Then again, Kansas State was a great university and offered him a wonderful opportunity.

I didn't tell Steve what to do—I just listened and asked questions and did my best to support him throughout this difficult decision. He eventually decided to stay at ECU. The fact that he interviewed later became public knowledge, but the details he shared with me during that difficult time remain private— locked securely in a vault of confidentiality.

That's the kind of promise you have to be able to make to anyone who shares sensitive information with you. It's the kind of commitment I expect before I'll tell someone something I might not want broadcast to all the world. The Law of the Vault can make or break relationships. We've all known someone in our personal and professional lives who leaked confidential information. On the other hand, when we're able to promise that level of trust and confidentiality, the power of the relationship grows exponentially.

Chapter 24

Curiosity: The Power of Asking Questions

We're born curious. Somewhere along the way, however, we settle into the comfortable routines of life, and we only ask who, what, when, where, and why when we need an answer or solution to a problem.

When I was only four years old, I was walking with my dad, and I was peppering him with all sorts of questions. Then I stopped and said, "Dad, am I asking too many questions?" He looked at me and said, "You can never ask too many questions, Tommy. That's how you learn."

When I was in elementary school, my sister Lisa—older than me by two years—was a Girl Scout Brownie; my mother was the troop leader. She took the girls to the courthouse, the fire station, the local dairy—wherever she thought they might learn something interesting. And she took me with them.

I'd sit in the back—the only boy with a troop full of girls—and watch and listen until the time came for the Brownies to ask questions. More often than not, I shot my hand up and asked something. Then I asked something else. And something else. The Brownies almost never got a chance to ask anything. But my mother never told me I was out of line. She echoed my dad's words: "Tommy, that's how you get smart," she said. "Never stop asking questions."

So I never stopped asking people questions, and I never stopped listening to the answers. Dad calls me an "intense listener." I believe that comes from my sense of curiosity—the desire not only to ask but to listen, understand, and remember the answers.

Building Penthouse relationships is more about the deposits we make than about the duration of our investments, and there's no easier way to make deposits than by developing—or redeveloping—a sense of curiosity. Building meaningful relationships is more about asking questions than about answering questions. When we ask questions and listen, we make deposits rather than withdrawals.

When I met the bartender while waiting for my turn to interview for the Rotary International Ambassadorial Scholarship, all I did was display my natural curiosity about who he was and what his life was like. Before I knew it, he had a family photo album opened on the bar and we were laughing about stories from his youth. When we had dinner with Mark and Kate, I didn't start off by asking Kate to tell me the things in life that had her troubled. I started with simple, open-ended questions. But then I didn't stop. We kept peeling back the onion until we got to what really mattered.

That type of curiosity paves the way for vulnerability and allows relationships to move off the lower floors and toward significance.

Chapter 25

Generosity: Acting on Your Awareness

The spirit of generosity leads to simple acts of giving to others in need—whether it's helping a co-worker finish a project, helping a neighbor shovel his sidewalk, or giving time or money to buy shoes for a child in Ethiopia.

In business, corporate giving is planned. But generosity can also involve empowering employees and taking the initiative to "do the right thing" when circumstances present themselves.

Acting out of generosity heightens our awareness about the needs of others (empathy) and builds trust with those around us. If we want our co-workers and customers and vendors to trust us, we have to show them that we care about them. But we also have to show them that we care about other people—people who offer us nothing but a heartfelt thank-you (and sometimes not even that).

This is the attitude Kurt and Brenda Warner embody when they go out to dinner with their seven children.

There was a time when the Warners scraped by from paycheck to paycheck, with Kurt stocking shelves at a grocery store when he wasn't playing quarterback in the low-paying Arena Football League. Then, in 1998, he got a call. The St. Louis Rams needed a reserve quarterback. Next thing you know, Kurt was on the Rams' roster. And when the starting quarterback suffered an injury in 1999, Kurt stepped in. The former stock boy was on his way to becoming a Super Bowl champion and two-time MVP of the National Football League.

After Kurt became an NFL celebrity, he and his wife noticed that restaurant managers often "comped" their dinner. This made little sense, given how much he made as an NFL quarterback. So the Warners turned things around, giving their kids a lesson in generosity in the process. Now when the family goes out, they buy dinner for someone else. They do their best to do it anonymously. They let one of the children pick the recipient.

After leaving St. Louis and spending a short stint with the New York Giants, Warner ended up with the Arizona Cardinals, where he led them to a 2009 Super Bowl appearance against the Pittsburgh Steelers. The Friday night before the Super Bowl, he and his family were eating out, so they held to their tradition and bought dinner for some folks at a nearby table—twenty Steelers fans.

I doubt that Kurt changed their allegiance for the Sunday showdown, but he probably bought some goodwill. More important, he honored his children's choice and set an example for how to give unconditionally—even to opposing fans.

Chapter 26

Humility: The Gift of Perspective

One of the funniest stories I've ever heard about humility is attributed to Don Shula, the Hall of Fame football coach. Shula coached thirty-three years in the National Football League, and his 347–173–6 record is the best in the league's history. Most of those years were with the Miami Dolphins, a team he took to the Super Bowl five times. His Dolphins won it all twice, once while going 17–0 to become the NFL's only undefeated champion.

Needless to say, Don Shula is a national celebrity. In south Florida, there aren't many public places he can go where fans don't recognize him.

As the story goes, one year while on vacation in a remote area in New Hampshire, Shula took his family to an old-fashioned single-screen movie theater. As they walked in and began taking seats near the back, the small group seated near the front stood and applauded for a few seconds.

"I can't even go to a small town in New Hampshire without being recognized," Shula whispered to his wife.

After the movie, he began talking to one of the locals as they exited the theater. Shula decided to ask him about the ovation.

"When I walked in, you all gave me a standing ovation," he said. "I was surprised you recognized me."

"Buddy, I don't know who you are," the man said. "I just know there were only eight people in the theater and they don't start the movie until the tenth person shows up."

When we take ourselves too seriously, something almost always happens to bring us back to reality! It's easy for success to go to our heads. When things are going our way, we tend to take the credit—especially if others are eager to give it to us.

Over time, however, arrogance poisons relationships.

People follow leaders who have humble hearts. If we don't have humility, others might respect our accomplishments, but they won't truly engage with us and follow us. And they certainly won't join us on the Fifth Floor. We might have positional authority, but we lack relational authority. And positional authority only takes us so far.

Staying humble isn't easy when we're climbing the corporate ladder, starting a company, and trying to make a name for ourselves in a world that often only pays attention to self-promoters and squeaky wheels. But the humbler we are, the better we can lead others.

This is particularly important in times of conflict and/or failure. How we deal with challenges demonstrates our humility as well as our character. Good leaders point their finger at their teams and co-workers when the team is successful. Great leaders point their finger at themselves when the team fails.

John Wooden, perhaps the greatest basketball coach in NCAA history, put it this way: "Talent is God-given; be humble. Fame is man-given; be thankful. Conceit is self-given; be careful."

Chapter 27

Humor: Living with Levity

Humility helps us take ownership of our mistakes and flaws, and we might as well do that with a healthy sense of humor. Why beat ourselves up over our failings, and risk losing our self-confidence? Why project a negative vision of ourselves? No one wants to follow Eeyore in the Hundred Acre Wood.

Seeing the humor in our shortcomings and in the world around us can act as a great stress reducer. It allows us to turn bad situations into something good, or at least something bearable. And it can be used as a tool to grow relationships.

During my time as leader-in-residence at East Carolina, I always stayed at the same hotel—the Hilton in Greenville, North Carolina. When you stay at the same place for a week each month for a year, you get to know the staff pretty well, and they get to know you.

During one stay, things didn't go particularly well. I always requested and got a nonsmoking room, but on this trip they assigned me a room that reeked of tobacco smoke. They moved me to another room, but, again, it reeked of smoke. By the time I found a truly smoke-free room, I'd changed three times.

The next month, I checked in and went to my room and noticed immediately that there was no lingering odor of cigarettes. Then I noticed something else—a gift basket on the bed.

The manager wanted to show his appreciation for me as a customer, apologize for the problems from my previous trip, and make sure everything was in order this time.

But he also showed his sense of humor. In the basket, along with the candy and fruit and other niceties, was a personal note from the manager, as well as an ashtray and a pack of cigarettes!

I laughed out loud. Then I called him to thank him. I now have a new friend, and he has a loyal customer.

Chapter 28

Gratitude: The Art of Being Thankful

I want to end this section on the "traits" of building relationships with what might well be the most important quality of all.

Building deep, meaningful relationships is simply not possible without a well-developed sense of gratitude. We're promised nothing in this world. Every relationship is a gift worth treasuring, as are the benefits that come from those relationships.

Bestselling self-help author Melody Beattie says, "Gratitude unlocks the fullness of life. It turns what we have into enough, and more. It turns denial into acceptance, chaos to order, confusion to clarity. It can turn a meal into a feast, a house into a home, a stranger into a friend. Gratitude makes sense of our past, brings peace for today, and creates a vision for tomorrow."

When we're thankful for each breath and each moment and each relationship, we don't take them for granted, and we don't abuse them. Gratitude allows us to make the most of them, not only for ourselves but for everyone around us.

I don't know anyone who lives out this idea more naturally and thoroughly than Joel Mauney. When I was in college at

East Carolina University, Joel and I worked as busboys at the same restaurant during our freshman year. We joined different fraternities, but we became fast friends. As seniors, I was elected president of the Inter-fraternity Council, and Joel was elected vice president. After graduation, I told Joel I was driving a couple of hours west to see an Up with People show so I could interview for a job as a staff member. Joel came with me, because he had never seen an Up with People show. After my interview, I looked all over for Joel. I finally found him— interviewing to become a cast member. He won a spot, and the next year I was on staff for the cast to which he was assigned. We traveled all over the world together for two years with Up with People. Joel ended up in Denver, where he worked with me at Up with People and helped me launch Leader's Challenge. He's one of the most gifted employees I've ever hired, and an even better friend. He's now vice president of the Spaulding Companies and the program director for the Spaulding Leadership Institute, the holding company for the four nonprofits I founded.

Joel has spent much of his life as my second-in-command. He knows we complement each other. And while the world might see me as the leader and visionary, I never take for granted what Joel has done and continues to do in ensuring the success of the organizations we've been involved in. Joel has been a huge part of the success of every organization I've ever started.

Whenever an opportunity has presented itself, I've tried to make sure Joel has shared in the rewards. We went to the Super Bowl and the Major League All-Star Game together. Joel's a sports fanatic—he loves anything that involves a goal, a net, an end zone, a ball, or a puck. I look for opportunities to invite him to travel with me to interesting places.

Of all the people who could look me in the eye and say honestly, "You owe me, Spaulding," none would have a better claim than Joel. Yet he's never asked for a favor. And he's never treated a favor or a gift as something that he deserved. He simply enjoys each moment, each gift that comes with life.

When I speak to audiences around the world, especially youth, one of the things I always talk about is the sense of entitlement—the opposite of gratitude. Especially in America, this is a virus that is spreading throughout organizations and eating away at our culture. By the time kids reach their teens, many have been taught that the world owes them pretty much everything—an education, a job they love that pays well, a fancy title, a luxurious car, the corner office.

Those things are all there for any of us, but they aren't promised. They require hard work and perseverance.

So, I'll tell you the same thing I tell those kids: grab your dictionary and look up the word *entitlement*. Stop reading right now and grab your dictionary and mark out that word with a black marker. Remove that word from your vocabulary and remove it from your heart. Replace it with something no relationship can survive without—gratitude.

Relation*Shift*: Life in the Penthouse

Chapter 29

Journey to
the Penthouse

The easiest things in life are the safe things, the things that look and feel most obvious. They are the roads most traveled. But most of us are guilty of settling into the routine of the obvious. That's why we miss so much that life has to offer. We see a junior executive we could mentor, an entrepreneur who could use our advice, or a customer who would benefit from knowing one of our contacts, but we decide not to act because we are too busy or we just don't want to complicate our routine, safe life.

Relationships on the First Floor are routine. Relationships on the Second and Third floors are less routine, but they involve very little risk and, therefore, produce limited rewards. If our relationships stop at the Third Floor, or even the Fourth, we're missing the best things that life offers: the chance to make a difference, not only in our own careers but throughout our organizations and across our communities. These are our Fifth Floor relationships—the Penthouse, the best of the best.

I'm fortunate to have Fifth Floor relationships with many business owners, CEOs, and other executives. But the Penthouse isn't some exclusive country club. If it were, I doubt they'd let me in! Fifth Floor relationships are about *more than* who you know; they're about the relationship itself. The Penthouse is blind to race, gender, position, national origin, or social or economic status. It's open to anyone.

For instance, I have a Penthouse relationship with Mike Chambers—my wife's ex-husband. Mike and Jill went through a bitter, difficult, painful divorce, but a mentor of mine—Jerry Middel—gave me a key piece of advice: My job, he said, was to "love Mike Chambers."

My wife and Mike have a son together—Anthony—so I did everything I could to befriend Mike and show him that I cared about him and Anthony without wanting to take his place as Anthony's father.

Naturally, Mike was suspicious at first and it took time for us to get beyond the wounds. But Mike now spends the night at our home on Christmas Eve. He has a stocking that hangs on our mantel. We take Anthony to ball games together. My kids, Caroline and Tate, call him Uncle Mike. For his fortieth birthday he invited Jill, Anthony, and me to join him and his mother for dinner. Two years later, when Jill asked how I wanted to celebrate my fortieth birthday, I suggested a nice dinner with four other couples—including Mike and his girlfriend.

In 2008, Mike went into the hospital, and I went to see him every day. I'd sit with him, feed him, and talk with him. After he improved enough, I'd sometimes sneak in cheeseburgers and his chewing tobacco. I don't see Mike as an "ex" anything. I see him as family, and I love him like a brother.

Unlikely? Maybe. Impossible? No!

The worst mistake we can make in life is to close our hearts and minds to the potential of relationships simply because tradition and stereotypes tell us nothing good can come of them.

At times we have to become "relational contrarians"—rejecting the easy and the ordinary and the safe when dealing with the people who move in and out of our lives. We can't have Fifth Floor relationships with *everyone*, but we can have Fifth Floor relationships with *anyone*. The question is, which ones do we choose to embrace in that way?

Often we make that decision quickly, almost instinctively. We meet someone and there's a connection that's hard to explain, a click. We can feel it, and we know we want to invest more time and energy in building that relationship. Then there are those relationships that we know will be a challenge at the start—like my relationship with Mike. But we decide, for whatever reason, that we should take the chance anyway.

The problem is that all too often we limit ourselves to the quick and easy. We go for the low-hanging fruit. So any relationship that isn't microwavable gets left on the shelf. No time for that one. Too much work. Too much energy. But often the relationships that aren't low-hanging fruit have the sweetest taste.

The irony is that the only real way to find out which of those relationships we *should* try to take to the Penthouse is to invest time and energy in them.

Let me give you a couple of true stories that illustrate how we can take that journey from First Floor relationships to ones that move upward and eventually find their way to the Penthouse.

The first is the story of my relationship with Jerry Middel, the mentor who advised me to "love" Mike Chambers. It illustrates how someone can focus purposely on building a relationship, and how, over time, that relationship can develop into something incredibly special.

The second comes from Ron Hall and Denver Moore, two men I've never met, but whom I greatly admire. Their story illustrates the power of giving a relationship a chance even when conventional wisdom says the relationship stands no chance of getting off the First Floor.

These very different accounts can give you a sense of how Fifth Floor relationships can develop. But I also hope they expand your view of what the Penthouse looks like and what types of relationships can live there.

Chapter 30

The Ultimate Middel Man

Jerry Middel owns a vacation home in the Rocky Mountains, a rather large cabin right on the Blue River in Silverthorne, Colorado, not far from Breckenridge. The deck and large windows offer breathtaking views of the river, the valleys, and the snow-capped peaks of Buffalo, Red, and Keller mountains.

This "mountain shack," as Jerry calls it, is an ideal setting for the three Rs—resting, relaxing, recharging. Owning such a place is one of those pictures many of us envision in the slideshow of our own personal version of the American dream.

To all appearances, Jerry's living that dream. But it's all too easy to see the great big vacation house and miss the most important things about his life. His true measures of success are defined by the people he knows and the impact he has on them.

Jerry, or "Pops" as I call him, began his professional career as a door-to-door salesman, but he's always been in the full-time business of helping others. And as his business fortunes grew, so too did his giving. Even when he sold his business a few years ago, at the age of sixty-one, Jerry didn't retire. He still works, but now he gives away one hundred percent of what he makes. Jerry eats, sleeps, and breathes generosity—and not just the kind that comes from writing checks for worthy causes.

When I call him, he's often at the movies, at a ball game, fly-fishing, or playing golf. But it's almost always with some inner-city junior-high student that he's mentoring.

Jerry lives out everything I mean by *more than* relationships. He embodies relationship excellence the way Alex Rodriguez embodies a great baseball swing. Indeed, when it comes to relationship excellence, Jerry's the guru, the maharishi, the swami, the kingfish, the savant, the virtuoso, the . . . well, you get the idea. He's *really* good at it.

For Jerry, everything starts with relationships. Everything else—money, houses, and so on—are by-products, not for his personal pleasure (although he enjoys life), but for helping others and for building more meaningful relationships. He is passionate about people, not possessions. His life is a testimony of selfless significance in a materialistic world.

We can have Penthouse relationships with peers, protégés, and mentors. For me, Jerry falls into that last category. He's been a mentor in many different areas of my life, not the least of which is my understanding of relationships.

When I was younger, I relied on the Dale Carnegie strategy for winning friends and influencing people, but his message focuses mainly on how to use relationships for personal and professional gain. I eventually figured out that my personal and professional gain meant very little if I wasn't making a significant contribution to others. And Jerry helped me discover an even deeper truth: that my personal and professional gain actually increased when I focused on helping others.

That's the shift. Most popular books on networking or the power of relationships stop at the Fourth Floor—even those books that talk about the power of creating a close inner circle of trusted friends (which I'll discuss in more detail in chapter 32). That's because the end goal in most books on networking and relationships is all about advancing *you*. That's fine for Floors One through Four. The Penthouse is reserved for relationships that are totally selfless. It's a servant relationship—and it works both ways. This is true of all my Penthouse relationships.

The "what you do" tactics and strategies and the "who you are" traits combine to help us move relationships off the First Floor to greater places of meaning; some of those relationships can become so selfless that they define a Penthouse relationship.

Jerry taught me much of this mostly by doing just one thing: living it.

When I joined the Denver Rotary Club six months after moving to Colorado, I figured it was a good way to meet other leaders, serve in the community, and pay back the organization that had awarded me a Rotary Ambassadorial Scholarship.

With more than four hundred members, the club is one of the biggest in the world. That provided an enormous opportunity for me. In some ways, however, it also made meeting people a little harder than I'd expected. I walked in for lunch, looked at the sea of tables and sharply dressed men and women with their circular name badges, and wondered if I'd ever get beyond surface-level networking.

Then I met Jerry.

Shortly after I joined, I got a phone call from "Rotarian Jerry" inviting me to lunch. After I accepted, I checked the club's member directory to find out more about him. Next to "occupation," Jerry listed "insurance." So I prepped myself for the inevitable sales pitch.

Great to meet you, Tommy! . . . Tell me about yourself and

your family! . . . Great, great! . . . Now, Tommy, my friend, if
you were to die tonight, would your family be taken care of? . . .

Well, we met for lunch—I remember that we both had salmon
salads—and we talked about this, that, and the other, but the
topic of insurance never came up. Not once.

I expected a First Floor relationship in which Jerry would
push for the transaction like every other life-insurance salesman
I'd ever known. I figured I'd be the one who pushed the relationship in a different direction. But Jerry, I discovered, wasn't
building our relationship based on a transaction. My fork had
barely touched my salmon salad when I realized this was no
ordinary man and that we'd have no ordinary friendship.

His original purpose in inviting me to lunch, he later told
me, was that he thought I'd be a good mentor for Denver Kids,
a program for at-risk youth. But he didn't bring that up during
that first lunch, either. He wanted to get to know me—my passions, my hopes, my dreams, my story—and move our relationship off the First Floor.

A few weeks later we had lunch again; once again, no talk of
insurance, and no talk of Denver Kids.

We continued to meet and talk, and we developed a sense of
trust in each other as we shared more and more about our lives.
We must have met fifteen or twenty times, in fact, before Jerry
finally asked something *of* me and not just *about* me. It was
then that he asked if I'd consider helping with Denver Kids.
(Still nothing about insurance.)

By that time, Jerry knew we had the potential for a deeper
relationship.

How did he know? Because he listened.

If you ask Jerry about his business relationships, he'll tell
you that most of them reside on the Third or Fourth Floor—
right where they belong. Some relationships simply can't stay

professional if they become too deeply intimate. They can— and must—have mutual trust and respect, but not necessarily intimacy. The only way to figure out whether a relationship can go deeper is to get to know the other person as much as possible. That comes not only from asking the right questions, but from actually paying attention to the answers.

Jerry likes to say that most people, especially most men, don't really listen when they ask a question. Usually they're already formulating their next response. So when they ask, "How's your family?" they don't listen to the answer; they start thinking about their own family or what they want to share when the other person stops talking.

When you listen, you find out the little things that let you know if there's a chemistry that will help a relationship blossom into something more intimate. It's a kind of soul-searching.

Jerry's involved in a Christian ministry, the founder of which likes to tell people to "ask meaningful questions, listen intently, and fall in love with someone's soul. Then share your faith with them out of love, not duty."

Let me stop for a second and mention that Jerry's been a spiritual influence in my life, but he never tried to sell me on religion any more than he tried to sell me insurance. My point isn't about evangelism or proselytizing, but about building relationships by listening intently and discovering someone's soul so that you can share your life with them out of love, not duty.

"I think that's the key to relationships," Jerry says. "Asking questions and listening intently to what people are all about— their problems, their concerns."

Because Jerry listened intently to my challenges, he recognized the voids in my life. And, when asked, he offered his insights, sometimes by sharing stories from his own life, such as when he was struggling to start his business, and sometimes by recommending books. And, frankly, sometimes by making fun of me. I was single when I met Jerry; he loved to tease me about the women I dated. As he got to know me, when I'd tell him about a new girlfriend I was seeing, he'd simply hold up a number of fingers to represent how many weeks he thought the relationship would last.

More important, he modeled what it looks like to love and respect other people—including his wife and adult children, which helped inspire me to approach my life a little differently. I had strong relationships with people in my life—except for the people I dated. It made no sense, and Jerry helped me see it. Because of Jerry's influence, I reevaluated my values and began to take dating relationships more seriously. If I hadn't, Jill never would have given me the time of day!

Jerry doesn't let me get by with the surface-level niceties. He wants to know not just what I'm doing or what I believe, but why. As Socrates said, the unexamined life isn't worth living. Jerry helped me examine my life. Whatever the subject, Jerry gets to the real heart of the matter, whatever that is.

I go into most relationships with a desire to be positive about myself—I want to share my strengths. Most of us are like that, and there's nothing wrong with it. But Jerry was one of the first people I knew who didn't want to hear just the good stuff. The more we got to know each other, the more probing questions he asked. He wanted to know what was going on with me. And I felt very comfortable sharing my fears, my anxieties—my darker side—because Jerry has a gift of not treating others like he's judging them.

Jerry does this by living out the concept of giving without expectations. I do things for Jerry all the time, and sometimes it's because he's asked. But he never tries to get something *from me for himself.* When he asks a favor of me, it's almost always for something that will serve someone else.

When I asked Jerry what he gets out of our relationship, here's what he said: "I've never thought of it that way. I never intended to get something out of it." So he gave it some thought and added, "I get a sense of pride in seeing someone grow. You were kind of wild when I met you, and you've ended up with a great wife and a great family. I feel a sense of pride in watching a person I care about grow to great levels."

It was *four years* into my relationship with Jerry before insurance came up. And even then it only came up when I looked him in the eye and said, "I can't stand it any more. When are you going to try to sell me some life insurance?"

That's when he told me about his products, and I bought a policy that I renew each year.

By that time, Jerry had become a trusted friend. He was one of the original board members of Leader's Challenge, the non-profit I founded in 2000, even though I never asked him for a dime for the organization. But every now and again we'd have lunch and at some point, in an almost oh-by-the-way manner, he'd hand me a large check and say, "Don't tell anyone."

The growth in our relationship occurred over weeks and months, and it did so in ways so subtle as to go almost unnoticed. One day we were meeting for salmon salad, and the next thing you know I'm volunteering for his charities, he's helping me launch a nonprofit, and we're having discussions about what I want in a long-term relationship with a woman. In retrospect, I see his vulnerability, his selflessness, and his willingness to ask probing questions and listen to the answers as the critical steps along the way.

I can't put a time and date on when our relationship reached what I would describe as the Penthouse level, but I can look back and say when I realized it was there.

When I was running Leader's Challenge, the husband of one of our staff members was the CEO of the Major League Baseball Alumni Association. We were always looking for ways to honor our donors, so he donated some tickets to that year's All-Star game in Chicago. I took Jerry Middel.

By that time, Jerry and I had developed a relationship in which we knew intuitively when the other person was struggling or in need, and our mutual respect and trust allowed us to ask the toughest of tough questions. We also celebrated each other's victories. When something positive happened in Jerry's life, I felt that I'd won as well. And he felt the same way when things went well for me.

We had different things to offer each other, because we were in different stages of life and came from different backgrounds and had different skills and experiences. But our values and principles were closely aligned. When Jerry and I spent time together, I always left feeling like I was a better person. And his needs became as important to me as my own.

During that trip to Chicago, Jerry and I had dinner at Mike Ditka's restaurant. As we talked about our friendship, I found I had no reservations in telling him that I loved him. It was the sort of mutual love that marks the most meaningful relationships. Later I'd give that love a label: a Fifth Floor or Penthouse relationship.

Chapter 31

Moore than Meets
the Eye

R on Hall first encountered Denver Moore on a Tuesday evening at the Union Gospel Mission, a homeless shelter in downtown Forth Worth, Texas. Ron, a middle-aged white man and a successful art dealer, was volunteering alongside his wife, serving food for the evening meal. Denver, a six-foot-two, 230-pound black man, caught the couple's attention because he was throwing a chair across the room, screaming obscenities, and promising to "kill whoever stole my shoes!" as he swung his huge fists at anyone who lacked the good sense to get out of his way.

As Ron looked around for someone who might intervene, his wife, Deborah, leaned over and told him that she thought he ought to try to make friends with him.

Ron, understandably, wanted no part of that relationship.

"Probably in his sixties, he looked younger and, somehow, older at the same time," Ron recalled. "He dressed in rags. A loner, the whites of his eyes had gone an eerie yellow. He never smiled and seldom spoke. Nor did we see anyone acknowledge him. But it wasn't as though others at the mission ostracized him; it was more like they kept a respectful distance, as one might give wide berth to a pit bull."*

For weeks after that first encounter, Ron would see Denver in or near the mission. Denver waited until everyone had gotten their food, then he walked up and asked for two plates, one for himself and one for an old man who lived nearby. Ron figured Denver just wanted extra food, and he knew giving out two plates was against the mission's policy. But he figured he wasn't the mission police, so he'd simply give Denver two plates and tell him he was glad he'd stopped in.

Ron still had no desire to befriend the man, but he honored his wife's continued request and reached out to Denver from time to time. The risk seemed minimal, since Denver clearly didn't want to spend time with Ron any more than Ron wanted to spend time with Denver. When Ron spoke to Denver, he usually got no response. And when he did get a response, it usually came as three one-word sentences: "Leave. Me. Alone."

Ron and Deborah Hall heard about a free concert at the Caravan, a swank theater in downtown Fort Worth, so they decided to take anyone from the Union Gospel Mission who wanted to attend.

---

* Ron Hall and Denver Moore chronicle their story in their *New York Times* bestselling book, *Same Kind of Different as Me* (Thomas Nelson, 2008). It's a book that changed my life, challenging me on many levels. It is a book that I'll give to my children and insist that they read. My abbreviated description in this chapter is told in my words, not theirs; only the dialogue is quoted from their book. And while I'm giving you a good bit of the story, it's far from the full telling. So please, read their book.

It had been a few months since they began volunteering at the mission, and they'd gotten to know several of the regulars. But not Denver Moore. So Ron was surprised to see Denver standing off to the side of the group of men who were waiting for Ron to drive them to the concert. After the others loaded into the back of Ron's Suburban, Denver stood nearby, staring at the car for several minutes, before eventually getting in the passenger seat next to Ron and sitting stone-faced and silent as they made their way to the theater.

When everyone else went in the theater, Denver stayed outside smoking a cigarette until Ron came back down and asked if he wanted to come inside.

Denver didn't speak. He stood silently for several minutes, then walked past Ron and into the theater without a word. Ron followed him in, sat next to him, and later patted him on the knee, smiled, and told him he was glad that he had decided to come along.

Denver got up and moved to another seat, alone.

After the concert, everyone loaded into the cars—the women with Deborah in her Land Cruiser and the men with Ron in his Suburban. Everyone, that is, but Denver. As usual, he hung back for several minutes. Then he approached Ron—with an apology.

"You and your wife been tryin to be nice to me for some time now, and I have purposely avoided you," he said. "I'm sorry.

"Next time you is at the mission," Denver added, "try and find me and let's have a cup a' coffee and chat a li'l bit."

Ron made sure the "next time" was the very next morning. The outing seemed simple enough. But when he picked up Denver Moore and took him to breakfast, it was the first time

Denver had eaten in a restaurant in his sixty-plus years on earth.

At breakfast, Denver Moore sought permission to ask Ron Hall a personal question, and Ron said, "Ask away."

"What's your name?" Denver said.

That was it? That was the "personal" question? In his circles, Denver explained, you don't ask people their names. You just don't.

Ron shrugged, smiled, and told him his name.

Denver ate slowly, but he began to share a little about himself. He had escaped the cotton fields of Louisiana, where the plantation system had kept many black men like him tied to poverty on the farms of wealthy landowners. One day a train had rolled by and he'd hopped aboard. Then he had carved out a life in the concrete jungle. It was all he knew. When he finally finished his meal, which took well over an hour, Denver looked at Ron with another question, this one a bit more penetrating: "What you want from me?"

"I just want to be your friend," Ron said.

Denver raised his eyebrows in disbelief and paused for several seconds.

"Let me think about it," he said.

As they drove back to the mission, Denver began to laugh out loud for no apparent reason, and Ron helplessly looked at him in hopes that he'd eventually reveal the joke. After a few blocks, he did. He told Ron that he and the others at the mission thought Ron and his wife were from the CIA.

"Most folks that serve at the mission come once or twice and we never see em again," Denver explained. "But you and your wife come ever week. And your wife always be askin everbody his name and his birthday . . . you know, gatherin information. Now just think about it: Why would anybody be wantin to know a homeless man's name and birthday, if they ain't the CIA?"

Several weeks after Ron Hall had treated Denver Moore to his first breakfast in a restaurant, the pair went out again. This time, Denver told Ron he'd been giving some thought to the question Ron had asked during their previous outing.

"What did I ask you?" Ron said.

"'Bout bein your friend."

What Ron saw as a somewhat offhanded comment, Denver saw as a defining point in their relationship. He didn't take it lightly, and he wanted to be sure. So to be sure, he asked Ron a question about fishing.

That's right—fishing.

He told Ron he didn't understand why "white folks" did something called "catch and release" when they went fishing. Why did they go to the trouble of catching a fish and then let it go? It was more a statement than a question, and he let it hang in the air a bit so that Ron could grasp the deeper meaning.

"If you is fishin for a friend you just gon' catch and release, then I ain't got no desire to be your friend. But if you is lookin for a real friend, then I'll be one. Forever."

After Denver and Ron officially became friends, they began spending more and more time together. Ron would take Denver to museums and nice restaurants, and Denver gave Ron insider's tours into the lives of Fort Worth's homeless population.

Denver's life took the fast track to change. He began drinking and cursing less and less, and he began helping out around the mission more and more. Mentally and spiritually, he began to see the world differently—not as a lone wolf who had grown up as a virtual slave on a Louisiana plantation, but as a person with intrinsic value who had something to offer those around him. Before long, the same man who'd once thrown chairs in the mission was singing at its chapel services.

He grew closer and closer to Ron and Deborah Hall, learning from them as they learned from him. Some lessons were deep spiritual and philosophical lessons in life. Others were overtly practical. But even those lessons eventually delivered some greater meaning.

For instance, Denver, at sixty-two, had never had a driver's license, so Ron helped him get one. And a few weeks later he put it to good use. Ron and Deborah's daughter, Regan, had taken a job with a youth camp in Colorado, but most of her possessions were still at her apartment in Dallas. So Ron asked Denver if he wanted to drive solo to Colorado to take Regan her things.

Ron was half-joking with the question, but Denver liked the idea—especially when he learned the trip would take him through the city for which he was named. So Ron and Denver spent three days planning the trip, with Ron drawing out maps because Denver could read a hand-drawn map but couldn't read the atlas. Then they loaded up Ron's nearly new Ford F-350 crew-cab pickup with Regan's clothes, furniture, and electronics, and Denver drove off in search of Winter Park, Colorado. As he drove away, Ron wondered if he'd just acted in great faith or great foolishness. Denver wondered the same thing. He knew he could be trusted, "but Mr. Ron didn't know that."

Denver knew Ron was a smart man, but he didn't understand why anyone would hand him $700 in cash and the keys to a $30,000 truck loaded with electronics, clothes, and furniture.

"Bein smart don't mean he'll ever see his truck again—that takes faith," he said.

Ron didn't hear from Denver until he showed up back at his house several days later, the truck washed and waxed, Regan's belongings delivered. He handed Ron the keys to the pickup and a handful of wadded-up cash—about $400. Denver had slept in the truck and eaten only at fast-food restaurants and convenience stores.

When Ron suggested that Denver keep the money as payment for the trip, Denver refused.

"I ain't for hire," Denver told him. "I did that to bless you and your family. Money can't buy no blessins."

Two weeks later, Ron hired Denver to drive a rental truck to Baton Rouge, Louisiana, to deliver paintings and sculptures valued at more than $1 million. And when tragedy struck Ron's family, Denver was among their closest friends, seeing them through day after day and week after week. Ron kept his promise not to make Denver a catch-and-release friend. And Denver kept his promise to be Ron's friend—forever.

These two unlikely men, one white and one black, one well-off and successful, one homeless, one from an educated upbringing, one illiterate and from a family of plantation workers, had achieved a Penthouse relationship together.

Chapter 32

Collecting What Matters

When I was a kid, I collected baseball cards. Nothing unusual about that. But I collected them in classic *How to Win Friends & Influence People* style. I went for the numbers. Just as I wanted more friends, I wanted more baseball cards. More was always better.

Of course, I was wrong. In baseball cards, as in relationships, quality is more important than quantity. It's easy to fill up a Rolodex or Microsoft Outlook with contacts, but that's mere networking; it's just name-collecting. What matters is collecting things of lasting value. When it comes to baseball cards, what we need is a 1933 Babe Ruth or a 1952 Mickey Mantle. We need a 1914 "Shoeless" Joe Jackson or a 1951 Willie Mays.

We need a 1909 Honus Wagner.

When the American Tobacco Company released its 1909 baseball cards, the great Honus Wagner complained that they had used his image on one of the cards. Some say it was because he wanted to be paid for it; others that he didn't want his image used to promote smoking. Regardless, the result was that the company stopped producing that card. Only around one hundred Wagner cards were made that year. Fewer than sixty exist today, and only about ten of those are in excellent condition. All of them are valuable, but one such card sold for a record $2.8 million in 2007, making it significantly more valuable than the shoeboxes full of cards collecting dust in my parents' basement.

I've never counted them, but there are hundreds, perhaps thousands, of cards in those boxes. Of those, none are worth thousands, much less millions, of dollars, and only fifty or sixty really ever meant something to me. I treasured the cards of Johnny Bench, Mike Schmidt, and George Brett, but most of all I loved the baseball cards of the New York Yankees.

I'll be a Yankees fan until the day I die. I'll never forget Reggie Jackson's three homers in Game Six of the 1977 World Series against the Dodgers, which earned him the name "Mr. October." Or Bucky Dent's home run over the Green Monster on October 2, 1978, to beat the Red Sox for the American League pennant. And I was depressed for months after Thurman Munson's plane went down in Canton, Ohio, on August 2, 1979.

When we found out they were going to tear down Yankee Stadium and build a new ballpark, Jill and I took our son, Tate, to the old park as an infant just to make sure he soaked in some of that Yankees tradition.

No baseball cards mean more to me than my Yankees cards, and no Yankees card means more to me than my Phil Rizzuto—the five-foot-six Hall of Fame shortstop who helped the Yankees to nine World Series titles between 1941 and 1956. My dad got the card when he was a kid, and passed it along to me.

All of those cards, however, remain in a box in a basement. My point? They can't compare to flesh-and-blood relationships. And my most treasured relationships are the ones that make it to the Fifth Floor. Those are the ones worth collecting.

I'm blessed at this point in my life to have an all-star Fifth Floor team. That team is the equivalent of what some people call their "inner circle" of friends, their "kitchen cabinet," or their personal board of directors. It's that group of most highly trusted friends with whom you work through your life. When I'm working through challenges at work, when I'm faced with big decisions at home, when I have to sort through the chaos that threatens to take me off track spiritually, I turn to one or more players on my Fifth Floor team. Some of them don't even know each other. They have diverse backgrounds and skills and gifts.

I know these mentors and friends will give me honest feedback and counsel. They tell me what I need to hear, not what I *want* to hear. And they know that when they need a listening ear, a gentle nudge, a firm push, I'll be there for them. We love each other unconditionally. Most important, we're fiercely loyal to one another, through the good, the bad, and the ugly.

These very different people bring different things to our relationship, but in every case we're committed to doing everything we can to lift each other as high as possible—in our work, with our families, and in our spiritual lives.

That's why the Penthouse is such a special place. You can't get to this level if you focus on what the other person can or will give to you. When you find yourself in one of these relationships you discover that you're giving more than you ever realized you had to give, and getting more than you possibly could deserve.

My all-star Fifth Floor team is sort of like the roster for the 1977 Yankees, except instead of having Chris Chambliss at first base, I have Linda Childears. Instead of Willie Randolph at second, I have Steve Farber. Rather than Bucky Dent at short, I have Scott Bemis. Graig Nettles isn't at third; instead, I have Mark Urich. My outfield doesn't include Reggie Jackson, Roy White, Mickey Rivers, and Lou Pinella; it has Dick

Eakin, Joel Mauney, Kerry Caldwell, and Chris Hennessy. My DH is Keith Wegen, rather than Carlos May. Thurman Munson isn't my catcher; it is Scott Lynn. My pitching staff, instead of including Ed Figueroa, Mike Torrez, Ron Guidry, Don Gullett, Catfish Hunter, Dick Tidrow, and Sparky Lyle, has Mark Burke, Rob Harter, Steve Demby, Cynthia Madden Leitner, Humberto Lopez, Doug Miller, and Jim Warner. And my coach is Jerry Middel, not Billy Martin.

Rizzuto didn't play for the 1977 Yankees, of course, but I can't have an all-star Fifth Floor team without a Rizzuto.

That would be my father, Tom Spaulding Sr.

Everyone should have a Fifth Floor all-star team—not so much for what that team can do for you, but for what you and that team can do together. That's the power of relationships in the Penthouse.

Who makes up your Fifth Floor all-star team and why?

At this stage, you might be tossing a ball up in the air and catching it yourself. Or perhaps you have one or two people you *really* classify at this Penthouse level. Or you might have an entire Fifth Floor roster.

When you make a list of the members on your all-star team, remember that it's not a list of your best buddies or even everyone who is on your Fifth Floor. These aren't the friends you hang out with for drinks or to watch the big game. Some of those people may be on your team, but some won't. It's more about the roles they play in your life and that you play in their lives. My team includes mentors, my attorney, employees, board members, pastors, my life coach, my business partners—and some of my buddies.

Take some time to really think about your team. Who is on it, and why? What are they giving to the relationship? What are you giving to them? Do they hold you accountable? I break my team into three life categories: spiritual growth, family and health balance, and professional growth. Pick the categories that are important to you. Put the names of those that fit into each category. Next, talk to those people about how you can serve a greater purpose in each other's lives. If they don't already know they're on your team, they really aren't on your team.

There is no roster limit, nor is there a minimum. How many Fifth Floor relationships can you nurture? Most likely, more than you think. And almost certainly, more than you now have.

I treasure Fifth Floor relationships the way some people treasure vintage baseball cards. But that doesn't mean I only value relationships that end up in the Penthouse. Baseball card collectors wisely care for all their cards because they don't always know which ones will turn out to be the next 1933 Nap Lajoie and which one will be the rookie who gets one at-bat and never sees the big leagues again. The same is true of relationships— you don't always know which ones will be the most important.

Of course, good things can come from relationships at all five levels or floors. Lifelong "you have my business and loyalty no matter what" relationships only live in the Penthouse. My relationship with the bartender I mentioned early in the book never really went that far, because our interaction lasted only a few hours. Today I can't tell you the man's name. But he absolutely changed my life for the better. And all because neither of us dismissed the relationship before it had a chance to begin.

We even benefit from the relationships that seem forever

stuck in the cellar. I have a handful of basement relationships with family members, past employers, and former friends. Base relationships can motivate us to become better people, and provide lessons that will enable us to improve our lives and our work.

So although we can't always control where a relationship ends up, we *can* make the most of every relationship. It starts with treating everyone as a potential roommate or teammate in the Penthouse. A conversation with the woman who sells us our morning coffee can be purely transactional, or we can reach out to the other person and strive to make it a personal connection.

Our first words should be more on the order of a heartfelt "How are you today?" instead of a monotone "Cream and sugar, please." Ask one or two questions that might give you a little insight into who the other person *really* is and what she wants out of life. Two or three minutes of our time. And who knows, one day you might have a Second or Third Floor relationship, with the potential for even more. She might someday invite our family over for Christmas dinner—and we'd go!

When we do this in our personal lives, we make friends. When we do it in our professional lives, we build genuine relationships *and* great organizations. We build a culture that's motivated toward excellence. A culture that's off the charts when it comes to generating employee loyalty, customer loyalty, revenue, innovation, profits, brand identity. All that ROR comes from an investment in taking relationships toward the Penthouse.

Picture an organizational culture where the entire staff strives to facilitate Penthouse relationships, not only with customers, clients, and vendors, but also with one another. Tell me employee morale wouldn't go up. Tell me sales wouldn't increase. Tell me customer service and retention wouldn't improve. Tell me relational competence wouldn't become a hallmark of the organization.

The Relation*Shift* we must make, therefore, is to stop approaching others with a self-focused agenda that asks only how the relationship can help *us*. We must start with the intention of not only helping that person in some basic way but advancing his or her well-being.

This is no easy matter for most of us, in large part because it goes against much of what we've learned growing up. But it's not impossible.

It wasn't impossible when Jerry Middel, a successful businessman, began investing in a young Rotarian.

It wasn't impossible when I began investing in a relationship with my wife's former husband.

It wasn't impossible when Ron Hall began serving meals at the Union Gospel Mission and agreed to patiently invest in the angriest, loneliest, scariest person in the room.

And it won't be impossible when you invest in the relationships that surround you—co-workers, neighbors, vendors, customers, supervisors, and, who knows, even the angriest, scariest person in the room. That person might not only become your greatest customer, but your closest friend—forever.

Chapter 33

Fifth Floor Givers

The 1984–85 famine in Ethiopia, one of the worst of many in that country's history, brought Noel Cunningham to tears. But what really broke his heart was the response the crisis drew from his employers at the posh Los Angeles restaurant where he worked. While the restaurant raked in profits from its wealthy patrons, the owners gave very little back to the greater community and nothing to the starving Ethiopians halfway around the world.

"I couldn't do anything to get them to help," Noel told me. "But I made myself a promise that when I got my own restaurant I'd do something."

Individual giving is important, but Noel felt strongly that businesses should give as well. So in 1986, when the Irish immigrant moved to Denver and opened Strings Restaurant, he followed through on his promise.

Strings quickly became the uptown hot spot for the city's movers and shakers. For Noel, whose culinary career began at age fourteen and included a stop as an apprentice chef at London's famed Savoy Hotel, owning his own restaurant was a dream come true. But it also was an opportunity to use fine dining as a tool for extraordinary giving.

Growing up in Dublin, Ireland, in the 1950s, Noel learned about giving from his mother's example.

"She was always bringing people in," he says in his thick Irish accent. "I'll never forget Harry Lemon. He was a huge man with a big beard—the epitome of a homeless man. She'd bring him in and put him by the fire and give him some food. At first we all were afraid of him. But we came to understand that he was just another child of God."

As the owner of Strings, Noel quietly went about serving great food to the well-to-do and serving hope to people in need. Mother's Day, for instance, is typically one of the busiest days of the year for an upscale restaurant, but Strings is closed to the public on that Sunday. Instead, for nearly twenty years, Noel has thrown a Mother's Day party for two hundred elderly women who take part in the area's Meals on Wheels program. It's their day to eat at the nicest restaurant in town—for free.

His passion for helping impoverished Ethiopians took center stage from the day Strings opened its doors, but his giving always incorporates and adds value to the local community as well. Programs like Quarters for Kids and Four Quarters for Kids not only raise thousands of dollars each year for food, clothing, and educational supplies in Ethiopia, but they've also taught elementary, middle, and high school students around Denver lessons in leadership and the value of giving.

The children learn that their quarters can add up in a hurry. They see it—and hear it—when all that loose change is poured into a huge bucket during a special event each year at Strings. And many of those students, as well as nurses and other professionals, end up traveling to Ethiopia with Noel and his wife, Tammy, through the foundation they started in 2003.

"There's nothing we're going to do that's going to substantially change Ethiopia," Noel says, "but *we* will be substantially changed."

I know this firsthand because I joined him for one of those trips.

I initially resisted going to Africa. So I zigged and zagged away from a commitment whenever Noel brought up the idea of my traveling with him.

Finally, Noel just told me flat out, "You're coming to Africa with me. And bring some of your kids from Leader's Challenge. Bring some from the inner city and some who are affluent. This will change their view of the world. And yours."

So I finally said yes. Noel turned around and helped with the fund-raisers that paid for my Leader's Challenge students to go with us.

I had learned a lot about people and cultures while backpacking across Europe, South America, and Asia, and by traveling with Up with People, both as a young cast member and later as its president and CEO. But few things have touched my heart like walking a dusty road in Ethiopia with a child clinging to my finger, knowing that the money raised by students involved with Leader's Challenge put shoes on that child's feet and food in his stomach, and helped build a hospital and school to improve his life. Nothing compares to seeing the joy-filled face of a boy crippled by polio, simply because I lifted him into the air so he could dunk a basketball for the first time.

For this, I must thank Noel Cunningham—not just for insisting that I join him on the trip to Ethiopia, but for playing a key role in the creation of Leader's Challenge.

I had lived in Denver about a year when I left my job with Up with People in 2000 to start Leader's Challenge. I still didn't know many people in the area, so I counted heavily on referrals as I went about raising the money to launch my dream. One name that continued to come up in my conversations with people was Noel Cunningham. Noel had a quiet reputation as a man who loves kids and almost never says no to good causes that help young people.

At the time, I'd never eaten at Strings, because I couldn't afford five-star restaurants on my nonprofit budget. So when I arrived for my meeting with Noel, I was glad that the first thing he said was that lunch was on the house. Then Noel looked at me and said four words every fund-raiser loves to hear: "How can I help?"

I shared my vision for Leader's Challenge. I told him I wanted to build a statewide high school program that inspired and equipped young people to lead through acts of service. I told him I wanted to partner with the schools, private and public, and make the program available to kids regardless of race, academic performance, or social status. I told him I wanted to create a program that developed servant leaders and would motivate the next generation to change the world. And I told him I wanted to cast this vision to as many people as possible who might be able and willing to make it happen.

As I looked around Noel's restaurant, I realized many of those people were sitting around the room. High-profile leaders from just about every sector—business leaders, political leaders, and celebrities—lunched together at nearby tables. The potential donors of Leader's Challenge's future were the customers of Noel's present.

Noel knew this. He also knew that Leader's Challenge hardly had two pennies to its name. So he said, "Tommy, you now have a house account at this restaurant. Anytime you need to have lunch or dinner to share the vision of Leader's Challenge, you can do it here on me. And you don't have to tell them. Just sign the ticket."

I probably ate in that restaurant three or four times a week for a year, and I never paid for a meal. I raised hundreds of thousands of dollars while eating Strings' famous cashew-crusted sea bass with saffron couscous and vanilla *beurre blanc*. I built dozens of great relationships. And I gained about twenty pounds!

When Noel was there during one of those meetings, he'd always stop by my table and say that he endorsed Leader's Challenge. And, of course, I always told the person who was with me that Noel Cunningham was picking up the tab.

"That wasn't the idea," he says. "The idea wasn't for me to look good, it was for you to look good."

A typical Noel Cunningham response.

Noel shares a common quality in what I call Fifth Floor givers—he cares more about results than about getting credit.

When I was a kid, my mother often took my two sisters and me to the Woodbury community pond to swim during the summer. The pond had diving boards, and I vividly remember standing on the high board, despite my fear of heights, and calling for my mother's attention. "Watch me! Watch me!" I'd scream until she looked up and encouraged me. Then I'd do a cannonball into the water.

Many of us give like we're that preteen on a diving board—*Look at me! Look at me!* But the greatest givers I know—true Fifth Floor givers—go almost unnoticed until someone else points them out.

That selfless quality sometimes takes such givers onto some risky ground. Noel, for instance, never sacrificed the quality of food or service at Strings because of his Fifth Floor philanthropy, but there came at least one time when it looked as though his giving might cost him a golden opportunity to make a sound business move.

Noel had been leasing the building for Strings, but he had crunched the numbers and knew he'd be much better off financially if he owned it. The owner of the building offered to sell if Noel could meet the asking price with three payments over a six-month period. Noel knew he couldn't meet those terms, given that so much of his normal cash flow went toward charities. Giving away food and paying a staff to feed nonpaying customers "isn't always bottom-line profitable for business," Noel points out.

The answer, he decided, wasn't to decrease his giving but to increase business. So he put a note in his menu telling customers that the more they spent on wine and food, the more it would help him buy the building. And he called me, and who knows who else, and asked if I knew any businesses that might want to rent Strings for a holiday party.

Of course, I went to work spreading the word; holding a holiday party there would be a nice payback to one of the most unheralded philanthropists in the city. Enough people bought enough food and drank enough wine that Noel was able to buy the building and never decrease his giving.

When the economy took a turn for the worse in 2008, Noel figured his business would suffer as more and more people cut back on things like dining out. But several customers went out of their way to tell him they had made a commitment to keep eating at Strings—not just because they loved the dining experience, which they did, but because they knew how much Noel helped others with his profits. He had earned their loyalty even in tough times because his business was more than a business. It was a Fifth Floor business. It changed lives for the better. By becoming a Fifth Floor giver, Noel Cunningham created Fifth Floor customer loyalty.

That's the thing about the Fifth Floor matrix—it's a model for excellence for just about anything, not just relationships. What do you do professionally? Is it merely transactional, First

Floor work, or are you producing Fifth Floor outcomes? Are you a Fifth Floor banker, a Fifth Floor salesman, a Fifth Floor pastor, a Fifth Floor teacher, a Fifth Floor CEO, a Fifth Floor business owner?

What's your level of customer service? Is it Fifth Floor customer service? If not, why not? What type of team are you on? If it's not a Fifth Floor team, why isn't it, and how can you change it? And how are you addressing the community's needs? Are you a transactional soup-server, or are you and your organization on the Fifth Floor of outreach? What can you and your organization do to become Fifth Floor givers?

You can't have a Fifth Floor culture that isn't giving—as individuals and as a group. If you want to build successful organizations, increase sales, develop loyal customers, improve employee retention, impact your community, and change the world, you have to become sold out to a Fifth Floor culture. As Mahatma Gandhi put it, "Be the change you want to see in the world."

Chapter 34

Living Give/Get from the Outside/In

Noel Cunningham and Jerry Middel both understand the power of pouring themselves into the lives of others in a way that, frankly, doesn't always make sense to people who don't *get it*. That's because many people can't fully embrace two critical but paradoxical realities that work in the lives of Fifth Floor givers and that affect our ability to move relationships from the First Floor toward the Penthouse.

First, **the Law of Give/Get**: Investing unselfishly in the lives of others is *the most important* thing we can do for the health and success of our personal lives, our professional lives, our organizations, and our communities.

Second, **the Law of Outside/In**: By moving *outside* ourselves in service to others, we can begin changing who we are on the *inside*.

The Law of Outside/In sounds counterintuitive because we're all taught early in life that lasting, meaningful change happens from the inside out. And that's true. But stopping with that leaves the process incomplete. It doesn't address an important conundrum most of us face: that human nature often gets in the way of our best intentions. In other words, we're sometimes selfish, lazy, indifferent, fearful, or just plain unable to see what we need to do if we want to make a lasting change.

Let's face it, there's a reason why most Americans are overweight, and it's not that we have no desire to shed a few pounds; it's that we eat and drink too much of the wrong things and exercise too little. And there's a reason why we don't serve the underprivileged more often—or even serve those around us in our work. It's the same reason we find it hard to "love our enemies."

The reason: that stuff is hard!

It requires things like focus, discipline, energy, time, and commitment. Furthermore, the payoff often stands far away in the foggy distance, while self-gratifying rewards dangle immediately in front of us.

It's hard enough to selflessly serve the people we like at work and in the community, much less the people we don't know or don't like. And because it's hard, there's a part of us that resists doing it. Our emotions and our feelings set up roadblocks to our actions.

So sometimes we have to act even if our heart's not fully engaged, trusting that something good will come of it— something good for others and, ultimately, something good inside of us.

We have to go "outside"—we have to leave our offices or our normal workspaces to view our work through a different lens. Other times it's more of an emotional journey—we have to leave our comfort zones in order to experience an internal change.

That is why executives have to leave the spreadsheets on their desks from time to time and go visit with front-line workers or personally investigate customer complaints or shop in the stores that sell their goods. By getting "out there," they can relate to their employees and their customers in fresh, important ways that help them make smarter decisions when they return to those spreadsheets.

Sam Walton, the founder of Walmart, famously walked the aisles of his stores. Because he was a private pilot, he often flew unannounced to stores all around the country, learning volumes about what customers and associates thought, while also sharing his vision for the stores and the company. He also sent his executives and buyers out on store visits—Walmart stores and the stores of competitors. And his buyers were required to work at least five days a year in a store. "You can't 'merchandise the world' by sitting in your office," he'd say.*

The same is true when developing any type of attitude of service, whether it's in-house or in the community.

Ron Hall certainly left his comfort zone when he tagged along with his wife to volunteer at the Union Gospel Mission. And I had to leave my emotional comfort zone when I went with Noel to Ethiopia, an act of service that led to a changed heart.

During my trip to Ethiopia, I saw just what a difference sacrificial service makes in the world. My friend Doug Jackson, president and CEO of PROJECT C.U.R.E., a nonprofit that collects and delivers millions of dollars' worth of donated medical equipment and supplies to developing nations, came with us on the trip. Doug has a law degree and a Ph.D. in business administration; he's been successful in the academic and business communities. But he left that behind to run the nonprofit his father started.

During our Ethiopia trip, I took a side trip with Doug to

---

* Michael Bergdahl, *The 10 Rules of Sam Walton: Success Secrets for Remarkable Results* (John Wiley & Sons, 2007).

Addis Ababa so he could do an assessment of the needs of some of the hospitals and clinics. Those hospitals had dirt floors and used antiquated equipment. They recycled syringes and gloves, and often did without what Americans would see as the basics of care. I'd never seen anything like it. What he's doing is totally changing the world.

Doug says he's in the business of second chances. Many of the donated supplies would have been thrown out in North America. He gives them a second chance. And that gives the sick and hurting in the poorest parts of the world a second chance at life.

Doug's nonprofit saves lives, but it also changes the lives of the people who volunteer to make it happen. That's because when we pour ourselves into something that helps others, our attitude about who we are begins to change for the better. At a very basic and essential level, we develop a greater sense of self-worth.

Mimi Silbert, who operates a rehabilitation program for ex-convicts in California, put it like this: "You don't get it by someone helping you. You get it by helping someone else. It's being the helper that makes you like yourself."*

The more we do this, the easier it becomes to do it again. That's because when we start serving others and putting others first—even when it isn't the easy thing to do—those

---

* Silbert founded and runs the Delancey Street Foundation in San Francisco. For more than thirty years her foundation has operated a variety of businesses staffed by hardened ex-convicts who, in many cases, are third-generation gang members. This quote is from the book *Influencer* by Kerry Patterson, Joseph Grenny, David Maxfield, Ron McMillan, and Al Switzler (McGraw-Hill, 2007), which chronicles some of the unconventional techniques she's used to foster some amazing life change.

outside actions create a change within us. As the saying goes, it's sometimes easier to *act* our way into new ways of *feeling* than to *feel* our way into new ways of *acting*.

The Law of Give/Get involves a proactive approach to relationships that's built on a foundation of noble motives. It starts with "investing unselfishly in the lives of others." That requires an action (investing in others) driven by specific motivation (selflessness). But what this law makes clear is that we "get" rewards from our selflessness.

Focusing on others, for instance, doesn't mean abandoning our own motives and strategies. There's nothing wrong with helping ourselves by helping others.

When I went to Noel Cunningham with Leader's Challenge, I made no assumptions about what he might do to help. And he had no expectations for how he might benefit from our relationship. Noel never expected anything in return, no matter how much sea bass I ate for free. And he didn't stop helping Leader's Challenge because I initially refused to go with him to Ethiopia. He saw me as a friend who was championing a great cause, and that was enough. And getting me to go with him to Ethiopia was never a condition for his support of Leader's Challenge.

The selflessness I'm talking about simply means there is no quid pro quo. It means going into it with the understanding that we are doing the right things, even if the personal benefits never materialize. (Remember the Law of Mother Teresa: results, while important, are secondary to doing the right thing the right way.)

Think about the donation Warren Buffett made to the Bill and Melinda Gates Foundation. His overall gift, depending on stock values, is estimated to reach around $37 billion before all is said and done. Bill Gates must have given him some sales pitch, right? Not really. "I actually never spoke to him about the gift," Gates said. "It was completely a surprise to me."*

Gates cast his vision of helping others in his speeches in hopes that other people would catch that vision and join in making it happen. Buffett jumped in because he believed in that vision, and because he had a long-term relationship with Bill and Melinda Gates. He literally trusts them with *billions* of dollars because of the Penthouse relationship he has with them.

I've been involved in fund-raising for nonprofits for more than ten years. The five-, six-, and seven-figure gifts that have come in almost always have come without an "ask" from me. They were all about relationships. The donors believed in the vision of the organization, believed in me, trusted me, and responded. That doesn't mean you never ask; it means you seldom *need* to ask if you've built a strong relationship.

There are no guarantees in life, we're told. But I can tell you this with confidence: investing unselfishly in the lives of others is *the most important* thing we can do for the health and success of our own lives, our organizations, and our communities. And the more we practice this, the deeper it embeds itself in the soul of a culture.

Ken Blanchard, the bestselling co-author of *The One-Minute Manager* and the founder of one of the world's top leadership training organizations, once put it this way: "My own experience about all the blessings I've had in my life is that the more I give away, the more that comes back. That is the way life works, and that is the way energy works."

I know Ken as an authentic Fifth Floor giver who fully lives out the Law of Give/Get.

---

* *The Rotarian*, May 2009.

I had first met Ken when I approached him to speak at an Up with People fund-raiser, during a trip I took to Southern California in 2008. Afterwards he invited Jill and me to come back to San Diego that June and go to dinner with him and his wife, Margie. It was the weekend of the U.S. Open golf tournament, which was being played nearby at Torrey Pines Golf Course. Ken got me two tickets to the tournament for the next day, and gave them to me when we had dinner that Friday night at his country club.

It had been less than a year since a series of wildfires devastated that area of California, burning Ken and Margie's home to the ground. Yet he and Margie had the most upbeat attitude of anyone I've ever met.

When we talked about the golf tournament, Ken kept telling me that I needed to stop by the American Express tent. All I had to do was show them my American Express card, he said, and I could use one of their high-tech satellite monitors to follow the action all over the course, no matter which group I was following. It sounded great, except for one thing: I didn't have an American Express card. To be polite, I didn't say anything, but he kept talking about how neat it was and how I had to use one of those monitors.

Finally, I sheepishly confessed that I lacked the proper credit card. Without another word, Ken pulled out his wallet, slid out his American Express card, handed it to me, and said, "Use this to get in the tent and mail it back when you're done."

We'd met twice!

Several months later, we both spoke at the Up with People fund-raiser—it was my last event before I left my job as CEO there to start my own company.

The following morning, Ken and I played golf. The night

before he left town, my wife and children joined us for dinner together.

At dinner, Ken looked over at Jill and said, "Are you nervous about your husband leaving Up with People and starting this new career?" She was, she admitted. Given that I'd spent so much of my career in the nonprofit sector and that I was leaving without a severance, Jill had every reason to be nervous. "Don't be nervous," Ken told her. "Your husband has an incredible gift to communicate with people. He's going to make a huge impact on the lives of people." His words were an incredible comfort for Jill, and they renewed my own confidence in my decision to leave Up with People.

When I drove him to the airport the next day, we talked about the challenges of starting a new venture. The biggest challenge for most entrepreneurs, and certainly for me at that time, is cash flow. We had a plan, of course, but money was going to be tight. The next week, to my surprise, Ken sent me a check to help fund my startup. And it wasn't a few hundred dollars to cover groceries. It was a significant amount. And here we'd known each other for only a few months. But it made a huge difference in getting the Spaulding Companies off the ground.

My point? Ken lives the things he teaches in ways that go far, far beyond the ordinary. He gave me his time, his energy, his encouragement, and his financial support—all without a thought about what was "in it" for him.

Not every gift or act of giving can be returned in kind. But putting the needs of others first always has an enormous, long-term positive impact on people and organizational cultures. The seemingly most insignificant encounters with people—like my encounter with the bartender—often become the highest-paying investments in life, if we'll only let them.

Tom France, Ken Blanchard, Jerry Middel, and Noel

Cunningham have all invested unselfishly in me, even when reason indicated that such an investment might not pay any dividends. They did it because they saw it as the right thing to do. And when I see potential in others and a chance to invest in their success, I jump at it. I can only hope it has a fraction of the impact on someone else that it had on me.

Do organizations benefit as well?

The short answer is yes. Sometimes the "get" was measurable—increased customer loyalty and revenue, deeper employee loyalty and lower turnover. And sometimes that "get" falls into the "soft" side of the balance sheets.

"The real return," Noel says, "is knowing in your heart that you've helped inspire people to make a difference in the world. I knew in my heart, Tommy, that you'd never be the same after that trip to Ethiopia. And I can't describe what it feels like to see a group of high-school kids organize a fundraiser at my restaurant to help the children of Ethiopia. To see them put in that kind of work and take that kind of pride as they raise three thousand bucks. Those are the paybacks. When you see the glint in their eyes."

I don't know that Noel or any of my other Fifth Floor giver friends have ever verbalized the Law of Give/Get or the Law of Outside/In, but I can say with confidence that they make those laws a part of who they are and how they live. I also can say with great certainty that the multitude of opportunities they've taken to invest in other people—people like me—have made the world around them a better place.

Tom France made his Rotary Club better because he lived out Give/Get and Outside/In. Ken Blanchard makes the Ken Blanchard Companies better because he lives out Give/Get and Outside/In. And Noel Cunningham makes Denver and Ethiopia better because he lives out Give/Get and Outside/In.

—ᴏᴇᴏ—

When Fifth Floor givers lead large organizations, you get Fifth Floor organizations. And throughout Fifth Floor organizations, you'll find the spirit of Give/Get and Outside/In.

For example, Jim Click is a Fifth Floor friend of mine who lives in Tucson, Arizona. Jim runs one of the nation's largest automobile dealer groups. The thirteen full-service dealerships that make up the Jim Click Automotive Team bring annual revenues of more than $315 million. But he's equally well known for his philanthropy—a trait he learned from his father, Jim "Boompa" Click. The Jim Click Automotive Team, the Click Family Foundation, and the Click Charitable Contributions Program have a nearly forty-year track record for supporting worthwhile charities. No other name in Arizona is more synonymous with giving than Jim Click.

One of those charities is Linkages, a nonprofit Jim helped found in 1996 as a resource for connecting the community's disabled workers with employers. Linkages has developed partnerships with around forty-five agencies and more than 160 employers, because Jim understands the intrinsic value people feel when they hold a job.

Before he helped launch that program, Jim began modeling Outside/In and Give/Get at his dealerships. Jim's dealerships are one of the state's largest employers of disabled workers.

During one of my Tucson visits, Jim took me on a tour, and we stopped in several of his dealerships. A friendly employee would open the door. Another was pouring coffee for customers in the service department. Another was on the lot washing cars. All had some physical or mental handicap, but all had something productive to do.

Jim leads by example; his employees and customers

understand that his business represents something far greater than itself. It's a way of life for him, not a program or a PR campaign.

Jim and I once walked into an ice-cream shop for a quick snack, and he left after paying the tab for everyone in the store. Another time, when a young boy admired his Colorado Rockies baseball cap, Jim took off the cap, adjusted it to fit the boy's small head, and gave it to him. Jim Click's love for people is contagious.

But you don't have to be a successful business owner to make Outside/In and Give/Get a part of your organization.

Consider the management approach of former naval officer Michael Abrashoff. In 1997, as the newly appointed captain of the USS *Benfold*, Abrashoff inherited a crew with horrible morale and a ship with a sinking reputation. Uninspired and lightly motivated, the sailors had grown weary of an oppressive management style that had them all looking forward to the end of their tour and the chance to rejoin civilian life.

The *Benfold* was Exhibit A in the United States Navy's failed attempts to recruit and keep great sailors.

So Abrashoff took a radical leadership approach (especially for the military) that involved trusting his crew and treating them with respect. It's often referred to as "grassroots" leadership, although it's tough to have roots or grass on a guided-missile destroyer.

Over two years, however, Abrashoff proved that a leader could practice Give/Get and Outside/In without sacrificing discipline or chain-of-command respect. Indeed, Abrashoff was beloved by his crew, and they became as disciplined as any crew in the Navy. Soon the ship that outsiders ridiculed and insiders worked hard to leave became the ship that sailors longed to join and commanders trusted with the most difficult of missions. It developed a reputation for efficiency, creativity, and excellence. As Abrashoff (and his crew) put it, the *Benfold* was "the best damn ship in the Navy."

One way he turned things around was to make an effort early on to interview his crew, learning not only their names but something personal about them—all 310 of them in one month. That's one of those ideas that sound great—for other leaders! And it's easy to imagine a fast start and a quick fizzle. Somewhere around that 200th interview, Abrashoff had to second-guess this particular tactic. But he stuck with it. He went about building solid relationships with his officers and crew, from the lowest rank to the highest.

Long after those initial interviews, Abrashoff would regularly eat meals with the enlisted men, talk to them about their lives and their work, send notes to their parents praising them when they did things well, and encourage them to take responsibility for improving their ship in any way possible.

Abrashoff believed in his crew, trusted them, and did everything within his power to help his crew succeed, even when it meant risking his own advancement. The approach not only helped change the culture of his organization and the performance and morale of the crew, but it changed him, as well.

"How can you treat people poorly when you know and respect them?" Abrashoff wrote in his 2002 book *It's Your Ship* (Warner Business reprint, 2009). "How can you put people down when you realize that the journey they are on will not only improve the workplace and help you, but will improve society as well? I enjoyed helping them figure out what they wanted in life and charting a course to get there."

A few years ago I realized that Jerry Middel, despite forty-some years of Fifth Floor giving, had gone largely unrecognized by the larger community. This was no surprise, really, because Jerry gives money anonymously and does much of his charitable work behind the scenes or on the front lines, not on the stage.

So I led a campaign to present Jerry with the Denver Foundation's prestigious Minoru Yasui Community Volunteer Award. I also co-nominated him for the 2005 Outstanding Volunteer Award given by National Philanthropy Day of Colorado.

Championing Jerry was a simple way of showing my appreciation for all he has done—not just for me, but for everyone around him. Not only was he worthy of the honors, but I knew his winning them might heighten awareness for the causes he supported.

What I didn't know was that the Minoru Yasui award came with a significant cash prize. What do you think Jerry did with that award money? He gave it away, to Leader's Challenge, the nonprofit I'd founded. It was my turn to be humbled and honored. This was no quid pro quo—just a Fifth Floor giver living out the laws of Outside/In and Give/Get.

Chapter 35

Elevation: Advance, Link, and Lift

Steve Farber, the president of Extreme Leadership, earned his stripes by running his own financial services company, working as director of service programs at the international training consultancy TMI, and then serving for six years as vice president and official mouthpiece of the Tom Peters Company. Now he's one of the top corporate speakers in the country and a bestselling author on leadership.

I got to know Farber, as I call him, in 2006 when he spoke at the Leader's Challenge annual business breakfast fundraiser. Two friends whom I have great respect for connected the dots. Terry Pearce, author of *Leading Out Loud* (Jossey-Bass, 2003), told me Steve Farber was the most authentic person he had ever met—a huge compliment coming from a guy who regularly coaches Fortune 500 executives on authentic leadership. And Patrick Lencioni, author of *The Five Dysfunctions of a Team* (Jossey-Bass, 2002), and the speaker at our Leader's Challenge event the previous year, also recommended Farber.

So Jill and I went to Las Vegas to hear Farber speak. I was blown away by his message. I could tell right away that he and I shared many of the same values about leadership—in particular, the contrarian notion that love plays a key role in leadership excellence. In fact, he was the first person I'd ever heard who so clearly articulated what I had always seen as a missing message in the corporate world.

Steve agreed to speak at our fund-raiser for Leader's Challenge. In the course of getting to know him, he told me that his son, Jeremy, was about to graduate from high school, but wasn't really ready to start college. Jeremy wanted to see some of the world before settling in to his studies. At the time, I was playing the dual roles of president and CEO of both Leader's Challenge and Up with People. So I suggested that Jeremy join one of the casts of Up with People. And he did—for eighteen months. Eventually, Farber, at my urging, became a member of the international board of directors of Up with People.

One evening when we both had speaking engagements in Vancouver, we went out to dinner together. I told him how much I admired his career as a speaker and author, and expressed a desire to take my own career down a similar path.

I was an accomplished speaker, but not in the corporate arena.

Steve looked across the table at me and said, "Tommy, not only can you do it, but I'm going to do everything I can to help you get there."

Steve calls this GTY—Greater Than Yourself—and he explains it in detail in his book by that title (Broadway Books, 2009). His first two books—*Radical Leap* and *Radical Edge* (Kaplan Publishing, 2009)—were bestsellers, extremely creative business fiction stories that used narrative to teach a larger lesson about what he calls "extreme" leadership (and life). For those same reasons, *Greater Than Yourself* hit the *Wall Street*

Journal bestseller list within a month of the time it was released.

Steve believes everyone should mentor another person with the goal of intentionally making that person "greater than yourself." That's a much bigger idea than just helping someone improve his skills. When he was writing his book, he asked himself a challenging question: "Who is my GTY project?" Steve gave it some thought and realized I was his GTY project. Steve was a more accomplished corporate speaker and author than I, and building those skills was a major goal of mine. So he gave me a call and we formalized what to that point had been an informal mentoring relationship.

But Steve doesn't just want to help me succeed—he wants me to become more accomplished as a speaker and writer and thought-leader than he is. And he wants me to find my own GTY project and do the same for that person. It's an approach we see often with parents and their children, teachers and their pupils, coaches and their athletes, but almost never in the competitive world of the marketplace. Too many people live in fear that their own careers will inevitably sink if they elevate another person above them. Not Farber.

So Steve started giving me every contact he had in the speaking and publishing worlds. He introduced me to his business manager. He introduced me to his contacts at the top speakers' bureaus. And one evening when we were in Boston for a conference at Harvard, he introduced me to his publisher.

"If there's anything I've learned, I've shared it with him," Steve says of our relationship. "Nothing's a trade secret. I'm not trying to be helpful. We should all try to be helpful. What I'm doing is everything I can to make Tommy greater at this-stuff than I am. My fulfillment is going to come from looking up and saying, 'There he is. He did it. And I was able to help him with a boost here or there.' That's the pot of gold at the end of the rainbow for me.'"*

Steve's able to win the battles we all have with our egos so that he can take pride in achieving this goal. We've got a long way to go, to be sure. But unlike some previous mentors in my life, I know Steve won't bail on me if my success begins to outshine his. Nor will he give up on me if that success isn't immediate.

Steve's approach works because it's based on sincere, authentic love for another person. When that exists, ego doesn't go away, but it's relegated to its proper place. When we love someone, his or her success is more important to us than our own. And we realize that no matter how much of ourselves we give away in helping make that happen, we never get drained of our own success.

Steve lives out in a very intentional way what I like to call **the Law of Elevation**—the idea that we're making the most of our relationships when we're intentionally lifting others to places they can't go alone. There are three essential components to the Law of Elevation—Advancement, Link, and Lift.

At its basic levels, the Law of Elevation means pointing another person in the right direction or introducing her to the right person, and then getting out of the way. It means being helpful. But that's not enough. What really elevates this idea into something that makes for transformational relationships is the follow-through—the part where we do *more than* what's "nice and helpful."

GTY fits squarely in that first component: Advancement. GTY's a high-end version of mentoring, so it's not for every relationship. It works for Farber with me because he's been

---

* http://greaterthanyourself.com

successful in some arenas in which I'd like to succeed, and because he's confident I have the skills, abilities, and passions to succeed in those arenas, as well. So he can replicate himself—or at least those parts of himself—in me by sharing information and resources, by helping me overcome my flaws and weaknesses, and by encouraging me through the difficult transitions that inevitably come with personal and professional growth.

But the Law of Elevation carries applications for all relationships, not just those in which we're committed to teach, train, and mentor someone to become greater than ourselves. The advancement component also means helping another person reach their full potential when it has nothing to do with our skill levels or abilities.

For instance, as a manager, I've always seen it as part of my responsibility to know the dreams and aspirations of the people who work with me. I want to know where they want to be in five or ten years and what goals they have professionally. I also want to know, to the extent they want to share that with me, what's going on in their personal lives. What are their goals for their marriage and for their kids? What aspirations do they have away from the office?

Part of my job is to help them achieve those goals. But I don't limit that approach to my employees—or even my co-workers. In fact, I see it as something I can and should do with everyone I meet, including my customers, clients, and vendors.

If you work in sales, you no doubt understand the concept behind "Solution Selling." The idea is to find the needs of your customer and then figure out how your products or services can serve as a solution to those needs. It's a good model that, more often than not, benefits both the buyer and the seller, because it starts with the question of how one person or organization can help another. During my time with Lotus Development, the entire sales staff took a weeklong training course on Solution Selling.

But what if my products or services aren't the solution to your problems? Do I try to retrofit them in order to make the sale? Or what if your biggest challenges have nothing to do with my business? Do I just walk away and hope that our roads cross at some future date?

No!

I would argue that we should do everything within our power to help others find a solution. That's what pushes *advancement* beyond Solution Selling. In the end, Solution Selling is still about me making my sales quota. Advancement is when we help others get where they want to go and achieve what they want to achieve. Sometimes there's personal gain and sometimes there's not.

When we provide solutions without regard for our own gain—think of it as "solution giving"—we're creating more than a network of clients and customers. We're creating life-long, loyal relationships. We become part of the rising tide that lifts all boats.

If we want to really help people, we have to become the *link* that brings them together.

I became such a link for Jim Click and Charlie Monfort.

I mentioned Jim earlier—he's my friend who owns several automobile dealerships in southern Arizona. Charlie Monfort, also a good friend, is the owner of Colorado Rockies baseball franchise.

About a year after Jim and I met, he called to say the civic leaders of Tucson had asked him to help convince the Colorado

Rockies to keep their spring training site in Tucson. The Rockies and the Arizona Diamondbacks were the only teams based in Tucson still playing in the Cactus League—the league made up of Major League teams that hold their spring training in Arizona. The others were moving to Phoenix. The Tucson leadership was concerned about the impact those moves were having on their economy and community.

Jim knew I had close ties with business leaders in Denver, so he asked if I knew anyone with the Rockies. I told Jim that Charlie Monfort and the Rockies organization both were friends and supporters of Leader's Challenge, the nonprofit I had founded.

At that point I could have given Jim a phone number for Charlie and told him to be sure and say that "Tommy said to call." That would have been helpful. Instead, I called Charlie directly and arranged a meeting where I flew to Tucson and I took Jim and some other leaders to a spring training game with Charlie.

During the trip, I set up a dinner for me, Jim, Charlie, and my pal Keli McGregor, who was president of the Rockies organization. We spent several hours talking at one of the city's nicer Italian restaurants. And, of course, Jim brought up how important it was for Tucson to remain the spring training home of the Rockies.

At that meeting, Jim and Charlie began the process of working out the details that would allow the Rockies to remain for the following year. A year later we all met again for dinner, and, once again, the Rockies agreed to stay in Tucson.

My part in it? Not much. I had nothing to gain or lose no matter where the Rockies decided to play their spring training games, or whether or not Jim and Charlie became friends. I just saw an opportunity to introduce two good friends with mutual interests. And they became friends with each other. In fact, the Rockies decided that 2010 would be their last spring in Tucson before moving to Scottsdale, a suburb of Phoenix. Jim and Charlie, however, remain friends. They share similar values and interests, and each appreciates and trusts the other.

It's always a home run when you can connect two people where they both benefit. I constantly try to connect people across the world who stand to gain professionally by working together and personally by knowing each other—people who can make a tremendous influence on their organizations, their communities, and the world.

There's a third component to the Law of Elevation. This might not seem as practical on the surface as *advancement* and *link*. But *lift* plays an important if all-too-often undervalued role in elevating others and, in the process, elevating our relationships.

We lift others when we honor them in some way, publicly or privately, depending on the circumstances of the situation, with some form of praise or recognition—in other words, when we act on the instinct that tells us we're thankful for something the person has done, either for us as an individual or for our organization.

Management gurus have long beaten the drum of honoring employees, especially in public ways, for doing good work. In fact, some employers have run so quickly with this idea that they've charged right off a cliff. They have established all sorts of rewards programs without thinking through the potential negative consequences. For instance, how will the "non-winners" view the rewards? Will the rewards become an expectation? What happens to productivity if the rewards are removed?

I see rewards and recognition as part of a genuine relationship and, therefore, as an expression of the heart, not a program. That doesn't mean rewards programs can't work, but that it is simply a different discussion. A rewards program typically honors someone for something he's earned and might reasonably expect to get because of his good work. It's sort of like an airline's frequent-flyer program—calculated and transactional, not an authentic response of gratitude. The type of lift I'm talking about honors the deserving person at a time when she might not expect it and wasn't striving to achieve any special recognition.

Lift knows no limits. It's open to everyone we know. Again, the management gurus are quick to push us to recognize people on our staff for their good work, but I contend we need to take that another step (or two or twenty). When opportunities present themselves, we need to recognize and honor people outside of our organizations—vendors, clients, customers, and anyone else who contributes to our success or the success of those around us.

Many of us lift others every day in classic Dale Carnegie ways by sending them thank-you notes or calling just to say thanks, or by walking by their desks and offering some encouraging words of gratitude.

One way we can take that a step forward is by offering "third-party" compliments, where we sing someone's praises to another person. If I tell you that you did a great job, that's powerful. But it's even more powerful if I tell five other people.

For instance, I have a Fifth Floor relationship with Scott Bemis, the long-time president and publisher of the *Denver*

Business Journal. Remember my all-star Fifth Floor team? That was Scott Bemis playing shortstop. He's my Bucky Dent.

The first time I met Scott, the *Business Journal* had come out with its annual "Forty under 40" list that recognized up-and-coming leaders in the Denver area—forty emerging leaders under the age of forty. As the thirty-two-year-old founder of Leader's Challenge, I had made the cut, and had been featured in the *Journal*. As a result, I had been invited with the other winners to an awards luncheon in our honor.

When they announced our names, each of us came to the front table to shake hands with Scott. He handed us a plaque and a $100 gift certificate to Morton's Steakhouse. After he called my name, I gave him a bear hug, tucked the certificate in my pocket, and headed back to my seat. Later, when I was back at my office, I pulled out the gift certificate and noticed that it felt odd—it was too thick. Scott accidentally had given me two certificates that were stuck together.

When I wrote Scott a thank-you note, I included the extra certificate with an explanation of how I'd ended up with two of them. And when he got the note, he gave me a call.

"That was very good of you to send that back," he told me. "Lots of people would have just kept it. Who would know, right?"

The certificate, he went on to say, was an extra and he suggested that we use it on a nice lunch together at Morton's. Before you know it, I had a new friend. And the more we got together, the closer we grew. Before long, Scott was a mentor and an all-star player on my Fifth Floor team.

One day I was having breakfast at Ellyngton's in the Brown Palace Hotel and saw Scott at one of the tables, so I walked over and said hello. It turned out he was meeting with his boss,

Whitney Shaw, the president and CEO of American City Business Journals in Charlotte, North Carolina. We exchanged a few pleasantries and I left. But as I walked away I wondered if Mr. Shaw had any idea how truly valuable Scott was to the *Denver Business Journal*—not just for his business acumen, but as a leader and ambassador throughout the Denver community. So I sent him a handwritten letter singing Scott's praises.

I didn't want Scott to know that I had done it; I just wanted to make sure his boss knew how people in Denver felt about Scott. I mention it now only because Mr. Shaw mentioned it to Scott, and Scott mentioned how much he appreciated it.

We never know how much such private acts of honor might mean to others.

My father spent his career teaching junior high school English, and he was involved in all sorts of activities in the school and the community. He directed school musicals, served as the adviser for the school newspaper, was head of the teachers' union, taught piano lessons, and coached the ski team. He had a huge impact on countless students during nearly forty years in the public schools.

But one of his most prized possessions is a letter he received about ten years before he retired from the director of admissions at MIT.

Dear Mr. Spaulding:

Each year we ask students admitted to MIT to share with us the name of a teacher who has been especially influential in that student's development.

We congratulate you on being named this year by: Bandita N. Joarder.

More importantly, we thank you for the time, patience, expertise, love, discipline and all the other qualities which have had such an important impact on your students. You do the work from which we all benefit.

Congratulations again on the respect you have earned from your students.

Sincerely,
Michael C. Behnke
Director of Admissions

The fact that this student singled out my dad was a great source of encouragement for him. That small initiative on the part of MIT provided a reminder to the students that they didn't get into a prestigious university without help, while no doubt providing encouragement to teachers all across the country. To my dad, those kinds of letters were special.

We never know when a letter or note of encouragement we've written will provide a lift to someone when they need it most.

Dr. Jim Bearden, the longest-serving professor at East Carolina's School of Business, approached me after I had given the commencement address at ECU's 100th Anniversary graduation. He and I shared a common vision, he said, to see ECU create a culture that made leadership a core competency of every graduating student. The more we talked, the more I appreciated the years he'd spent in the front-line battles of creating that culture. So when I returned a book that I had borrowed from him, I included a handwritten note on a six-by-nine piece of paper torn from a steno pad, telling him,

Dear Jim,
You're changing the university one student, one staff member, and one faculty member at a time.

Love,
Tommy

A year later I was visiting him in his office, sharing the challenges of trying to make meaningful change as the leader-in-residence at ECU. I was working to create the very type of leadership program he envisioned for the school, and I knew he could relate to my challenges.

"Tommy, I want to show you something," he said. And then he picked up a frame from his desk and handed it to me. It was the note I had sent him, framed and given a place of honor in his office. My attempt to lift *him* had come full circle—what I had used to honor and encourage him, he now used to honor and encourage me!

There are times, however, when thank-you notes or third-party compliments simply aren't enough. We need to do more. That's why I nominated Jerry Middel for an award honoring his charity work, and that's why I campaigned to help him win it. It's also why I flew Tom France and his wife to Denver.

Tom France was the Rotarian from my hometown who seemed to be there at every turn to help me along the way.

As you'll remember, Tom nominated me to attend the Rotary Youth Leadership Academy (RYLA) when I was fifteen, helping me get a spot even though I lacked the required grades. He organized a Rotary fund-raiser to help pay for my travels with Up with People. When I applied for the Rotary International Ambassadorial Scholarship, I needed someone from my local club to nominate me. Tom did it. He also was my biggest advocate on the selection committee, and he was the one who later told me how the bartender had cast the deciding vote. When I applied for a congressional internship in Washington, D.C., Tom not only wrote a letter of recommendation but made a call on my behalf to our congressman. And when I became president and CEO of Up with People and wanted to bring a cast to Suffern High School for a benefit concert to raise money for Lori Nolan's scholarship fund, Tom France got his Rotary club to sponsor the event.

Tom wasn't what most people would consider a high-profile leader, but he had a Fifth Floor relationship with his community. The decorated World War II pilot returned to his home state of New York after college, started a heating and air service in Suffern, became active in Rotary and other worthy organizations, and raised a family that learned (as did I) by his examples. He wasn't wealthy by the world's standards, but he gave away things that can't be measured in a bankbook.

So I went through life thanking Tom France for his impact on me. As I traveled the world after high school and college, I constantly sent postcards to Tom.

"Here I am in Italy. Thanks for making this possible. I love you."

"Business school in Australia is awesome. I never could have made it without you. Thanks so much."

"Japan is fascinating. I wish you were here to share it. Miss you and think of you often. Thanks for changing my life."

I wanted him to know how much I appreciated all that he had done for me. I sent him dozens of cards, and I found many special ways to thank him over the years. But there's a difference between thanking someone and honoring him. I send fifty handwritten thank-you notes a week to people I know and respect. I've been doing this for nearly twenty years. We thank

Second and Third Floor relationships. We *thank and honor* Fourth and Fifth Floor relationships, and I wanted to honor Tom.

I found my big chance in 2004 when the Denver Rotary Club asked me to give the keynote speech at a banquet honoring the graduates of the Denver Kids program (the mentorship program in which my pal Jerry Middel was deeply involved).

Tom's wife, Lu, grew up in Denver, and Tom had a degree from Denver University. They met while he was in school there, but it had been years since they had been back. So I called Tom and told him I wanted to fly them to Colorado so they could visit family and attend a special Rotary event.

John Schafer, who at that time was the general manager at the Denver Hyatt-Regency, donated a hotel room for Tom and Lu for their stay, and Jill and I took them to dinner one evening. At the Rotary banquet, I had them seated at a table at the front. It wasn't until he saw I was sitting at the head table that he realized I was part of the program.

The Denver Rotary Club has more than four hundred members, and the banquet hall was full for this event. Around fifty kids who had been through the Denver Kids program were graduating from high school, so Rotary was honoring them and the mentors who had made a difference in their lives. My keynote focused on mentoring and on the importance of Rotary in our communities.

I told the story of this Rotarian I knew who exemplified the "service above self" motto of Rotary. Then I told the audience all the things Tom had done as a mentor to me, without mentioning Tom's name.

"I've had a twenty-year history with Rotary," I said, "and this one Rotarian has been the thread in that experience. In my opinion, he's the greatest Rotarian I've ever met. And he's with us today. Ladies and gentlemen, I want you to meet Tom France—the greatest Rotarian in the world."

And I asked him to stand in front of all of these people who didn't know him.

"All these Denver Kids had mentors," I said, "and Tom France was my mentor."

Tom was crying as he stood, holding his wife's hand. The audience gave him a standing ovation. The entire place rocked for Tom. And when it was over, Tom was swarmed by people who wanted to shake his hand.

Three years later I sat with Tom France at the Up with People benefit concert for Lori Nolan. That was the last time I saw Tom. He died a month later, in December 2007, just a few weeks after his eighty-fourth birthday. And that's when I realized how important it is to recognize people, publicly, whenever the opportunity presents itself.

Tom France has been one of the three most influential mentors in my life (along with my father and Jerry Middel). He didn't help me through life to gain recognition. He helped me because he cared. He literally changed my life.

Chapter 36

Serving the Stakeholders

Stephanie Wilmer, James LaFrenz, and Officer Christopher Hudak live in vastly different worlds. They don't know each other, and it's unlikely that they'll ever meet. But these three people—a bookkeeper at a nonprofit organization, a customer service manager for an airline, and a small-town police officer—represent some very important ways relationships become *more than* ordinary. They also represent the three distinct categories of stakeholders we encounter in our pursuit of Fifth Floor relationships.

Everyone within an organization, from frontline workers to managers to the CEO, board, and owner, needs to understand and pursue *more than* relationships with three distinct groups—internal stakeholders, external stakeholders, and community stakeholders (or, as I've come to see them, the "forgotten stakeholders"). We hold a stake in every relationship, and all relationships fit within one of those three groups, including relationships with people we hardly know or we've never even met.

As a bookkeeper at Up with People during my tenure as that organization's CEO, Stephanie Wilmer was an "internal stakeholder." She reported to someone who reported to me, but we all were part of the same team. Everyone within your organization is an internal stakeholder—your peers, your boss, your direct reports, your indirect reports, just to name the most obvious.

James LaFrenz met my wife and me as we raced to make an international flight on one of those days when destiny seemed out to get us. As customers of Frontier Airlines, we were external stakeholders in James's world. Like all customers, vendors, clients, shareholders, donors, investors, and partners, we didn't work with or for him, but he played a huge role in something that mattered greatly to us—getting on that flight.

Officer Christopher Hudak and I have never met, and yet we still have a relationship. We have a relationship because we live on the same planet. We're part of a global community that, when it operates at its best, serves each other in times of need. We become aware of those needs and respond to them by putting ourselves in a position to see them and respond to them, and that's how Officer Hudak and I connected.

A community is a living, breathing organism made up of stakeholders from all spheres of life—religion, business, education, nonprofits, the government. Knowing these stakeholders isn't enough—we have to develop *more than* relationships that produce a bigger benefit for them and everyone around them. That's where Fifth Floor relationships become out-of-this-world powerful—not to mention fulfilling and fun!

Internal Stakeholders

The messages we send to our internal stakeholders—management, employees, peers, and so on—is the message they will send to each other and to the outside world. If we tell them we're all about the money and the market share, that's the message they'll communicate to each other and to their clients, although most won't do it overtly.

If we communicate (with actions and words) that we have to make a profit and grow market share to survive, but that our approach to those goals starts with building transformative Fifth Floor relationships, then that's the message they'll communicate.

When we develop a culture in which relationships matter, innovation and productivity increase, trust becomes foundational, turnover drops, and morale skyrockets. Our organization benefits, and so does everyone within it. But we have to put forth an intentional effort to make these relationships matter, and not just with the people around us who are in an obvious position to help advance our careers.

Our vice president of finance at Up with People came by my office one day and suggested I treat Stephanie Wilmer to lunch, to show the organization's gratitude for the fine work she'd been doing as our bookkeeper. It seemed like a great idea, so I sent her an e-mail asking her about her favorite restaurants, and then scheduled a time for us to go.

Part of me, however, wasn't too jazzed about the appointment, and it had nothing to do with Stephanie. One of my biggest responsibilities at Up with People was managing relationships with our board, sponsors, and donors, and the opportunities to nurture those relationships usually revolved around meals. From a financial standpoint, it made much more sense to have lunch with a donor who gave thousands of dollars to our organization than with someone who helped keep track of those dollars.

We make choices every day about where we invest our time and energy when it comes to managing relationships within

our organizations. Most of us split it into at least three categories: we manage *up* (with the people we report to), we manage
down (with the people who report to us), and we manage *around*
(with the people who are our peers).

They're all important. It's often tempting, however, to sell out
to the "kissing up" culture—that all-too-frequent pull to pucker
up only with those who can advance our careers because of their
influence over things like our salary, our bonus, and our job
security. Sincerity knows no greater enemy than a "kissing up"
culture. Instead, we need to invest in a "loving down" culture—
one that equally values the people who work with us and for us.

I kept my appointment with Stephanie, and it was one of
the best lunches I had that month. I got to know someone I
didn't know particularly well, and I walked away feeling like
I'd "won" something because of the time I'd spent with this
single mother who was working so hard to make ends meet.
She encouraged and inspired me. And the investment of one
lunch showed her that we valued her as a person, as well as for
the work she did.

Every person has something of value to offer every other
person—Stephanie had something to offer me and I had something to offer her. There are times when that "something" is
obvious and big, and other times when it's subtle or when it
might take weeks, months, or years to fully appreciate it.

If we only focus on the people who are above us on the organizational chart then we limit our view and our opportunities for growth. We have to look all around us, giving what we
have to give and soaking in what others have to offer, whether
he or she is a bartender, a janitor, a bookkeeper, or a CEO.

Any doubts about whether Stephanie appreciated the lunch
were put to rest during my going-away party a few months
later. I was stepping down as president and CEO, and I had

built many great friendships as we shared in the struggle to breathe new life and energy into a great organization. Lots of people respected my leadership skills—vision, inspiration, my ability to build a board and a donor base—but the sincere tears on Stephanie's cheeks as she gave me a hug provided more joy than any of the money I'd helped raise or, really, any other accomplishment I'd achieved. She cared about me because she knew I cared about her.

When I was told about her stellar job performance, I could have sent Stephanie a personal note—I absolutely love writing notes to people, and I highly recommend it—or we could have given her a gift of some sort. There are lots of ways to show our appreciation for people, and there's no need to see them as either/or propositions. But few things have more impact than sitting face-to-face with someone and giving them your time, your attention, and your encouragement as you learn a little something about who they are as a person.

Now at this point you might be thinking, *That's all well and good, Spaulding, but did that lunch really make this employee a better bookkeeper? Did it have any measurable impact on your organization?*

Well, she already was a great bookkeeper—that's why I took her to lunch! But I think she was an even better employee because she knew we cared about her. I think she was happier and more energetic and that others around her benefited from that, as well.

But here's what I know for sure: If you're only "kissing up" in your organizational culture, then the people around you never feel empowered and loved. And over time, that affects their performance and their morale. It begins to show up in every nook and cranny of the organization, usually in the forms of boredom and cynicism. Instead of a "why not?" attitude, people embrace a "why bother?" approach. The goal becomes to get through the day with as few hassles as possible—a self-focused agenda rather than one that instinctively serves the customers, the organization, and the community.

When we create a culture that pursues Fifth Floor relationships among internal stakeholders, we're creating a culture that ultimately best serves the organization's bottom line. It sounds counterintuitive, but it's a proven model.

For instance, while most airlines struggled for survival over the last few decades—and some of them didn't make it—Southwest Airlines made itself a front-runner in large part because of its commitment to its internal stakeholders. Consider that from April through June 2008, while the other major airlines lost a collective $6 billion, Southwest showed its sixty-ninth consecutive profitable quarter. It also was the only major airline to report a profit in the first quarter of 2009.

It began with challenging the traditional view that the customer is Number One. In the Southwest Airlines organizational chart, the employees are the Number One constituents. Southwest understands that if you take care of employees and build a culture of trust and respect with them, then those employees will work hard and serve customers better. That, of course, leads to repeat business from the customers and to greater efficiency from the employees, two key factors in growing market share and revenue.

Southwest's mission statement, crafted in 1988 when the airline still was an up-and-comer, makes no mention of profits or market share. It focuses on service to the customer and to its employees:

The mission of Southwest Airlines is dedication to the highest quality of Customer Service delivered with a sense of warmth, friendliness, individual pride, and Company Spirit.

To Our Employees—we are committed to provide our Employees a stable work environment with equal opportunity for learning and personal growth. Creativity and innovation are encouraged for improving the effectiveness of Southwest Airlines. Above all, Employees will be provided the same concern, respect, and caring attitude within the organization that they are expected to share externally with every Southwest Customer.*

That's all warm and fuzzy, you might say, but does Southwest Airlines really live that out and, if so, does it really work? Yes and yes.

Southwest lives it out in all sorts of ways, at all levels. You hear it in the voices and see it in the attitudes when you check in for a flight, get ready to board a flight, or listen to the flight attendant go through the announcements.

A company can *tell* its employees to behave that way, but how does it *create* a culture in which they do it naturally? There is no one prescription or program, but a multitude of actions and attitudes that add up over time.

Southwest Airlines, for instance, doesn't cover the walls of its corporate headquarters with portraits of its executives and board members, or with works by famous artists. Instead, it frames photos of its employees and their families. It might seem minor, but it's a powerful message about the things the company values.

Or consider Chick-fil-A's long-standing policy of closing on Sunday. Think about it: in 2008, sales at Chick-fil-A's 1,428

---

* http://www.southwest.com/about_swa/mission.html

stores topped $2.96 billion without taking in a dime on what's historically the third-most-productive day for its competitors (only Fridays and Saturdays are bigger).

The simplistic view of the Chick-fil-A policy is that it's nothing more than the owner's personal religious values and that it has nothing to do with "good business." But Truett Cathy, the founder of Chick-fil-A, believes that the concept of the Sabbath—an intentional time off—is good business, in part because of the impact it has on his internal stakeholders. It tells them the company values their time away from their jobs and that it wants them to invest in friendships, faith, and family. And it tells them that rest is important—to their personal health as well as that of the company.

"As leaders we have the responsibility of managing the energy that's within our people," Dan Cathy, Truett's son and the company's president and COO, once said. "Particularly in today's knowledge-based economy, we're really managing innovation and creativity. And innovation and creativity come from a rested mind."*

I serve on a national board with Dan Cathy, and he's one of the most genuine and generous people I know. He shares his dad's values and lives them out each day, not just when he's taking Sunday off. The way he and his dad and the other members of their leadership team respect and care for their co-workers filters down and throughout their organization, all the way to the teenager handing you a soda at the drive-through.

Building "rest" into its corporate culture is just one way that Chick-fil-A "gives" to its operators and employees. And, more important, it's not *the* way. Leaders in organizations like

* *The Life@Work Journal*, July/August 1999, vol. 2, no. 4.

Chick-fil-A and Southwest Airlines understand that valuing internal stakeholders isn't a program but a mindset. Programs and policies ultimately reflect that mindset and reinforce it, but they seldom, if ever, create it. The mindset inspires and shapes a thousand little decisions each day. Most of all, the mindset creates something that's vital to the success of every organization—the most effective motivational tool in the world: relational authority.

In organizations with a high level of relational authority, people rise to the challenges they face in ethical, creative ways. They support each other and grow together as a team with common bonds and common goals. Without it—well, in most cases the results include poor relationships, weak sales, decreased customer satisfaction, high employee turnover rates, and declines in repeat business.

The internal stakeholders of an organization are its life-blood, because the health of those relationships always shows up in how the organization presents itself to the outside world. A sick, anemic internal culture eventually shows itself to clients, customers, donors, vendors, and stockholders as pale and hollow.

Just about every industry has seen at least one outwardly healthy company crumble, or even die, from these types of internal wounds—Enron, WorldCom, Fannie Mae, and Freddie Mac—and those are just the high-profile examples. Not every company or organization that sacrifices long-term health for short-term results ends up meeting such an inglorious demise, but few survive without the need for some serious surgery.

Leaders—regardless of where they are in the organizational chart—have a choice about what they want spreading throughout their ranks. They can go with the cancer of greed or the tonic of relational authority. Either way, they shouldn't be surprised by the results.

External Stakeholders

We were heading to the airport in a heavy snowstorm, but that didn't matter because sunny Mexico awaited! A week-long pre-Christmas vacation at a friend's home in Cabo San Lucas—what could be better?

Well, one thing could have been better: driving to the airport *with* our airline tickets, passports, and my wallet.

We usually leave for such trips in a rush typical of a family with small children, but on this day everything had gone eerily smoothly. That was great for me, because I'm a creature of order and routine. I'm the sort of guy who likes to leave the house clean when we go on vacation, so I'm always the last one out. I do a last check to ensure everything is in its place, and then I grab my briefcase from the kitchen barstool, lock the door as I walk out, and off we go.

Not this time. This time the briefcase with our airline tickets and passports remained on the barstool, and we didn't realize my mistake until we got to the Denver airport, some forty-five minutes away.

I've made thousands of flights, including international trips to more than sixty countries, so I know the ropes, and I know how I need to adjust when I'm with my family as opposed to traveling solo. So I pulled up to the terminal a solid two hours before our flight to drop off Jill and two of our three children, Caroline and Tate. I had plenty of time to park the car and catch the shuttle back so we could all check in. That's when it hit me: for the first time in all my years of traveling, I not only had forgotten something, I had forgotten something we couldn't travel without!

No wallet. No passports. No Cabo.

We had no chance of making it home and back and still making our flight, so I drove and Jill began calling some of our Fifth Floor friends. The first one she reached—our neighbor Jon Pardew—immediately went to our house, retrieved the briefcase, and met us halfway to the airport for a ten-second hand-off in a parking lot just off one of the tollway exits. I'm not sure his vehicle or ours ever fully stopped as we rolled down our windows, made the exchange, and headed back for the highway.

Still, time worked against us. There now wouldn't be time to drop off Jill and the kids, park the car, and ride the shuttle back to the terminal. And taking the shuttle with our luggage and the kids wasn't an option. So we called Tim and Cheryl Sheahan, two friends who lived near the airport. They agreed to meet us at the terminal, help us unload, take my keys, and do something—we really didn't care what at this point—with our car.

As we made our way back to the airport, our mental calculators produced nothing but bad news. The wet snow made road conditions poor and travel slow. So when my phone rang, Jill answered it so that I could focus on the slick highway. Later I'd learn that the call was from James LaFrenz, the customer-service manager with Frontier Airlines.

"I'm just checking on you," he said. "Your flight to Cabo is on time. Are you still planning to travel today?"

Jill made our long story short and told him we were still twenty minutes away. A few seconds later she was reading all the passports and checking us in over the phone.

When we got to the airport, Tim and Cheryl were

there—and so was James. He loaded our luggage onto a cart, handed us our tickets, and sent us to the gate. "Don't worry about your luggage," he said. "You'll see it in Cabo. Get to the gate."

We zipped through the security line—one advantage of frequent flying—but Jill's bag got pulled, and the security agent was not too happy to find the always suspicious "baby food" in the bag of a mother with a ten-month-old boy on her arm.

"We're going to be in a remote area, and I don't know if the baby food there will be OK," Jill explained.

"We'll have to open all thirty jars and check it," the agent said.

Jill, as you might expect, began to freak out, while her normally calm husband was insisting that we leave the baby's food and go to the gate. Just then, from the corner of my eye, I saw James LaFrenz and began yelling his name. He walked over and I started explaining our newest plight. He stopped me in midsentence, grabbed the bag of food, and said, "Don't worry. I'm going to make this happen."

So off we went to the gate, trusting James to keep his word. And he did. We got on the plane just in time, and the four of us, our luggage, and our baby food all made it to Cabo.

Did I mention that First Floor relationships are important? My family needed nothing more from the customer-service agent at the airport than a good and smooth transaction—we need to get checked in and get to our flight. For that to happen, though, he had to treat us as something *more than* a transaction—and he treated us like we shared space on his personal Fifth Floor.

James and my family found ourselves in a relationship between external stakeholders, and while the circumstances were unique (I hope!), we all deal daily with external stakeholders—

clients, vendors, shareholders, donors, investors, and partners. And they base their opinion of us largely on how we treat them. Part of that involves the quality of what we deliver, but the quality of the human interaction always plays a paramount role.

Many fine companies build their entire brands on the concept of great customer service. Whenever some business magazine releases a list of the best of the best in customer service, you'll see such stalwarts as USAA (insurance), Four Seasons (hotels), Nordstrom (retail), Wegmans Food (supermarkets), Edward Jones (brokerage), and Starbucks (restaurants).

For them, it's all about the relationship with the client, customer, investor, and others. But this requires a Fifth Floor focus with internal stakeholders that produces the type of motivation and enthusiasm to generate *more than* relationships with external stakeholders.

"Despite their differences, most of the names on our list share a few important traits," *BusinessWeek* wrote the first time it released rankings for the top twenty-five customer service companies. "They emphasize employee loyalty as much as customer loyalty, keeping their people happy with generous benefits and perks."*

Happy, motivated, committed, and loyal internal stakeholders become ambassadors who produce happy, motivated, committed, and loyal external stakeholders.

The former chairman and president of Frontier Airlines was a friend of mine, but knowing him—or even the current president—wasn't going to get my wife and me on our flight any sooner. That one employee's dedication to the company's vision for customer service certainly did.

---

* *BusinessWeek*, March 2, 2007.

External stakeholders, of course, aren't always so short-term. We also have long-term relationships with vendors, with donors, with investors, and with partners, and it's critical that we earn their trust and loyalty over time by seeing them as potential Fifth Floor relationships.

When I took over as president and CEO of Up with People, the organization was making a comeback from near bankruptcy. The thirty-five-year-old organization closed in 2000, and then relaunched in 2004 and hired me in 2005. I had been a cast member and I had worked in the organization for a year when I first moved to Denver. I believed in the organization and knew most of its strengths and weaknesses.

The near-death experience, however, left many board members, donors, host families, and twenty thousand alumni around the world more than a bit queasy. But those groups represented the key to any possible rebirth and survival. I knew the only way to turn the ship around was to get the external stakeholders to buy into our new vision. I also knew in my heart that to move forward as an organization we had to own the mistakes of our past. That was no easy task. In some cases, it meant cutting ties with longtime supporters who weren't willing to change.

Many of the problems that caused the organization to close its doors left wounds on the thousands of external stakeholders who lovingly supported its great works. Creating a new vision, a new financial model, and new strategies was only part of my challenge. They would take us nowhere without buy-in from the right people.

So for my first two years as CEO, I lived in airports. I traveled to more than a hundred cities on three continents, speaking to hundreds of alumni and constituent groups, sharing the new vision and owning the mistakes of the organization's past, giving them hope that we would rebuild the organization, and cultivating relationships to ensure our success. I often stayed with host families to save the company money, and I rebuilt bridges with our essential external stakeholders.

Few organizations intentionally neglect their external stakeholders, but there's often a huge gap between where those relationships are and where they could or should be. Too often, these relationship stay on routine transactions of the First or Second floors. Taking them to the Third, Fourth, and even Fifth floors generates unmatched loyalty and creates partnerships that become the rising tide that lifts all boats—yours, theirs, and everyone's around you.

The Forgotten Stakeholders

My father is among the humblest, most unassuming people you'd ever encounter, and he's also among the least "networked." He taught me to have goodness in my heart and to love others at every opportunity, but he never said anything about using relationships to help grow a business or raise money or collect on favors. He only told me that I had an obligation to make a contribution to the world. That, he said, was the price we all paid for living in a free society.

And even though I've been blessed with Fifth Floor relationships with many wealthy and influential people, my dad never asked me to leverage one of them on his behalf—until March 2009.

"Tommy," he said when I answered his phone call that day, "I have a favor to ask you."

If I had a dollar for every time my dad called and asked a favor, I'd have a dollar, so I figured something important was going on. It turned out that one of our neighbors in Suffern, New York, was helping with a fund-raiser for Christopher Hudak, a police officer in nearby Ramapo. Officer Hudak's wife, Michelle—the daughter of a retired police chief and the sister of a state trooper—had died earlier in the year during the birth of the couple's fifth child. The Ramapo Policeman's Benevolent Association held an auction and party to raise money for the now single-father with five young children.

My dad said, "Tommy, I want to do something to help this police officer. Our next-door neighbor knows this officer very well and says he's a wonderful person."

As it turned out, Officer Hudak was a huge New York Jets fan who greatly admired Brett Favre. The longtime Green Bay Packers quarterback played the 2008 season with the Jets. Since I have a relationship with Woody Johnson, the owner of the Jets (we met in 1996 while working together on Bob Dole's presidential campaign), I called his assistant and explained the officer's story.

A few days later I got a phone call from my dad, who was nearly in tears. He had just received two footballs. One was signed by the entire New York Jets team to auction off at the fund-raiser. The other had a signed personal message of encouragement for Officer Hudak from Brett Favre.

This is the hidden value of Fifth Floor relationships, or what I call **the Law of Influence**: relationships reach their greatest potential when they elevate others without regard for personal gain.

As this story unfolded, everybody won. My father won because he was a hero to his next-door neighbor. His neighbor won because he got an auction item of significant value to donate to the worthy cause. Nothing, of course, could lessen the tragedy of Officer Hudak and his family. But the money from auctioning the football helped him keep his job and raise his family, while the other football offered encouragement and a fond memory of an event that showed him how much the people around him cared for him and his children. And the New York Jets won because they did something great for the community of New York. I won too. I won the joy that came from using my relationship with Woody so that he could serve others.

If I had abused my relationship with Woody over the years—if I had only called asking for box seats or for a signed football for my son or some other personal favor—then our relationship never would have had an opportunity to impact Officer Hudak's life. Woody's assistant would have sent my call to voice mail's version of the dead-letter department. But if we're known for calling in favors that benefit others with no expectations for ourselves, we'll have a whole different outcome with those relationships.

That doesn't mean we can't expect a return on our giving. Unconditional giving and ROI—or ROR—aren't mutually exclusive; there are times when you can expect results. Indeed, responsible giving requires that we give strategically of our time, talents, and money so that the greatest benefits are realized.

John D. Rockefeller created a legacy of Fifth Floor philanthropy anchored on the idea of giving that addressed what he saw as "inefficiencies." Crime, for instance, was an "inefficiency" within society, so he helped fund programs that addressed crime, but he made sure they were well run and effective. He wanted a return on his investment.

The organizations that are having the greatest impact, whether they are small, privately owned businesses or giant public companies, are the ones that find creative ways to leverage their giving for the greatest return.

In my role as a consultant, I teach companies how to build Fifth Floor relationships with their customers and vendors, and how to generate Fifth Floor customer service. But I also help them transition from the old model of community giving plans to the new business model of community investing. These plans are strategic and targeted, and they offer the greatest potential benefits to the company and the charities. Nonprofits have to leverage their outreach to benefit companies. And companies have to leverage their relationship with nonprofits so they can create a return on their investment that includes

- more marketing exposure
- more brand awareness
- greater employee engagement
- stronger customer retention
- more effective public relations
- and higher sales and profitability

Sometimes organizations need innovative ways to create and implement giving strategies. Or they need help building relationships with nonprofits that are accustomed to simply holding out their hands and asking for money rather than seeing companies as strategic partners. Or they need help learning what it means to turn all of that focus on corporate social responsibility into something that's meaningful to the individuals throughout their organization.

The Spaulding Companies not only help figure out creative partnerships between for-profits and nonprofits, they also offer team-building and community service programs centered around what we call the Give/Get Challenge. No more ropes courses. We've set up a "day of service" for organizations, and we have a "build a bike" program that teaches teamwork, quality management, and customer service—all while providing new bikes for underprivileged kids.

As often as anything, however, an organization needs to figure out the causes that make the most sense given the company's mission, vision, and values. Not long ago, for instance, Coca-Cola adopted "water stewardship" as one of its primary targets for giving. Why? Because water is a key ingredient in its product.

I learned the thinking behind this approach during a visit with Thomas Mattia, Coca-Cola's senior vice president for worldwide public affairs and communications. Thomas explained how CEO Neville Isdell had led an effort that helped the company change from a vast and various giving strategy to a focused and intentional community investment strategy. Coca-Cola, like increasing numbers of other responsible companies, is looking for a return from its community investments, and not just a feel-good proposition. It wants to be strategic, efficient, and effective—whether it's investing in a new factory, a new advertising campaign, or water stewardship initiatives.

Many companies—very generous companies—have a "giving list" that looks like my baseball card collection. It's a shoebox or two full of causes that aren't connected in any particular way and that don't bring any significant return back to the company, its partners, or its employees. More and more companies, however, are moving away from the vast and various strategy of giving to a focused and intentional strategy for community investment.

The most giving corporation in all of Colorado, in my opinion, is Coors Brewing Company. Either through the corporate giving program or its foundation, the brewery headed by Pete

Coors is known for giving to just about every worthwhile cause. Pete was on the international board of directors of Up with People and remained a strong supporter of Leader's Challenge, so I've gotten to know him personally. I know how strongly he feels about helping others. Coors gives to literally hundreds of worthy causes.

So, not long ago, while I was having lunch with Al Timothy, the vice president of community affairs for MillerCoors, I asked him a question: "When it comes to your corporate giving, what do people say you stand for?" Al is charged with redefining their corporate giving strategy. When the answer was everything, the answer was nothing. You can't just give money to all the chirping birds; you have to be more strategic.

So MillerCoors is in the process of defining what the company stands for with its philanthropy—defining it not as giving, but as investing. But that's a much greater initiative then simply calling a board meeting and asking the leadership team for a list of their pet projects and causes. A deep, meaningful corporate investment program seeks the opinions of the employees and aligns with their interests, not just the interests of its executive leadership. And it involves not just the checks that are written, but the way companies engage their employees and customers in the community.

Every employee of an organization should be loyal to three things: the mission of the company, the customers or constituents they serve, and the welfare of the community. If an organization's giving fails to generate loyalty in those two areas, its corporate investment program isn't much better than a boxful of baseball cards taking up space in the basement.

This is where you can take the philosophy and ideals of building Fifth Floor relationships and being a Fifth Floor giver out of the personal realm and infuse them into a company's programs, activities, and strategies in powerful, world-changing ways.

Some returns on relationships are measurable, such as the value that an organizational brand gets from the goodwill that comes with selfless giving. And there are tax benefits to giving, as well. But most of the benefits are less obvious, or perhaps harder to quantify, and are at their greatest when the giving comes without expectations.

That's why this type of giving is important to the culture of an organization. When employees team up to volunteer at events, to serve on boards, to work on committees, or to donate money, there's a return in the quality of life throughout their community and there's a return in the way those employees see themselves and, therefore, in how they approach their work.

This is an essential building block in what Bill Gates likes to refer to as "creative capitalism"—the idea that the business community can and should harness its collective resources for the greater good of mankind. "The vast majority of the power, innovation, and ability to execute in the world is in business," Gates says. "If each company can think about how 5 percent of their innovative power could focus on the needs of the poorest and how we could tap more scientists, more resources, more abilities, it would be great."*

The importance of corporate financial giving isn't going away, but those dollars are supercharged when a corporate culture values community stakeholders and backs up that commitment with action.

These things work together for leaders who seek creative, innovative ways to combine them. For instance, *more than* leaders see service as a privilege rather than as a punishment.

---

* *The Rotarian*, May 2009.

How often do you hear about someone being "sentenced" to community service? Judges "sentence" criminals to community service. School principals "sentence" troubled students to community service. What kind of message is that?

We must send a message—to individuals and organizations—that community service is a privilege and not a punishment. That's the essence of Leader's Challenge, the nonprofit I founded a decade ago, and today it's the essence of the National Leadership Academy. We have to teach our youth that volunteerism is what you do when you are doing something right, not a punishment for doing something wrong. And it's a message we have to learn and live out as adults.

Shirley Chisholm, the first black woman elected to Congress, called service "the rent we pay for the privilege of living on this earth," and I grew up with my dad echoing those words in my ears.

The question, for individuals and organizations alike, is this: Are we paying our rent?

Chapter 37

Warnings

My father and my grandfather had a relationship that spent decades in the basement. Gordon Spaulding left his wife (my grandmother) one day without so much as a see-you-later and started a new life that didn't include his one-year-old son. He came back to New York to visit his parents, but he seldom saw my dad over the next twenty-five years.

My parents invited him to their wedding in 1966, but he didn't show up. About five months later, however, he stood at my parents' apartment in New City, New York, to ask for a favor: He wanted help getting out of his $100-a-month alimony payments. My dad politely declined to help.

Growing up, I knew very little about my grandfather. We knew he lived somewhere in Michigan and that he got his mail from us at a post office box in Toledo, Ohio. Every year my parents sent a Christmas card to him, and they occasionally sent pictures of my sisters and me. But we didn't know where he actually lived.

My sisters and I had no interaction with our grandfather. No visits. No phone calls. No letters. No Christmas cards. Then one day, when I was a sophomore in high school, my dad answered the phone and heard a voice he hadn't heard since the day his father left his apartment in New City.

"My wife's dying," Gordon Spaulding said. "I have no other family beyond her, and I'd really like to start having a relationship with you and my grandchildren."

It took a huge act of courage and grace for my father to forgive his dad and welcome him home for the visit that began an incredible healing process. Had he not done that, I probably never would have met my grandfather, much less gotten to know him.

Two years later, when I was eighteen and traveling with Up with People, my grandfather flew to Orlando and spent two days with the cast and me. It was the most unbelievable two days of my life. We had a wonderful time together, but I later learned my grandfather had big concerns when it came to my future.

After our visit, he sent my dad the most beautiful handwritten letter telling him that my dad's greatest accomplishment was the tremendous job he had done raising his children. He sang my praises, but he also wrote something that broke my heart.

"Tommy has an unbelievable love and trust for human beings," he wrote. "And this world is filled with jealousy, cynics and critics—people who will surely take advantage of him and not appreciate his kind heart."

Having worked for years in security for Ford Motor Company, my grandfather understood the darker side of human nature. I was idealistic and trusting and giving—fresh, raw meat, in his view, that couldn't survive for long in the dog-eat-dog world. And in many ways he couldn't have been more right. As I mentioned in earlier chapters, I have been hurt many times. Mentors have let me down. Employees have stabbed me in the back. Family and friends have betrayed me. People don't always return a kind heart with kindness. The world isn't perfect because people aren't perfect—including me.

This reality has provided me with opportunities to learn many hard lessons through the years, and from those lessons I've identified some valid warnings when it comes to building relationships—especially relationships with the potential of reaching the Penthouse.

Warning No. 1: Choose Your Teams and Closest Relationships Wisely

We can start off treating every relationship as a potential Fifth Floor relationship, but we can't have a deep relationship with everyone we meet. We have to decide which relationships merit our time and energy from a business perspective, which ones we want to pursue even if they don't connect to our business interests, and which ones we won't follow up on.

There are all kinds of valid reasons for choosing not to build a relationship with some people. But the harder thing is to recognize when to back away because the relationship is potentially destructive. The values we talked about in previous chapters need to run both ways for a relationship to move beyond the lower floors. Wisdom allows us to evaluate where a relationship is headed and decide where we want it to go.

All relationships start with a set of boundaries, and wisdom helps us define those boundaries and know what to do when they're pushed or when lines are crossed.

Sometimes the boundaries are partly defined by the positional authority of our professional relationship. A CEO with a hundred employees, for instance, should have a relationship with all of those workers, and she might even have a Fifth Floor relationship with a few. But she can't, and probably shouldn't, be close personal friends with every one of them.

We need to learn when to walk away from a relationship.

If a person has proven himself untrustworthy, cynical, jealous, or manipulative, or if he doesn't share our values, then we're wise to walk away.

We can maintain relationships on the first three floors with people who don't share and live out our values. And if they're open to it, we can coach, mentor, and guide them toward new ways of thinking and living. But we can't force our values on others. Leadership isn't just about what relationships we say yes to; more important, it's what relationships we say no to. There are people we shouldn't trust and just don't like very much, and, hard as it is to believe, there are people who won't like us. There are times when it's best simply to move on.

Knowing when to walk away comes from wisdom, which is honed by experience and knowledge but also by the counsel of our all-star Fifth Floor teams. That same wisdom can allow us to heal basement-level relationships with the type of grace and forgiveness my father extended to his father.

This is my biggest weakness. When I feel people have wronged me, I tend to put the relationship in the basement, lock the door, and throw away the key. Forgiving those who have wronged or betrayed me doesn't come easily. It's something my wife and my mentors constantly challenge me on and hold me accountable to, but it's an area I'm always struggling to improve.

Warning No. 2: Know When to Say No

We need wisdom to understand when we should develop a relationship and when we should walk away, but we also need the discipline to say no when we're in a relationship. The temptation, good-intentioned though it might be, is to embrace every request and every need until we look up and realize our good intentions have written checks that our minds and bodies simply can't cash. We have over-promised and inevitably we'll under-deliver.

When we say no in the right ways at the right times, we're staying true to ourselves. And we're staying true to the people around us—clients, customers, co-workers, and anyone else who is depending on us to keep our promises.

I call this **the Law of No**: It's better to say no to something you can't deliver than yes to something that you don't deliver on. Few things wreck a business or personal relationship like consistently failing to keep a promise, whether it's missing a deadline or coming in over budget on a project or falling short of standards of excellence.

In business, our ability to say what we'll do and do what we say reveals something about us to our customers, clients, and other associates, regardless of whether we're telling them yes or no. It adds power to our "yes" because they know we're not prone to overcommitments. They know we'll deliver. And it lets them accept our "no," because they understand and trust that we have genuine, honorable reasons for not saying yes.

Warning No. 3: Beware of Relationship Cancer

Unhealthy habits can keep a relationship from reaching the Penthouse, or knock the best relationships down to the lower floors. And, in fact, the higher you climb in a relationship, the deeper the pain when it falls. So if we're going to experience the joys of living out relationships on the Fifth Floor, we also need to understand the risk that those relationships can end with searing pain.

I've had valued relationships crumble because of gossip, overcompetitiveness, narcissism, self-agendas, insecurities, selfishness—all the negative traits that eat away at our souls. It's impossible to have a Fourth or Fifth Floor relationship when any of these traits exist, and the worst of these relationship cancers is jealousy.

Nothing kills more relationships than jealousy—that dark passion which predates even Cain and Abel. When we let our insecurities drive us to envy and jealousy, we start acting out of bitterness and anger—often toward the very people who care the most about us or who are in the best positions to help us. We become reactive, petty, small-minded, and weak. We let the world around us define our value at a rate far below our true worth.

I learned a hard lesson about the ugliness of envy when I was in high school, and it totally reshaped the way I viewed and responded to the success of people around me.

I mentioned early on that my childhood sweetheart was Lori Nolan, but Lori and I dated other people during our junior and senior years of high school. During the spring of my junior year I was dating Jenn Cesca, and that's who I took to the junior prom. Everything was going great that evening until the time came for the final song—"Come Sail Away," a ballad by Styx that fit with the prom's "sailing" theme.

As vice president of the junior class, I was responsible for helping to organize the prom. I was dealing with some now-forgotten official duty when the final dance of the night began. That was when I looked up and saw Jenn on the dance floor with Corey Turer, my best friend.

Corey was the most loyal friend a guy could have. He'd never do anything to hurt me. Neither would Jenn. I should have been thrilled that my best friend—someone I totally trusted—was dancing with my date while I was occupied with "prom business."

Instead, I was livid.

Overcome by my insecurities, a jealous anger filled my heart. When the final song, and the prom, ended, I quietly gave Jenn the cold shoulder. We got in the car to go to an after-prom party, and I turned into the biggest jerk you've ever met. Jenn had no idea why, because, of course, I wasn't telling her.

Finally she insisted that I tell what was going on, and we got into an argument. I wanted to know why she didn't come find me for the last dance. And I gave in to the temper that I like to blame on having an Italian mother and an Irish father. In fact, I got so upset that when we got to a stoplight, I got out of the car and walked away. Jenn, who was driving, followed me for several blocks and tried to persuade me to get me back in the car, but I kept walking—all the way home.

"How was the prom?" my dad asked when I walked into the house.

"I don't want to talk about it," I said, and went straight to my room.

To my father's credit, he gave me some space. He didn't push, or lecture. He let me go cool off, knowing the time would come for us to talk.

About thirty minutes later I heard a knock at the front door. I looked out my window to see Jenn's car in the driveway. Then I heard her talking to my dad. Then I heard her crying.

I stayed in my room until my father came up and knocked on my door. He came in and sat beside me on the bed, his arm around my shoulder. Because he never lectured me and seldom offered advice, his words carried special weight.

"Tommy, everyone lives with jealousy in their hearts," he said. "It's a normal, natural thing. But jealousy is the ugliest quality that somebody can have. The sooner you work on this and understand how ugly it can be and how it ruins relationships, the happier you will be in your life."

Then he told me I was totally wrong in the way I had treated Jenn, and that I owed her an apology.

And he was right.

I knew then that I was wrong, and I made a vow that I would never give in to that ugliness again. And I can't recall a single time since then that I've sabotaged a relationship because I was jealous. I feel it at times. We all feel it. But we all have a choice about whether to control it or let it control us. And if we want to build and maintain relationships that matter, we have to control it.

Unfortunately, our human struggle with jealousy isn't something that goes away as we mature beyond our high school years. It's the stuff of headlines; it can drive otherwise rational people to irrational behaviors. Professors falsify research. Coaches pad their résumés. Accountants cook their books. Salesmen spread rumors about their teammates. People lie, cheat, steal, and even sometimes kill because they are consumed by jealousy.

Clearly, there's no place in a Fifth Floor relationship for this cancer. So the first thing we have to overcome as we build meaningful relationships is our insecurities. Then we can embrace the success of others, even when it's greater than our own success.

In my Fifth Floor relationships, there is no jealousy. The more successful those friends are in life, the happier I am. I get great joy from seeing them succeed, and they view my success the same way.

Many of my Fifth Floor relationships are with people who are more successful than I. And that's fine. Who better to learn from? I love playing golf, but I'm not particularly good. My handicap is about a 25, but I love playing with low-handicappers because they make me better. And I like to hang out with successful people. I'm not threatened by their success; I'm inspired by it.

If you're in sales and others on the sales team are pulling in better numbers, learn from them. If you get passed over for a promotion, give that other person her due and self-reflect on the things you need to improve to get the next promotion. If the regional vice president flies in and takes a handful of people to dinner but you aren't one of them, don't assume it was personal. Evaluate what you might have done to get an invite, but also consider the strategic reasons she might have picked the people who went.

When I examine my unhealthy relationships, I never struggle to find faults. I can own them because they are mine. I don't need to create or allow another one, and that's all I'm doing when I allow the ugliness of jealousy to control me.

Warning No. 4: Not Every Relationship Lasts Forever

Sometimes bad habits kill even the best of relationships. Then there are the relationships that lose some of their meaning either because we don't give them enough attention or simply because circumstances change. Sometimes we feel the urge to cling to those relationships, despite the degree to which they've changed, but often I've found it is best to release them.

There are studies that claim most of us have no more than three close friends, and that those friends change over the course of about seven years. I've been fortunate to defy those statistics. I think most of us can do much, much better than that. I believe we can have dozens of Penthouse relationships, and that most can last a lifetime. But I also understand that some of our Penthouse friends today might be Third Floor friends ten years from now, just because each of us changes to a degree over time.

We take new jobs, move to new cities. We move into new stages of life. Circles that once overlapped may no longer even touch.

Some relationships can withstand any change in circumstances. But Penthouse relationships can't be forced. We have to *work* to keep them healthy. We have to invest in them and value them and never take them for granted. But we can't make them something they're not. I have some great Third Floor friendships that once were Penthouse relationships, but circumstances kept us from regularly investing in each other. They are still friends I can count on in tough times, and they can count on me.

Evaluate your relationships with clarity and honesty. Know that you're doing what you can to keep them healthy. The objective is to cultivate relationships—with employees, co-workers, vendors, clients, and customers—as if they can become Penthouse relationships, but to value them wherever they are.

Warning No. 5: Learn from Your Critics, but Don't Become Their Slave

My time as president and CEO of Up with People wasn't always filled with "ups."

Outwardly the organization provides great opportunities

for young people to see and serve the world, learn lessons about leadership, engage in different cultures, and build bridges of understanding. The program absolutely changed my life. Of all the nonprofit organizations I've been involved in, including the ones I've founded, I know of none with a greater mission than that of Up with People. And the casts and crews and staff are great at living out the mission as they travel the world.

Inwardly, however, the organization has long struggled with leadership problems at its highest levels. The higher up you went, in fact, the more the organization struggled with narcissism and jealousy and hidden agendas. The senior leadership, frankly, wasn't living out the mission. When it shut down in 2000, it was more about a sickness within the leadership culture than its ability to balance the books.

When I took over as president and CEO in 2005, my stated goal was to "cut the cancer out." But it kept on growing back, partly because I allowed it.

Our efforts to build Penthouse relationships, especially in work settings, can create a tendency to give too much authority to the voices of our critics. We want to be understanding and empathetic, and, of course, we often learn the most from those who disagree with us. But we need the wisdom to separate constructive criticism—the feedback that's delivered with good intentions—from the people motivated by selfish agendas and not the goals of the team.

Tom France, the Rotarian who mentored me in my youth, told me there were three types of people in the world—leaders, followers, and critics. The world is starving for leaders and it needs followers, he said, but it has way too many critics.

Those critics often are the ill wind that blows into the face of a leader. And the higher you are on the flagpole, the harder the wind blows.

When I was president and CEO of Up with People, there were times when I listened far too much to the 5 percent on our board, within our alumni, and throughout our staff who criticized loudly and frequently. Some fired arrows that were right on target, but most, frankly, just wanted to hear their own voices or get their own way or counter the plans of others.

When I led defensively—focusing on countering those voices—the organization suffered. I lost opportunities to create a genuine Fifth Floor culture among the 95 percent that had the organization's best interests at heart.

I'm proud of many of our accomplishments at Up with People while I was in the CEO chair, and I'm certainly proud of how well the host families, alumni, staff, and cast members lived out the organization's new twenty-first-century vision we created together. But I learned a great deal from my failings while there. In my nearly four years at the helm of Up with People, what I learned most was that there's more to leadership than just protecting the mission of the organization—you have to protect the culture. A cancerous culture can sabotage a healthy mission—and eventually sabotage your heart.

Putting Purpose First

Chapter 38

Relationships +
Vision = Impact

By this point I hope I've built my case for the importance of deep, meaningful relationships and provided a few significant lessons on how to build them. Collecting relationships isn't enough—even if those relationships are in the Penthouse.

The greater question is this: What will you do with those relationships?

When you map out the business plan for your life, how do your relationships fit in? In other words, what's your vision for your relationships?

Consider this simple formula for changing the world:

Relationships + Vision = Impact.

The phrase "changing the world" might come across as a little intimidating, but it shouldn't. We change the world one relationship at a time. We change the world by having relationships that impact our family, our friends, our church, and our business/work. If our relationships impact those things, they will impact our community, our city, our state, our country, and the world. We might travel to Ethiopia to deliver medical supplies, or we might never leave the boundaries of our hometown—but if we're guided by a vision for our relationships, we can change the world.

To give our relationships with others the opportunity for the greatest impact, they have to include a shared vision.

A shared vision isn't some worn-out and seldom-read statement that defines an organization's purpose and mission. A shared vision is, quite literally, a shared picture of who you are as a person, where you're going, and where you and those around you want to take your relationship. It's not about an organization. It's about people.

A shared vision is vibrant, filled with bold colors and dynamic brushstrokes that fuel the imagination, inspire hope, and empower action. Vision is that *thing*—that wonderful, beautiful, almost indescribable *living thing*—that makes our hearts pump just a little faster and lifts our spirits in ways that nothing else can. It might live within the context of a plan and mission, but it breaths creativity and spontaneity into a relationship.

We tend to think of vision in organizational terms. But there's so much more. We need vision in our personal life, in our spiritual life, in our career, in our friendships, in our professional relationships, in our teams, in . . . well, in just about every human encounter.

In fact, vision is critical to Fifth Floor relationships. In our closest, deepest, most transformative relationships, it's essential that we share in each other's vision. We have to know where we're heading, individually and together. And we have to be committed to helping each other get there.

Shared visions give power and meaning to Fifth Floor relationships. But there's significant power in shared vision with relationships at all levels.

When Up with People hired me as its president and CEO,

we had to create a new vision for a proud, forty-year-old organization that had been forced to close its doors five years
earlier. We didn't need a new mission statement. We needed
a fresh way of executing that mission statement. It was my responsibility to help create that vision and then to share it with
others so we all could live it out.

The first big test came in Los Angeles around a conference
table in the office of Baron Hilton, the head of Hilton Hotels
and the son of that company's founder. J. Blanton Belk, the
founder of Up with People, and I were paying a visit to Mr.
Hilton and his son, Steve Hilton, who is the president and CEO
of the Conrad Hilton Foundation.

This was the first stop on a worldwide tour for Mr. Belk
and me. We needed to raise $3 million to relaunch Up with
People, so we were starting with the people who had helped
make it so great during its first forty years.

When we arrived, Mr. Belk and Mr. Hilton shared story
after story about those first four decades and all the great
things they'd seen Up with People accomplish. They talked
about how Up with People was the first international organization to go into the Soviet Union and Communist China, and
about all the thousands of lives that had been touched by the
host families, cast members, and staff. I found it humbling;
the shared love and respect between the two men was visible.

Then Mr. Hilton looked at me.

"Mr. Spaulding," he said as he chewed on his cigar, "I know
we didn't come here so Blanton and I could reminisce. We've
talked about the last forty years, and those were great years.
But what's your vision for the next forty years?"

It was a great question, because it went to the heart of Up
with People's challenge. As much as he loved Up with People's

past, he wasn't going to invest more money in it until he was sold on its future. His long relationship with the organization and with Blanton wasn't enough.

"Mr. Hilton," I said, "Up with People didn't go bankrupt financially back in 2000. It went bankrupt of vision. Up with People had such wonderful vision when it was founded in the 1960s. The next generation of leadership, however, didn't have a twenty-first-century vision. It was living on a twentieth-century vision, and it needed something new. The world changed, and the vision didn't change with it."

Then I walked him through our vision for Up with People in the twenty-first century.

When we own our mistakes of the past, it adds credibility to our plans for the future, and I think Mr. Hilton saw that. He saw that we weren't going back to the same old ways that were no longer relevant. He saw that we had vision. And he gave us a million dollars to help bring it to life.

We have to share vision not only with our clients, customers, and other external stakeholders, but with our internal stakeholders as well.

When Keli McGregor took over as president of the Colorado Rockies in October 2001, he knew the climb out of mediocrity for a small-market team in Major League Baseball was as steep as the mountains that surround Denver.

When the Rockies became a franchise, owners Charlie and Dick Monfort had pledged to run the team like a business, not a hobby. But when Keli became president, the Rockies were losing money. For one thing, they had poured around $190 million into a couple of high-profile pitchers (Denny Neagle and Mike Hampton) who didn't work out. Season ticket sales were low and playoff appearances were rare—they'd been to the post-season only once in team history.

Keli had been with the organization since its beginnings, and he knew that losing had become an all-too-easy option—not just for the team but for the organization. There were all sorts of excuses. The Rockies were an expansion team, playing their first big-league game in 1993, and some said they needed more time to build. And it's hard for pitchers to get batters out in the high altitude of Denver. And on and on.

But Keli had a vision of how to change things. It started with a mission statement to "embody the principles and practices of a championship organization in both the sport and business of baseball. In the rich tradition that has made baseball America's pastime, we are committed to conduct our business with integrity, service, quality, and trust."

But having a great mission statement wasn't enough. Keli needed everyone to *really* catch the vision—what it meant, not just what it said—and he needed them to live it out. So he met individually with everyone in the organization—from scouts to accountants to maintenance workers—to personally share that vision.

The goal was to get to the World Series, he told them, but things were going to have to change for them to get there. It wouldn't be easy. In fact, at times it would be painful. But the reward—a trip to the World Series—would be worth all the hard work and sacrifice. They all had a role to play in getting the team where it wanted to go. They all had to share the vision. They all had to live the vision.

Keli gave every leader in the organization a bottle of champagne. He handed out around fifty bottles, and every leader kept a bottle of champagne on his or her desk as a reminder of the organization's vision to everyone who came by.

He also took a photo in spring 2002 of two large buckets filled with iced-down bottles of champagne in the Rockies' locker room. In the background, plastic sheeting covers the lockers. And across the photo it says, "One thing at a time. One day at a time."

That photo remains framed in the Rockies' locker room at Coors Field and in offices throughout the organization. Keli even created postcards with the image.

"All of the hard work," he says, "everything we're doing is going to help us get the cork out of that bottle."

Keli had built strong and trusting relationships throughout the organization because people believed in the vision and believed they were a part of it. And they were.

In 2002, for instance, the Rockies became famous for storing baseballs in a humidor prior to their games to protect the integrity of the baseballs against the effects of the altitude. Some believe balls travel farther when hit in higher altitudes, and pitchers claim it makes the ball harder and slicker and thus more difficult to grip. Storing the baseballs in a climate-controlled environment prior to games levels the playing field for pitchers at their home park in Denver, and Major League Baseball eventually adopted the practice league-wide.

Where did they get the idea? From Tony Cowell, an electrician at Coors Field who was inspired after returning from a hunting trip with dried-out leather boots.   .

The fact that his idea was heard and implemented stands as a testimony to the relationships Keli built throughout the organization—a vision for openness and respect, not just a vague goal of "winning."

And winning hasn't come easily. In 2005 the Rockies finished in last place in the National League West. They had, to that point, made it to the playoffs only once in franchise history. But in 2007 the team caught fire at just the right time and went from fourth place in their division to National League

Champions and a berth in the World Series by winning a historic twenty of twenty-one games.

When they clinched the National League pennant, the Rockies were popping the corks on Keli's champagne—more than six hundred bottles of it before the celebration ended.

Keli had built the relationships and he had inspired them with a vision. Now they were celebrating the impact. They had changed their world.

As you go about building relationships, you have a choice. You can hold them tightly and reap the benefits that naturally flow from sharing life with other people. Or you can add a shared vision and watch as each relationship multiplies in power and impact. And the latter, my friends, ultimately will change the world.

As we were putting the finishing touches on this book, my good friend Keli McGregor passed away at the young age of forty-eight. Keli was an All-American tight end in college, played in the NFL, and was a rising star as a Major League Baseball executive. Several thousand people joined Keli's life-long sweetheart, Lori, and their four beautiful young children on a sunny April day for a memorial service at Coors Field.

What struck me the most during that service, however, was that the words "football" and "baseball" were only mentioned a few times, even by the famous coaches who spoke about Keli's accomplishments. Keli gained fame in sports, yet his legacy was something far greater: God, service, and relationships. I left his memorial service and immediately wrote a text message to my wife, Jill, who was out of the state visiting a friend: "I want to be more like Keli McGregor." And the thousands of people who knew and loved Keli feel the same way.

Chapter 39

Orion's Belt

In 1999, I stood on the convention hall floor in one of Orlando's finest resort hotels and watched money literally rain down around me. The incredible shower of cash, symbolic of my furious climb up the corporate ladder, left me stunned, and not just because I'd never seen anything like it. In fact, the money quickly became a blur as I came face-to-face with an undeniable, stark reality: my ladder was leaning on the wrong wall.

That ladder, as it turned out, stood on the Wall of the Transaction. The prize at the top was more. More power. More prestige. More money. More toys. More anything. More everything. And each transaction held the promise of more, more, more.

A king-sized chip on my shoulder had driven me to embrace success as the world around me defined it. My lifelong struggle with a reading disability had created a misplaced need for approval from others. I had a passion for helping people, but I also deeply desired the markings of success. Mostly, I didn't want people to see me as the "dumb" kid who could barely read. I had to prove I wasn't a stupid dyslexic. I wanted respect, and I saw material success as the best way to show the world I deserved it.

After years of earning it (without realizing it) by serving others, I finally found myself in a position to make some "real" money. So life had become all about getting "more" of whatever there was to get, and it didn't really matter what I was chasing—a job, sales, money, a cool car, a swanky condo, pretty girls, baseball cards, business cards—if one was good, more was always better.

After graduating from business school in Australia, I interviewed with five companies and took the job that paid the biggest signing bonus, the highest base salary, and the best commissions—without regard for any other considerations. As you know, I came from a family of modest means. I had never earned a six-figure salary. And at the time, that was the most important litmus test for me. So I moved to Boston, bought a nice watch (a Rolex Submariner) and my first home (a brownstone penthouse), and I went to work in sales for Lotus Development.

My passion for people served me well in this environment, and I quickly built relationships with customers that led to some great results. The salary was terrific and the commissions rolled in, but so did a gnawing awareness that something about my perfect life wasn't so perfect. Without realizing when or why or how, I slowly had given up the best parts of who I was.

Later these things became obvious. But because I took the job for the wrong reasons (money, pride, ego), it didn't immediately hit me that the product actually mattered. Lotus Notes was a great product and I worked with some terrific people, but I had no passion for technology or the software industry. Worse, this division functioned at that time in ways that valued transactions over relationships. And even though I took the job with my sights centered squarely on performance and results, something inside me knew that wasn't the life I wanted.

The epiphany came during our 1999 sales conference at the Walt Disney World Swan and Dolphin Resort.

The vice president of sales held court at the front of the convention hall, delivering a rallying speech to Lotus sales staffers from all around the country. We were at war with Microsoft Outlook, he reminded us. "We want more market share!" he screamed, his fist pounding on the podium. "More market share means YOU make more money!"

As the sales force applauded and cheered, someone somewhere flipped a switch or pulled a lever and one-dollar bills floated down from the ceiling like confetti on New Year's Day in Times Square.

Colleagues pushed and shoved, reaching and grabbing like children going after candy spilling from a piñata. But I stood in silence, almost as if I'd been pulled from my body to witness the scene from above—a fish out of water in the Swan and Dolphin Resort.

The message amid the chaos couldn't have been clearer: Money! Profit! Market share! Get ours, and you'll get yours! It was like a scene out of the movie *Wall Street*. I half expected the character Gordon Gekko (Michael Douglas) to step out and explain that "greed—for lack of a better word—is good." This was our high calling: To make more money!

For me, however, there came a very different clarity—that my ladder was on the wrong wall.

I went back to Boston and engaged in some intense soul-searching. Two months later I left my job and moved my ladder all the way to Denver, with a newfound purpose for turning all of my relationship skills toward something better than "proving" my self-worth by lining my bank account with cash and filling my home with all the latest gadgets and toys.

That transition, however, wasn't so simple, and I never would have made it without help from an unusual source— Lori Nolan.

Remember Lori—my first love? Because Lori's life was cut short by meningitis when she was only nineteen, I believe my relationship with her took on even greater significance.

When Lori and I shared our first kiss, we thought our love would last forever. And even though we didn't date each other exclusively as we made our way through high school, we were right. We went out with other people, but we were always best friends and cared for each other in ways that, no matter how you sliced it, could only be accurately defined as "love." So when Lori died during her freshman year in college, my heart broke. I thought I might never be able to bring the pieces together again.

Life went on, of course. I dated other women through the years before eventually meeting and marrying the ultimate love of my life, my wife, Jill. Lori was a big part of my past, but Jill became my present and my future.

In a way, it was Lori who led me to Jill, because it was Lori who led me to Colorado. You see, in that darkest period of my life—in that time of self-discovery following my epiphany at the Swan and Dolphin—Lori was my guiding star.

When Lori and I were dating as kids, we loved to find a peaceful spot away from the city lights where we could hang out and share our dreams while counting the night stars against the velvet sky. One evening, while looking together at Orion's Belt, we claimed the famed constellation as our own. Lori was the left star in the belt, and I was the right star. The middle star was us, our star.

When we talked on the phone at night, we'd look at those stars from our separate bedroom windows. When I was at the Rotary Youth Leadership Academy and Lori was at field hockey camp, I'd call her from the pay phone and we'd look together at Orion's Belt as we talked for as long as the counselors would let us.

In the years following her death, I often found it comforting that I could look at those stars and feel her presence, whether I was traveling with Up with People, attending college in North Carolina, backpacking in Europe, South America, or Asia, or living in a rural village in Japan. I missed Lori most when I was in Australia and other southern hemisphere countries where you can't see Orion's Belt.

She was there for me when times were great and when times were tough. And she was there for me in 1999 when I returned to Boston feeling empty, alone, and depressed.

It was right after the Columbine High School massacre, and my sister was living in Colorado. Life seemed so very fragile. And, of course, I had come to the realization that I was in the wrong job—a job I'd gotten in part because a very good friend had gone to bat for me.

When I returned to Boston, I had a heart-to-heart talk with my supervisor. She understood my dilemma and recognized that I needed something different. A change would be good for me, and, ultimately, for her as well. So she and Jeff Papows, the president and CEO of Lotus Development, gave me the freedom to visit other departments in the company in search of a better fit.

For the next two months I continued to do my best as a Lotus salesman, while looking throughout the company at other opportunities. I loved much of what I saw, but I really found no place where I thought I could contribute and thrive professionally.

I felt a bit trapped. If I left Lotus, I'd let everyone down. If I stayed, I'd be miserable.

How could I get my ladder off this wall? How was I going to change my life's direction?

All of this made for some sleepless nights. In the middle of the night in April 1999, I got up and went out on my deck—a rooftop patio atop my brownstone condo building. The view of Boston from that deck was unbelievable, but it only served as a reminder of how mixed up my priorities had gotten. I had it all—and there was the proof right there, in the spectacular penthouse view of the city. Yet, while I was living the life I'd dreamed of, I was no longer the person I wanted to be.

So I sat there on the deck at 3:00 a.m., tears rolling down my face. My whole life was supposed to be about people and service and relationships. I was going to change the world. And yet I found myself in the corporate world making lots of money and feeling totally empty. I had hundreds of friends, but I'd never felt more alone.

So I poured out my brokenness to the only friend I knew would listen: Lori Nolan. I'd become accustomed to talking to Lori when I had bad days, but this was the worst. This time I needed more than an empathetic ear to hear my troubles; I needed help. I needed direction. I needed someone who believed in me.

Sitting on my deck, all of Boston around me, I looked up at Orion's Belt, and told Lori that I was tired of trying to prove myself. I'd seen the emptiness of chasing after "things" just to have more things. "I feel so lost," I said out loud. "I want to make a contribution. I want to make a difference. I want to lead. I want to develop relationships that change the world."

I said, "Lori, I need you. I've never asked a favor and I've never questioned whether you were there. I need to ask that now. I'm so alone. I'm so scared. I need to know that you're here with me, watching over me."

I looked up at our star, sparkling like always in the belt of a warrior. And at that moment a shooting star flew out of the center of Orion's Belt, lighting up the Boston sky like the

Fourth of July. I had never seen anything like it before; my heart nearly stopped. Lori was there!

Call it an incredible coincidence if you want, but for me it was the tipping point; it gave me the confidence to change directions. I knew I wasn't alone.

Shortly afterward, I left my job with Lotus Development, and I sold just about everything I owned. Within a month I had packed my car and moved to Colorado, where I took a position in the headquarters of Up with People—thanks, in part, to a recommendation from Tom Sullivan, the same friend and mentor who had originally helped me to land a job with Lotus. Not only could I reconnect with my sister who was living in Boulder, but I could pour myself into the organization that had given me so much opportunity right after high school. I could move my ladder to the other wall. I could make a difference again, but this time in a much bigger way.

From that day forward, I realized that I'd treat every friend, every client, every customer, and every encounter in a different way. I'd always been a nice guy. I'd always done the things that would win friends and influence people. Now I wanted to do something more. My view of leadership and relationships shifted, and so did my approach to them. I had rediscovered myself, but also a greater vision for who I could become.

It no longer was about building my net worth or making friends and influencing people. Now it was about building relationships and organizations that would transform the lives of people.

I went from *proving* myself to *giving* of myself. I went from a *success* mentality to a *significance* mentality. From *networking* to *netgiving*.

I look at my life since that shift in 1999, and believe me, I've made plenty of mistakes. I've made bad decisions, taken wrong turns, and disappointed people who cared for me. But it's been the greatest phase of my life, because my priorities were back where they belonged—on others and not on myself.

People—authors, life coaches, friends, mentors, and the like—will tell you that you need a "network" of friends so that you can succeed in life. They'll tell you that you need a core group of advisers who can see you through tough times and critical decisions. And they're right—to a degree. We all need help in life. That's why I have an all-star Fifth Floor team. But if the only reason we're giving is because of what we can get, then we'll never get the most out of our lives.

This isn't just the heart of my message; it's the very soul of it.

When we really give ourselves away, we get plenty back—but what we really get is far, far greater than ourselves. We share in the success of our friends, we share in the success of our organizations, and we share in the success of our communities.

We share in Fifth Floor relationships.

We share in Fifth Floor teams.

We execute Fifth Floor performance.

We provide Fifth Floor customer service.

We become and help develop Fifth Floor givers.

We bring to life Fifth Floor philanthropy.

We help establish and define Fifth Floor cultures—cultures where people take care of their employees, their teams, their clients, their customers, and each other, all while making a profit *and* having a positive impact on their community.

We put our ladder on a wall that really matters—a wall that makes a difference.

Chapter 40

How to Make the World Spin Better

Michael Van Gilder is the CEO of a large family-owned company in Colorado. Not long ago he instituted a program he calls Trusted Business Partners, or TBPs. Michael understands that companies facing a big decision almost always consult with at least three groups of advisers— their accountants, their lawyers, and their bankers, a.k.a. their most trusted business partners.

So Michael's team makes it a priority to build relationships within those three sectors. They want those accountants, lawyers, and bankers to become their TBPs, so they do everything they can to get to know them and to help them succeed in their work.

The payoff, of course, has worked both ways. The sales force has sent clients to their Trusted Business Partners, and the TBPs inevitably have sent clients to my friend's company. They help each other's businesses grow.

That type of strategy, frankly, can work even if you have less than pure motives. You can apply that in a manipulative quid pro quo manner that's almost guaranteed to increase your market share and sales. Or, like Michael, you can go about it with pure hearts and honest intentions. It's your choice.

Most (if not all) organizations ultimately reflect the values of their leadership. They set the tone, and soon enough it becomes clear where an organization's ladder is leaning. Employees, clients, customers, vendors—people—eventually see through any business construct that's based on insincerity and manipulation.

If the ladder's on the wrong wall, sales and market share will increase for a time, but so will discord, dissatisfaction, and disillusionment. Unless things change, the organization will become as empty and unhappy as I was sitting by myself that night on the rooftop patio of my Boston penthouse condo.

I was fortunate to make the shift in my twenties. I knew all these things because people like my father and Tom France and Mrs. Singer had taught them to me when I was growing up, and countless other people had reinforced them for me. When I saw the folly of suppressing the values I had grown up with, I had something to fall back on: the lessons of my youth. When I felt that emptiness, those lessons came rushing back. They made it clear where I needed to move my ladder: somewhere that led to purpose and significance, and serving others.

The greatest lesson my father taught me—one of the things he said over and over as I was growing up—was that democracy isn't free. We have an obligation to make a contribution to the community around us. If we'll respond to that call to action, we won't have to wait until we retire to start building our legacy. We'll see community service and corporate giving as a privilege, not as a punishment or as the "cost" of doing business.

Life is about others. And it's about service. If you can make that shift, whether you're a broker on Wall Street, a teacher in St. Louis, a salesman in San Diego, a car dealer in Tucson, or a farmer in Nebraska, you will not only make money but change the world—not because of what you know and not because of who you know, but because of how you live. The most important thing in your life is not what you do or who you know; it's who you become.

Fifth Floor cultures result from Fifth Floor leadership. There's no excuse for any of us to wait on the top executives to show the way or institute programs. Ultimately, Penthouse relationships are about *more than* who you know or where you work or who you work for—they're about living out a spirit of loving and giving and service that no other person or organization can repress. ·

Fifth Floor cultures are a movement, not a mandated program. They begin with each individual who is willing to make a choice to put others first, to do the right thing.

Yes, the leadership sets the tone. But leadership doesn't reside only in corner offices. Leadership doesn't just stem from the boardrooms. Leadership isn't a position or a title; it's an attitude. It's a spirit. Leadership lives on the front lines, in middle management, in the administrative pool, anywhere one person is willing to step up and do what all great leaders do—serve others.

That's how Fifth Floor movements spread throughout an organizational culture—with one person showing the way to another, who shows the way to a third, until the organization breathes out service as naturally as it breathes in air.

It's the spirit that brings the heart and soul to life.

As many faults as we had at the highest leadership levels of Up with People, the traveling cast members and staff embodied that spirit. It was that spirit which whispered in my ear when I was a seventeen-year-old senior at Suffern High, watching the cast perform for the first time. It was that spirit which whispered in my ear at the Swan and Dolphin Hotel. And whatever success I've had and continue to have in living out that spirit will define the legacy of my life.

I want to close with a story about that spirit, a story that I hope demonstrates how any of us can make a difference by investing in others—if we'll only make that choice.

Living in a foreign country became a major goal of mine during my first few years with Up with People. My travels to more than sixty countries whetted my appetite for a longer, deeper understanding of some of the various cultures we visited. So after earning my undergraduate degree at East Carolina, I began looking for opportunities to live and work overseas before starting graduate school.

That's how I ended up in Japan in July 1994. With the 1996 Winter Olympics just around the corner, the Japanese government, through its JET (Japanese Exchange and Teaching) Program, was recruiting people from America, Canada, England, and other English-speaking countries to teach conversational English. I landed a spot in the rural village of Kisofukushima-machi, where I spent half my time working with junior-high and high-school students and the other half working with adults who would be volunteers during the Olympic Games.

I knew of only two other English-speaking foreigners among the eight thousand people in the village, and my first six months there were extremely lonely. The Japanese were gracious and polite, but quiet and reserved, especially with foreigners who didn't speak Japanese.

One day, however, I received a visit from Mrs. Etsuko Tanaka, a middle-aged mother of four who lived down the road from me. Three of her children were in the schools where

I was teaching, and she was in one of the English classes for adult Olympic volunteers. She stood at my door, bowed politely, and offered me a loaf of bread from the small bakery her family owned. Then she invited me to her home for tea.

The Tanakas' home became a regular hangout for me. I got to know her and her children as we sat in their kitchen and stumbled through conversations with hand gestures and broken English. But I quickly realized that Mr. Tanaka never joined us. He was always in the back room—or he would retire there as soon as I arrived. He wasn't rude, just absent.

At first I thought he was just shy and uncomfortable around me because he spoke no English. But it became apparent there was something more keeping him in that other room. So I finally asked Mrs. Tanaka why her husband never sat with us.

She bowed her head, her cheeks turned red, and tears rolled down her cheeks. "My husband does not like Americans," she said. "There's nothing you can do. But I'm honored to be your friend."

Mr. Tanaka, a thin, gentle-hearted man with graying hair and gold teeth in his ever-present smile, had lived long enough to remember the bombings of Hiroshima and Nagasaki in August 1945. As many as 140,000 people died in Hiroshima and another 80,000 died in Nagasaki. Most Japanese knew that America had caused the devastation that injured or killed so many of their countrymen, but they hadn't been alive when the bombs were dropped. Fifty years later, the wounds remained fresh for people like Mr. Tanaka.

On some level I understood Mr. Tanaka's distrust. I grew up during the Cold War, and many families lived in fear of a nuclear showdown between America and Russia. We lived close to a nuclear power plant—the Indian Point reactor—and close to New York City, two prime targets of any enemy attack. Our home included a bomb shelter stocked with food and water. Growing up, we regularly took part in school drills so we'd know exactly what to do if the Russians attacked—get on the floor under the desk and cover your heads. The Russians were the Evil Empire of our day, and it was impossible for me to meet someone from Russia without seeing them, at least initially, through that lens.

But my experiences with Up with People had fostered a deep spirit of understanding for people of different cultures and backgrounds, as well as a longing to bridge gaps and heal wounds like those of Mr. Tanaka. So I continued going to the Tanakas' house and tutoring his kids and his wife. I also helped with chores around the bakery. I'd clean the kitchen, shovel snow from their walk, and help in any way and every way possible.

And I did my best to understand. Hawaii and Hiroshima both marked the fiftieth anniversary of the bombings, acknowledging the tragedy that comes from war. So I visited Hiroshima to better understand the impact on the Japanese people. And when I returned from my interview for the Rotary scholarship, I stopped in Hawaii and visited Pearl Harbor.

Most of my time, though, I lived in Kisofukushima-machi, teaching conversational English and hanging out with the Tanakas. I was at the Tanakas' home at least three or four days of almost every week for nearly two years.

Eventually, Mr. Tanaka began joining us, sitting quietly at first and saying nothing. I started pouring him sake—it's amazing what sake will do for a relationship! Even though we couldn't understand each other's language, we began to communicate through actions. Over time, we built a level of trust and friendship through service rather than words.

When I left Japan in July 1996, the people I'd met and

taught filled the platform at the train station to say good-bye. Mr. Tanaka edged his way to the front of the group. It's rare in the Japanese culture for people to hug in public, but Mr. Tanaka hugged me as we stood on that platform. We both had tears in our eyes. He looked at me and said, in English, "I love you, Tommy-san. You are my American son."

I think that's why I loved Up with People so much. It's not a company or a program or an organization. It's a spirit—a spirit that builds bridges among people. I discovered that spirit as I traveled the world with Up with People, and it lived through me in Japan.

I learned that anyone could build those types of bridges with strangers, customers, vendors, employees, teams, and co-workers. I learned the power of relationships that focus on helping others, on giving, and on service. I learned how to take relationships off the First Floor, from the transactional, and move them toward the Penthouse, the transformational.

We all have Mr. Tanakas in our lives—in our neighborhoods and in our places of business. We all have a chance to leave a legacy with them that's *more than* who we know.

Dale Carnegie's *How to Win Friends and Influence People* taught me to ask meaningful questions and listen intently so people would fall in love *with me.*

But it's not about me; there is more, if we're willing to listen and ask meaningful questions. We can fall in love *with others.*

There's more if we're willing to live beyond an "it's not what you know, it's who you know" world. There's more if we're willing to live our life with a new spirit. A spirit that says, "It's not just who you know—it's who you *are.*"

I promise you, living out that spirit will change your life. It will change your organization. It will change your community. And it will make the world spin better.

Acknowledgments

In the summer of 2008, my wife, Jill, and I visited my father's hometown of Saratoga Springs, New York, where we watched the thoroughbreds run "the flat track." I love horse racing, and we had a great time, but I'm not an intrepid gambler. At the end of the day, it dawned on me that all my wagers had gone on the 2-to-1 favorites. As we watched a 20-to-1 long shot cross the finish line as the winner in the last race, I had to ask myself why I hadn't been a little more bold—why I hadn't put a little faith in a long shot.

A few months later, I was walking through the offices of Random House's headquarters in New York feeling very much like a 20-to-1 long shot at Saratoga.

Thankfully, Michael Palgon, the executive vice president and deputy publisher of Crown Publishing (a division of Random House), was willing to take a chance on me as a first-time author. His confidence in me and my message inspired and motivated me throughout the process, and I want nothing less than to give him a winner—in terms of sales, yes, but more, in terms of impact.

I believe this book can change lives for the better. And if I'm right, it's only because of the many wonderful and talented people who played a part in its creation. In a sense, this book is a case study of its message—the power of transformative relationships to produce something far greater than any individual.

Many of the people who shaped this book are referenced throughout its pages, but please indulge me this formal "thank-you":

To my Fifth Floor All-Star Team, for your friendship and mentorship; to my agent, Kevin Small, for your belief in this book from day one; to my editor, Roger Scholl, for pushing me and this book to a higher level; to my "*ghost*writer," Stephen Caldwell, who became my "*angel* writer" and good friend as we wrote this book together; to my business partner and friend of twenty years, Joel Mauney, for your loyalty and belief in my dreams; to my business and speaking manager, Kerry Caldwell, for your commitment and drive to make every client happy; to my business associates, Dan Streeter, Denise McMahan, and Linda Childears—I will never be able to thank you all enough; to Ken Blanchard, the most inspiring and loving man I know; to Steve Farber, my mentor and cherished friend; to the young men and executives I have the privilege to coach, guide, and mentor; to the young leaders who have participated in one of our leadership development programs over the last decade; to the twenty thousand plus Up with People alumni from more than eighty countries; to the companies, associations, organizations, and schools that I have had the honor of speaking to— thank you for making the world spin better.

There's a special category of thanks to my wife, Jill, for your unconditional love and unwavering support. I know no one on this planet who has a kinder and gentler heart than yours. I am a very lucky man to be married to you. To my children, Caroline and Thomas III (Tate), and my stepson, Anthony—thank you for teaching me what is really most important in life. To my cousin Sean Welsh, who shared in my life every step of the way. To Mike Chambers, for being an uncle to my children and a brother to me. To my parents, Tom Spaulding Sr. (and his wife, Angie) and Diane Marino (and her husband, Lou), for always believing in me. And to our heavenly Father—much will be required from everyone to whom much has been given.

Index

About the Author

TOMMY SPAULDING

Tommy Spaulding is president of the Spaulding Companies LLC, a national leadership development, consulting, coaching, and speaking organization. Spaulding rose to become the youngest president and CEO of the world-renowned leadership organization, Up with People (2005–2008). In 2000, Spaulding founded Leader's Challenge, which grew to become the largest high-school civic and leadership program in Colorado. He is also president of the Spaulding Leadership Institute, a nonprofit he founded that operates the Center for Third Sector Excellence, Global Challenge, Colorado Close-Up, Kid's Challenge, and the National Leadership Academy.

Previously, Spaulding was the business partner sales manager at IBM/Lotus Development and a member of the Japan Exchange and Teaching (JET) program.

Spaulding received a BA in political science from East Carolina University (1992); an MBA from Bond University in Australia (1998), where he was a Rotary Ambassadorial Scholar; and an MA in Non-Profit Management from Regis University (2005), where he was a Colorado Trust Fellow. In 2007 Spaulding received an honorary PhD in humanities from the Art Institute of Colorado. In 2002 he received the *Denver Business Journal*'s Forty Under 40 Award.

In 2006 Spaulding was awarded East Carolina University's Outstanding Alumni Award, the highest distinction awarded to an alumnus of the university. Spaulding is the chairman of East Carolina University's External Leadership Advisory Board and is the university's first "Leader in Residence."

A world-renowned speaker on leadership, Spaulding has spoken to hundreds of organizations, schools, and corporations around the globe. He and his family reside in the Denver metropolitan area.

To contact Tommy Spaulding, visit www.tommyspaulding.com.

SPAULDING COMPANIES

www.spauldingcompanies.com

SPEAKING
To hire Tommy Spaulding to speak at your next meeting or event, please contact your favorite speakers' bureau or contact Tommy's office at www.tommyspaulding.com.

WHOLE LIFE AND EXECUTIVE COACHING
Tommy Spaulding provides a limited number of one-on-one coaching engagements.

THE GIVE/GET CHALLENGE
The Give/Get Challenge is a community impact and teambuilding experience that engages corporate constituents—such as employees, customers, and stakeholders—with an inspirational day of service. Spaulding Companies partners with corporate clients of all sizes and tailors a community impact day that begins with a motivational keynote by Tommy Spaulding. After the service day, the group reconvenes for a wrap-up and inspirational closing ceremony.

DIALOGUE FOR TOMORROW
Dialogue for Tomorrow (DFT) is a leadership retreat inviting foremost thought-leaders from around the world to share friendship and best practices, and to have dialogue about important issues facing our nation and our world. Participants include corporate executives and leaders in the non-profit, educational, and political sectors, as well as world-renowned artists and authors. DFT is a private, bipartisan, nonreligious leadership retreat.

For more information on these or any other services and programs offered by the Spaulding Companies, visit www.spauldingcompanies.com.

SPAULDING
LEADERSHIP
INSTITUTE
www.spauldingleadershipinstitute.org

Spaulding Leadership Institute (SLI) is a Colorado-based 501c3 and is an umbrella organization that operates several unique statewide and national leadership development programs.

Our mission is to develop and implement cutting-edge leadership programs that inspire youth to be servant leaders, good citizens, and globally minded, as well as to motivate corporate and nonprofit leaders to achieve greater outcomes for the communities they serve.

National Leadership Academy (NLA) is a summer leadership academy for high-school students and recent gradsuates. Students experience an action-packed and intense five-day summer academy in Denver, Colorado, while engaging in leadership training, service learning, and civic engagement activities. Students meet fellow young leaders from around the country, hear from nationally renowned speakers, participate in leadership workshops, spend a day serving the community—and more! Session topics include service learning, civic responsibility, global understanding, and team building.

To sponsor a student or to download an application for a student, please visit www.nationalleadershipacademy.org.